Authentic Business

Authentic Business

HOW TO CREATE AND RUN YOUR PERFECT BUSINESS

NEIL CROFTS

© Neil Crofts, 2005

The right of Neil Crofts to be identified as the author of this book has been asserted in accordance with the Copyright, Designs and Patents Act 1988

This edition published 2005 by
Capstone Publishing Limited (a Wiley Company)
The Atrium
Southern Gate
Chichester
West Sussex
PO19 8SQ
www.wileyeurope.com
E-mail (for orders and customer service enquiries): cs-books@wiley.co.uk

CIP catalogue records for this book are available from the British Library and the US Library of Congress

ISBN 1-84112-649-7

Typeset in Adobe Garamond by Sparks Computer Solutions Ltd, Oxford
(www.sparks.co.uk)

Printed and bound in Great Britain by TJ International Ltd, Padstow, Cornwall
This book is printed on acid-free paper responsibly manufactured from sustainable forestry in which at least two trees are planted for each one used for paper production

Substantial discounts on bulk quantities of Capstone Books are available to corporations, professional associations and other organizations.
For details telephone John Wiley & Sons on (+44) 1243 770441, fax (+44) 1243 770571 or e-mail corporatedevelopment@wiley.co.uk

For Minnie
I hope that the ideas in this book are accepted as self-evident by the time you are old enough for it to matter to you.

Contents

Credits

Writing a book is an intense undertaking. At school my handwriting was deemed to be so bad that my teachers asked me to focus on shaping letters so that they could read them, rather than helping me understand how to communicate in writing. I did not start to learn written communication until I got my first Mac (an LC for Apple geeks) when I was 26. I was amazed by the depth and the potential of this machine and started to teach myself to write.

With a slight tendency towards dyslexia and having missed most of my writing classes, because I spent them shaping letters, I have never learned to spell or punctuate accurately. Not being able to write for so many years may actually have encouraged my development in spoken communication. My writing style is very much the same as the way that I speak and several readers have been kind enough to say that it is a clear and easy style to read.

Writing a book was a dream, for me. A dream so precious and seemingly so distant that I hardly dared to express it to myself, let alone to others. I spent a long time imagining I needed to co-author a book and trying, unsuccessfully, to engage others in my mission. Even after I started *Authentic Business*, the newsletter, I lacked the confidence to write a book. I was introduced to Mark Allin, one of the founders of

Capstone, and spent a year introducing him to everyone I met who said they wanted to write a book.

Eventually I realized what was happening and I wrote to Mark and told him that it was really me who wanted to write a book. Mark invited me for a chat and told me how to write a proposal and said he would help find suitable publishers. I was so excited I think I wrote the proposal for *Authentic* (my first book) on the train on the way home. When I spoke to Mark next I expected him to suggest changes to the proposal, instead he said that he thought they would like to publish the book.

Through a wonderful collaboration between the Capstone team, myself and Kat of Authentic PR, we organized a wonderfully success-ful launch for the book and our authentic ideas with seven authentic businesses. Thanks to Kat of Authentic PR and Jenny McCall at Cap-stone the press reception was remarkable, with coverage in the *Finan-cial Times*, the *Guardian*, the *Sunday Times*, the *Daily Telegraph*, the BBC, *Director* magazine and others. *Authentic* has sold extremely well and the feedback from readers has been marvellous.

Kat and I have now worked together for a year and a half and our collaboration has been inspiring, instructive and massively supportive for me. Her help in creating and promoting the books and the ideas to the media has been invaluable. Kat is the best PR person and com-munications strategist I have ever worked with, as well as a great and true friend.

Writing *Authentic* was more or less a solo effort, probably an unar-ticulated act of defiance directed at those teachers. Writing *Authentic Business* has been far more balanced with far more support. Big thanks to all of those who have collaborated to put this together, for all of their support, love and challenges, especially:

- Rob Best

- Atlanta Wardell-Yerburgh

- Byron Rose

- Ivan Favennec

- Craig Ritchie

- John Campbell

- Julia Glynn Pickett

- Mark Curtis

- Patrick Andrews

- Brett Sadler

- Simon James

- And to my wonderful wife Benedi for all her love and support.

Also, massive gratitude to those at Capstone who helped with the promotion of *Authentic* and those who will be helping with *Authentic Business*.

Introduction

Would you like to run or work for a business where everyone felt profoundly motivated and keen to get on with their work? Where decision making was a joy and always seemed to work out for the best? Where there was little need to manage because everyone was clear in their task and role and got on with it? Where customers, suppliers and staff all cared for and supported the business and wanted to see it flourish? Where everyone was happy and the results were excellent?

Businesses like this exist.

The post-industrial business world is now at a curious place where it operates without any real regard for the rest of society or the world.

Currently, the absolute norm is for businesses to be entirely engaged in the job of redistributing wealth from the population and the environment to a few senior executives and the shareholders.

The senior executives feel justified because it is their legal responsibility to make the best returns they can to shareholders. When you register a company you get a little booklet from Companies House, which tells you so. Of course the apparent altruism of the executives' 'shareholder value' mantra disguises the cosy corruption which leads to 'fat cat' salaries for those senior executives.

These companies do not, as they often claim, make money (unless they are banks, which actually do make money). All they do is redistribute wealth – everything else, including the 'products', is a by-product of that process. And most of those by-products are just pollution, including the products, the advertising and all the rest.

These companies are willing to experiment with all sorts of different fashions such as CSR (Corporate Social Responsibility), the Internet and coaching in various enlightened forms of management, but the truth is that unless these fads enhance the process of wealth redistribution they will never get past the next round of spending cuts and will be diluted out of existence.

Within this process, the employees in the companies (including most of the management) find the relentless focus on wealth redistribution more and more meaningless. Questions and doubt infect them as they struggle in to work on trains or in the traffic, and they long for holidays and distractions.

The corporate wealth redistribution machine is so effective at vacuuming the wealth out of the system that it drives cost cutting in public services as well. Under-resourced teachers, nurses and rail staff feel unable to deliver real value to others, or indeed meaning for themselves, for lack of money.

With the support of successive governments these businesses have become supremely successful at redistributing wealth. They have honed their talent and sold so many of us into their game that, as a society, we are successfully redistributing so much of what leading environmental thinker Paul Hawken describes as the 'natural capital' of our planet that, if everyone lived the way that we do in the West, it is estimated that we would need another five or six planets to live on.

This behaviour is unsustainable. And if you behave in an unsustainable way for long enough, you will not be sustained. A thousand years ago when people first settled there, Easter Island had diverse wildlife and plants, and was forested with palms and sophora, a small native tree. A flourishing and literate culture developed the skills to erect the famous stone statues or Moai. Over time the population of the island increased to perhaps 10,000 people. Maintaining the population and the heavy engineering work eventually deforested the whole island and exhausted its fertile soils. At some point the population overshot the carrying capacity of their island. As resources became scarce the order of the society came under strain leading to conflict, warfare and decline. When Captain Cook arrived in 1775 there were just 630 people scraping by; a hundred years later 155 islanders were left.

> *... if everyone lived the way that we do in the West, it is estimated that we would need another five or six planets to live on*

In our case, it is not clear which one of our support systems will disintegrate first; financial, environmental or social. But it is clear that if we allow business to go on behaving the way that it currently does, one of these systems will collapse. If it is the financial system, destroyed by corruption and debt, that goes first, it is likely that the social system will follow close behind. If it is the social system, destroyed by inequality and exploitation, it will take the financial system with it. The worst-case scenario is if it is the environment first, in which case all three will fail.

This is the scenario predicted by the Pentagon, who published a report entitled *An Abrupt Climate Change Scenario and Its Implications for United States National Security* in October 2003. The report predicts environmental collapse by 2020 and includes these consequences in the executive summary:

> *The report explores how such an abrupt climate change scenario could potentially destabilize the geo-political environment, leading to skirmishes, battles, and even war due to resource constraints such as:*
>
> 1   *Food shortages due to decreases in net global agricultural production.*
>
> 2   *Decreased availability and quality of fresh water in key regions due to shifted precipitation patterns, causing more frequent floods and droughts.*
>
> 3   *Disrupted access to energy supplies due to extensive sea ice and storminess.*

(For the full report see http://www.ems.org/climate/pentagon_climate_change.html#report)

The consequences of environmental collapse will be exacerbated by the stupefying and growing inequalities of our economic system, which the former counsel to the US Senate Committee on Finance, Jeff Gates, has detailed in his books *The Ownership Solution* (1998) and *Democracy at Risk* (2000).

Since 1985, economic decline or stagnation has affected 100 countries, reducing the incomes of 1.6 billion people.[1] For 70 of those countries, average incomes were less in the mid-1990s than in 1980, and in 43, less than in 1970.[2] In 1960, the income gap between the fifth of the world's people living in the richest countries and the fifth in the poorest countries was 30 to 1. By

1998, the gap had widened to 74 to 1.[3] Meanwhile, the world's 200 wealthiest people doubled their net worth in the four years to 1999, to $1000 billion.[4] Their combined wealth – 165 of the 200 live in Organisation for Economic Co-operation and Development (OECD) countries – equals the combined annual income of the world's poorest 2.5 billion people.[5] Three billion people presently live on $2 or less per day while 1.3 billion of those get by on $1 or less per day. The income of the top 1% worldwide (50 million people) now equals the total income received by the poorest 57% (2.7 billion people).[6] With world population expanding by 80 million each year, World Bank President James D. Wolfensohn cautions that, unless we address the 'challenge of inclusion', 30 years hence we could have five billion people living on $2 or less per day. The United Nations Development Programme (UNDP) reports that two billion people suffer from malnutrition, including 55 million in industrial countries. These trends suggest that, in three decades, the neo-liberal version of globalization could create a world where 3.7 billion people suffer from malnutrition, including 100 million in developed countries. UNDP's assessment: 'Development that perpetuates today's inequalities is neither sustainable nor worth sustaining.'[7]

With the demise of communism, capitalism seems to have been given the green light as the only game in town. Our capitalists are covertly or overtly running the western world through their power and influence over governments. Profit, competition and selling more are the policies of the day. People are paid vast amounts of money by companies to produce research showing their products are not harming us and our world. Further monies are spent on lobbying democratically elected politicians to ensure the corporate agenda is pursued.

The neo-liberals (those who promote what they euphemistically call 'free' trade) would have us believe that without their systems of provision we would all be immediately transported back to the worst *Monty Python and the Holy Grail*-esque mud and grind of the Middle Ages. They like us to believe that there is some evolutionary inevitability about their systematic exploitation of people and planet, and that the alternative is a return to the Stone Age.

It is of course true that we in the West are comprehensively addicted to our unsustainable luxuries and that we are busy working to make as much of the rest of the world as possible addicted to the same levels of consumption. It is also true that any hope that we might have for a return to a sustainable way of living without having to go through a societal collapse must involve finding a way to more or less maintain the lifestyle to which we have become accustomed *and* maintain the planet.

How can we as a society create a way of living which enables us to maintain our standard of living and the Earth's resources from which we live?

The big burning question is: how?

How can we as a society create a way of living which enables us to maintain our standard of living and the Earth's resources from which we live? What type of business is going to emerge that will generate the income and the jobs and create the products while protecting our planet and enriching our people?

Businesses that are pioneering new and more sustainable ways of trading already exist. These are authentic businesses. Authentic businesses are different because they make profits by pursuing a profound and positive purpose.

Authentic businesses have:

1 A purpose beyond profit.

2 A purpose that is profoundly held.

3 A purpose that is socially and/or environmentally positive.

4 Integrity between communication and action.

5 Respect for others and avoid exploitation of resources and customers.

6 Distinct and unique qualities and are not jumping on a band-wagon.

Authentic businesses are not the same as social businesses, which certainly have a positive purpose, but that purpose may not be profoundly held by the people in the business. Nor are they the same as ethical businesses, which may avoid negative ethical criteria but still do not have a positive purpose.

This book is about how and why you should set up and run an authentic business, or how and why you can turn an existing business onto the path of authenticity. It is also about why, as consumers, employees and investors, we should choose to support these businesses.

This book uses case studies of businesses that are already trading in this way, coupled with revolutionary business thinking and ideas that are being trialled in the businesses that my partners and I are founding, to illustrate the opportunities for budding authentic entrepreneurs.

> This book shares its title with a business and a Web site. The purpose of this book, the business and www.authenticbusiness.co.uk is to help change the way that business is done so that business creates happiness and security for us all.

NOTES

1   James Gustave Speth, 'The Plight of the Poor', *Foreign Affairs*, May/June 1999.
2   *United Nations Human Development Report 1999* (New York: Oxford University Press, 1999), p. v.
3   *Ibid.* p. 28.
4   *Ibid.*
5   *United Nations Human Development Report 1998* (New York: Oxford University Press, 1998).
6   Branko Milanovic, 'True World Income Distribution, 1988 and 1993: First Calculations Based on Household Surveys Alone', *Economic Journal*, January 2002, No. 476, pp. 51–92.
7   *United Nations Human Development Report 1996* (New York: Oxford University Press, 1996), p. 4.

What Makes a Business Authentic?

PURPOSE BEYOND PROFIT

Purpose beyond profit is the key to success for authentic businesses. Authentic businesses manage to maintain the perspective that their purpose is more important to them and to their success than profit. They understand that profits are like breathing
– you have to do it, but it isn't why you get up in the morning.

Purpose beyond profit is the key to success for authentic businesses

For an authentic business the purpose is also explicit and guiding. It is explicit because being open and clear about your purpose enables others who support the purpose to gather around. It also indicates to those who don't support it that there is no point in being involved. Without an explicit purpose it is assumed, in the prevailing business culture, that your purpose is to exploit resources to redistribute wealth as effectively as possible. So if an organization does have a positive purpose it is all the more important to make it clear. The purpose is guiding because every decision can be checked against the purpose to see if it contributes to its achievement or not.

Every one of us knows what our purpose is. It is only ever a question of how long it takes to articulate it. For some people it is a sentence, for others it may take them years to explain. Any purpose which takes more than a sentence or two to articulate is not very useable in any practical sense or very clearly understood by the individual. Ideally a purpose can be set out in a sentence or two and then it can be used in marketing as well as contractual material (see 'Integrity between communications, actions, beliefs and values', p. 17).

Juliet Davenport, CEO of UK-based renewable electricity supplier and generator Good Energy, speaks with tangible passion about their purpose of 'working to maintain a habitable planet'. Good Energy pursue this by generating electricity on wind farms, through small-scale hydro power (no dams) and through solar energy. Good Energy is also one of very few generators who buy back home-generated electricity.

Customers of Good Energy are so engaged with this purpose that 600 of them have invested £640,000 in the company, enabling them to buy their own wind farm and invest further in renewable energy.

Tim Mead, the energetic CEO of Yeo Valley Organics, a major UK dairy company, is so committed to their purpose 'to promote organic farming' that they have written this into their Articles of Association. This is the legal description of the nature of the business that all companies have to produce when they are incorporated. Their cows are the shiniest I have ever seen and I believe you can taste the company's commitment in their yogurt.

Purpose for Clare and Dave Hieatt, founders of iconic clothing company Howies, is 'to challenge the way people think about the world'. Howies use their Cardigan Bay headquarters, their way of working and most obviously the T-shirts, their catalogue and Web site to carry their message. Every aspect of the clothing carries the purpose too. Much of the fabric is organic. The clothes are well made in 'happy factories' to designs which are classic and stylish enough not to go out of fashion.

As consumers we generally know, at some level, which businesses inspire us and make us want to support them. Anyone who has thought about themselves and what they stand for will intuitively be able to pick out the products, brands and companies that make them feel uneasy, and those which they support. This is a mix of actual knowledge, even if it is not consciously held, and gut instinct. The knowledge comes from the media and just being aware of what is going on in the world, the gut instinct comes from our interpretation of the way the company presents itself, and our own spin detectors.

Whenever we pick any piece of communication from any source we absorb all sorts of subliminal information as well as the conscious information. These are innate senses developed way back in our evolutionary history. Today those same senses are deployed whenever we meet someone new or take on any piece of communication.

All the time we are assessing the authenticity of the message and the reliability of the deliverer. We apply exactly the same sensory skills when making other choices about products to buy or people to do business with. Why not give it a conscious try? Experiment with products in the supermarket and see how good you are at identifying those which are more authentic or more contrived.

To check your results go to the company's Web site and see what it says about purpose. If there is no explicit purpose stated, look for signs about what they focus on. In doing this remember that actions speak louder than words and that businesses, like people, give away their true intentions through the way they behave rather than the things they say. Authentic businesses do things that are positive; Howies have a library of inspiring books which visitors can borrow from. Happy give away their training manuals on their Web site. Ecover publish their product formulae on their Web site.

Marketing is now a highly developed activity where designers and copywriters know exactly how to communicate specific feelings in packaging, advertising and other material. Our senses are not foolproof and marketers spend millions working out ways to persuade us that their product is the flavour of the moment, but once we are consciously aware of the options and actively seek out the authentic, we can become expert at sifting the genuine from the fake.

PROFOUND PURPOSE

Many businesses come up with mission statements. The fashion today, certainly for quoted companies, is to have a mission statement which includes some reference to shareholder value. Many other mission statements talk rather blandly about serving customers. Far too many companies have no purpose at all, which begs the question – why do they exist?

For an authentic business the purpose is profoundly held and is not negotiable to those making the decisions in the business. If they found that they were unable to deliver on their purpose they would not be in the business.

Every decision they make is weighed against this greater purpose so their actions and achievements are guided by whether a particular decision or action delivers on their purpose and not just whether it will make them more money.

It is the profundity of the purpose that generates the motivation among the people within the company and the support of customers and suppliers. It is easy to say that you are in favour of authentic business; to really 'be' a supporter of authentic business requires a whole new level of commitment.

As Gandhi challenged us – 'You must be the change you want to see in the world' and 'To believe in something and not live it is dishonest.'

Being the change and holding your purpose profoundly may require significant personal investment and challenge. The first level of investment may be in research – in learning about the subject or inventing it if it is a new area.

It was their experience in the direct marketing industry that lead Doug de Freitas, Tim Harris and Julian Eagles to found permission marketing company Directive95. Doug, Tim and Julian were so appalled at the enormous waste generated by junk mail and decided to revolutionize direct marketing.

'You must be the change you want to see in the world' (Gandhi)

In the UK there are over five billion items and 78,000 tonnes of junk mail going to landfill at a financial cost of £2.14 billion just to get rid of it. Not to mention the environmental and social costs or the £20 billion annually spent producing it by companies trying to reach and influence all of us in our buying decisions (source: Directive95).

Directive95 set themselves the challenge of approaching direct marketing ethically. Their goal was to provide UK businesses with an environmentally sound, ethical method of communicating with people when they want a product or service. They set out to guarantee an advertiser that 100% of their messages will actually be read by people who want, need and are considering their offering now.

Their solution is to donate 50% of the revenue raised from advertisers to charity and 25% to the individual for sharing their information and receiving the message. Then with the individual's permission Directive95 invite selected advertisers to email or text special offers on the products and services that the individuals have specifically indicated they want to hear about. All communication is routed through Directive95 so advertisers never see details of an individual unless they contact them. Customers don't even have to buy anything to help charity or earn their reward.

Doug's, Julian's and Tim's commitment to their cause and their deep understanding of the issues of direct marketing is impressive. It is hugely challenging creating a new paradigm and Directive95 have persevered and evolved their model to create an inspiring business that facilitates true permission marketing.

For many authentic businesses their purpose is a direct challenge to a well-financed existing sector which will use all sorts of challenges and discrediting techniques to avoid being out-evolved by a newcomer with different ideas.

As Arthur Schopenhauer observed, 'All truth passes through three stages. First, it is ridiculed. Second, it is violently opposed. Third, it is accepted as being self-evident.' With respect to Schopenhauer, I would add a stage zero where it is ignored.

Unless you hold your purpose profoundly, it is unlikely that you will have the courage and determination to see your project through all these stages. And if you don't see it through, it is unlikely that the changes you hope for will occur.

The second investment is in being the change. This may mean changing your world view and your lifestyle. It may mean moving or adapting to a different way of living or working. A simple example is that Directive95 have an urgent need to grow their consumer base. However, since their purpose is to eliminate junk mail and pollution advertising, they are obliged to be creative about the ways in which they promote themselves. They also have a need to find good causes and charities to support. With typical creativity Directive95 have combined the two challenges and come up with a single solution.

They now promote the idea using local authentic franchisees. These are people who work in their local community through schools, youth and community groups, local fund raisers and local good causes. The franchisees earn in direct proportion to the good they do in the community in a business that has a purpose beyond just profit.

They promote Directive95 as a means of raising money for their own good causes whilst reducing junk mail and helping people realize the value in their personal information.

Having a profound purpose opens up the opportunity to be passionate about what you do, to be excited when you talk about it, to really care that it works and to engage, excite and inspire others with your message. Passion leads to creativity and commitment. If you are passionate about what you do you will have access to huge reserves of that creativity and commitment to overcome obstacles, to find solutions to problems and to persist. Without the passion, you might give up.

Having and working with your profound purpose gives meaning to your life and enables you to love what you do. Love is the ultimate test for any activity or relationship you enter into: can you love your life, your work, your customers, your colleagues? It is possible, so why settle for anything less?

BEING SOCIALLY AND ENVIRONMENTALLY POSITIVE

The purpose to which an authentic business is set is also positive in that it makes a positive social and/or environmental contribution. The advantage of the purpose being positive is the motivation of those within the company and support from outside the company; from suppliers, customers and even competitors.

To understand the scope of being positive, I use the Native American belief that our responsibility for our actions extends seven generations forwards. So simply offering uninspiring and exploitative jobs to people does not constitute a positive social purpose.

The purpose of an authentic business is positive by definition because authenticity is about the fundamental purpose of a human being. My belief is that humans are fundamentally good and that no one has an authentic purpose which is negative or destructive. Negative and destructive behaviour is symptomatic of some kind of dysfunction which, if resolved, will lead to positive behaviour.

I am often challenged on this definition of having to be socially or environmentally positive. Challengers believe that it is unreasonable to expect every organization to be socially or environmentally positive. The point is that if you are not able to make a contribution to society or to the environment, what are you doing it for?

You might say 'What about entertainment, fashion or financial services? How can they be socially or environmentally beneficial? Do they really have to be?' It is the same for any company – if a business wants to benefit from the support of customers, suppliers and others outside the company, their purpose must engage and motivate those people. If that purpose can offer benefits outside the company then it will enjoy the benefit of support. Entertainment is very often inspiring or uplifting so why could an entertainment company not be dedicated to inspiring people?

Larger-than-life founder of clothing company Hug, Nick Pecorelli, has a mission to make fair trade fashionable. As a follow up to his time as a speech writer for Gordon Brown, Nick's ambition is for Hug to be a major high street fashion brand which delivers social benefits to producers of the cotton.

After a career in the army and another at Barclays Bank, Charles Middleton, UK MD of Triodos Bank, took enthusiastically to their ethical commitment. Triodos Bank will only serve customers who offer a positive social, environmental or community benefit. This is beyond ethical: not just screening out negative behaviour but only actually working with positive behaviour.

For a business, industry or sector that offers no social or environmental benefit we have to ask whether we, as a society, want or need them to exist. The tobacco industry or the diamond industry are good examples of highly damaging industries we probably would not miss for long if they ceased to exist (this is not to say that diamonds are bad things in themselves, but the social and environmental cost of their supply to consumers is out of all proportion to their value). They only exist today because we, as consumers, continue to let them. We only let them exist because too many of us have had our confidence badly damaged and still believe that happiness can be bought from the outside.

INTEGRITY BETWEEN COMMUNICATIONS, ACTIONS, BELIEFS AND VALUES

A defining feature of an authentic business is that its profound and positive purpose shines through in every aspect of what it does, whether paying invoices, parting ways with a member of staff, or presenting at a conference.

In this way, everyone coming into contact with the business will experience the integrity of its purpose – the absolute congruence between what it says it stands for, what it thinks, what it believes, and what it actually does.

Everyone working in an authentic business lives and breathes what the company stands for, not because their job and profits depend on it, but because it's what they stand for too.

To arrive at this evolved yet simple state is never a coincidence. It takes a good deal of planning, care, energy and work. It's important that everyone has the chance in an open environment to explore what the business's purpose and values really mean to them.

As people voice their values, it's essential to continue to evolve the purpose in order to add fresh power and vitality to the existing energy. With complete alignment of purpose the energy will flow and it will be exciting to explore all the opportunities that exist within the business to express that purpose.

Everyone working in an authentic business lives and breathes what the company stands for ...

The outcome is a motivated, committed and inspired team, more so than any other within your conventional competitors. The integrity that an authentic business will then show to the world will not only win loyalty, but go on nourishing it and strengthening it to deliver its core purpose for all.

Their purpose will be explicit in marketing materials, in contractual and corporate documents and in their actions. Staff, customers, suppliers and partners will understand the purpose they are supporting through dealing with the business.

The starting point for ensuring the integrity of a business is to ensure that the purpose is enshrined in the articles of association if it is a Limited Company or the partners agreement if it is a Limited Liability Partnership (a Limited Liability Partnership or LLP is a new type of corporate structure that may be the most appropriate for an authentic business, see Chapter 2, p. 50 for more information) – the legal document created when the business incorporates that specifies the reason for the business to exist. The standard articles of association that you will be given by any solicitor prioritize value to shareholders but they can be changed, and that change can deliver greater value to the shareholders and other stakeholders.

With articles of association that are explicit about your profound and positive purpose, you will attract shareholders who support that purpose. These shareholders are more likely to stick by you and enjoy the social or environmental return for longer rather than simply basing their continued investment on their financial returns.

Contracts of employment, recruitment processes and induction for new staff all need to be adapted to ensure that every recruit explicitly understands and commits to the purpose. There is no point in recruiting anyone who does not, since that is the purpose of the business – so why would you recruit someone who did not want to support its core purpose?

Marketing materials and contracts with suppliers and customers can also explicitly state the purpose of the business, helping buyers and suppliers understand your business and choose whether it is one that they want to support or not. Being clear about your purpose can give a company a 'fan' base as opposed to just customers. Clothing company Howies and cool drinks company innocent regularly receive fan mail from customers.

The contracts and the documentation are the foundations of a culture of energy and behaviour which is committed to the purpose. Just as it is hard to stand out and display integrity in an environment of mistrust, so it is hard to stand out and be duplicitous in a culture of authenticity.

RESPECT FOR OUR COHABITANTS ON THIS PLANET

Exploitation has become the accepted model of modern business – it is apparent in language and actions where businesses seek to exploit customers, staff, suppliers and more; through genetic code, the law, basic human needs and so on. Authentic businesses are by definition respectful, honourable and non-exploitative. They seek to work collaboratively with suppliers, staff, customers and nature in pursuit of their purpose with profits as the outcome.

A business which respects rather than exploits its supply chain and customers is far more secure, because it has eliminated significant risk factors and built in a contingency of goodwill.

It is a curious anomaly that in the 'information age' and the 'knowledge economy' we are still largely stuck with work practices that were created during the Industrial Revolution

To many it will seem self-evident that one should respect customers and suppliers, but the current dogma of rationalist business practice is 'that which cannot be measured does not exist'. Even some things which can be measured but do not fit with our business plans (such as climate change) do not exist.

Respect is also about trust, and trusting colleagues or staff means not feeling a need to control them. In a great many cases offices are about control. Many companies have offices not so that they can work effectively together but to control staff and make sure they are doing what they are supposed to be doing with their time.

It is a curious anomaly that in the 'information age' and the 'knowledge economy' we are still largely stuck with work practices that were created during the Industrial Revolution. The idea of the nine-to-five day and of paying people for their time is rooted in social legislation to limit the exploitation of workers during the 19th century. Surely we are now capable of paying people not for their time, but for their accomplishments or energy! Surely we realize that nine-to-five is not necessarily the most productive way for most people!

Why do people need to make miserable commuting journeys every day just to send e-mails and talk on the phone – tasks that can easily be accomplished from somewhere else? We will often need to be in the same location as our colleagues – to collaborate on projects, to share ideas, to update each other on progress, to inspire, teach, learn, care for and to support. But we don't necessarily need to be in the same location to answer e-mails, write documents or to talk on the telephone.

Too often offices are about control. If you feel that you need to control your staff it means that you do not trust them and if you do not trust them why do you work with them?

This respect extends beyond people. An authentic business is also one which respects our environment and other living things, recognizing that we are all part of the same interdependent system, and that by respecting our cohabitants on this planet we also respect ourselves. A company that respects the environment will seek to minimize their environmental impact as well. They will use low impact packaging, renewable energy and recycle as much of their waste as possible. They will *reduce*, *reuse* and *recycle* wherever they can.

Yeo Valley Organics honoured their suppliers by helping to set up the Organic Milk Suppliers Co-operative (OMSCO), initially paying them a dividend based on Yeo Valley's profits. This is an interesting way to ensure that relationships are collaborative, by tying revenues of co-operating businesses together. Yeo Valley Organics also respect the cows who supply the milk and the environment in which they live by maintaining healthy hedgerows between fields and organic grazing and feeding for the cattle. They also respect their staff and have an accident rate on their farms and in their factories that is 75% below the industry average.

CEO Tim Mead sees nothing soft about this respectful attitude to business. His belief is that competitive advantage opportunities are everywhere and to make the most of them you have to care about everything.

BEING DISTINCT AND UNIQUE

Authentic businesses are created from a profound sense of purpose that comes from within the founders of the business. They are a reflection of the lifetime experience of the people who conceived and created them. Therefore they tend to be very individual, distinct and clear about who they are and what they do. They do not jump on bandwagons and copy others, but follow their own path.

Many exploitation-based businesses bemoan the 'commoditization' of their markets, and the lack of customer loyalty. The individuality of authentic businesses turns this on its head. Even when they are ostensibly in the same market as another business they have a distinct edge or flavour.

An authentic business has not gone down the path of diluting their message or product in an attempt to appeal to a wider audience. They understand that by communicating their message more strongly they may not appeal to the widest market, but they will appeal strongly to their market and that gives them a loyal customer base.

It is very hard, if not impossible, for anyone to excel with acquired talent. Those who excel are basing their performance on their own innate abilities. So why, in business, would anyone seek to create a 'me too' type of operation that was not based on their innate talents? For any of us to excel in any field it is far easier to follow our own path than to try to be like someone else.

Even where authentic businesses do compete with one another there is a distinct identity to each one, which means that they are not interchangeable for customers.

Few electricity customers would distinguish any brand personality for their mainstream electricity suppliers. Customers of renewable specialists such as Good Energy, Ecotricity or Green Energy will find it far easier to articulate the differences between them and identify their preferences.

For any of us to excel in any field it is far easier to follow our own path than to try to be like someone else

SUMMARY

These benefits are not easily quantifiable and those who follow their authentic path in business do not need to measure the outcome of deciding to behave in these ways. They do not work this way because they have spotted an opportunity, they work this way because it is the only way they can work.

I have not created these definitions of authentic businesses – I have simply observed them as common themes amongst the businesses I have worked with. I do not seek to classify businesses as authentic and say that only the ones I have identified are authentic. Authentic businesses are out there and probably always have been. I offer these distinctions simply to make it easier to tell the ones which are authentic from the ones which are not.

Starting an Authentic Business

2

IDENTIFYING YOUR PURPOSE

Is it for you? Most of us won't ever start an authentic business. If you are content with your life as a mother or as a teacher, doctor, vet, nurse, carer, fisherman, farmer, funeral director, secretary, IT expert, plumber, masseur or solicitor, that is wonderful and thanks for reading this book. I hope you live your life authentically and exercise your consumer choice by buying products and services from authentic businesses. And if someone you love starts an authentic business I hope you can support them unconditionally now that you understand their passion.

There is no point setting up an authentic business because it seems like a good money-making idea that is trendy and right-on. That won't get you through the hard times. People will see through your insincerity if you are not authentic, I promise you. No, to be an authentic business person you must want to do it so intensely that you *have* to do it. Read on.

Knowing and pursuing your purpose is what gives your working life meaning. Without our own purpose we are subject to the purposes of others, which may be fulfilling for them but are unlikely to be fulfilling for us. With no purpose at all we can end up distracting ourselves to oblivion.

For most of us our purpose is hidden from us in a cloud of conditioning. Our upbringing and education was designed more for conformity and to encourage us to follow of someone else's purpose in 'followership' than for individuality and self-leadership. This kind of individuality is absolutely not the same as the cult of individual greed that became fashionable in the 1980s. This is about identifying our individual place in the eco-system and the role that enables us to make our unique contribution.

We all know our purpose, in spite of the layers of conditioning that seek to hide it. For some it takes ten years to articulate, for others it takes a week, for others it takes ten minutes. The opportunity is that if you can encapsulate it in a sentence or two it becomes useful, inspiring, motivating and engaging. This is the challenge of this chapter – to help you to articulate your purpose in no more than two short sentences (preferably one), which you can use to find collaborators, customers and friends.

Imagine if instead of the standard nauseating 'So, what do you do?', we could ask 'So, what is the purpose of your life?' Just imagine the improved quality of conversation we would have.

Your purpose is your dream that you hardly dare to admit. It is the love which lies at the centre of your authentic ambition. You will only find it by searching within yourself and that means taking the time and making the effort to look.

It is important that what you do is based on your authentic purpose, because that is the challenge in your life for which you will sacrifice the most, compromise the least, work the hardest and never ever, ever give up – no matter what. When you hear those stories of perseverance about athletes, artists and even business people persisting and persisting and persisting beyond all reason, it is not because they are particularly dogmatic or uncompromising people, it is because they care and are utterly committed to their purpose.

Michael Schumacher and Lance Armstrong are not successful in their sports just because they happen to be better. They are able to succeed because they are more committed than anyone else. The stories of their commitment are legion;

It is important that what you do is based on your authentic purpose, because that is the challenge in your life for which you will sacrifice the most, compromise the least, work the hardest and never ever, ever give up – no matter what

how Schumacher will be in the pits discussing settings and strategy late into the night after all the other drivers have gone home; how Armstrong rides critical mountain stages again and again whatever the weather. It is no secret, so why don't their rivals do the same?

The answer is that you simply cannot fake that kind of commitment. You cannot access that kind of commitment for just any old purpose; you can only access that kind of commitment when it is your authentic purpose. No matter how challenging you may find commitment generally, once you understand what your purpose is you will find that it is the only path for you to follow and it is an easy decision to take.

I run an exercise for clients called 'Coming Out'. In the exercise we use physical spaces to stimulate the articulation of unconscious ambitions. In plain English, we choose a space that has a variety of different environments and is small enough to get to know quickly. A home is ideal – conventional offices and hotels don't work.

We walk around discussing how different spaces represent the person's past, present, future and destiny. We use the objects and items that resonate with the client to represent elements of each of those life stages. Through this process we are able to uncover and articulate ambitions that, in most cases, people have always known but have *never* articulated to anyone, not even to themselves!

In most cases this is their authentic purpose. The reasons for not having articulated it are connected with our conditioning: 'Having bold dreams is unrealistic and unacceptable. Better to just knuckle down and do what you are told, do something safe, something uncontroversial.'

Your purpose has been with you a long time, perhaps as long as you can remember. It will be supported by your innate talent, your natural languages; these are the things that you are good at anyway, without instruction or education, the things which you have a passion for learning and find easy to absorb.

Your purpose will find you, if you let it.

Seek out inspiration. Read, watch and discuss things that inspire you, and avoid distraction. All the time be conscious of your choices and your reasons for making them. Study yourself and your actions, notice when you are tense and when you are relaxed, notice when you flow and when you freeze. All of these will point towards your purpose.

- When do you feel at your most motivated?

- What are the times when you get lost in activity or thought and lose all track of time?

- What are the times when you feel alive, focused and engaged?

- What are you doing in those moments?

- What is the common thread between smiling at the rain, enjoying the earth in your hands, preparing a sumptuous feast and playing with your child?

- What is the focus of all of your flow activities? What is the pivot around which they turn, what is the outcome to which all drive?

- What is your non-negotiable dream? So precious that, so far, you have told no one for fear of it being compromised. What is the purpose to which you would commit body and soul if only you were allowed?

- What is your purpose that is profound for you and positive for life on Earth?

Say it.

Write it down.

Discuss it with people. If your regular friends won't discuss it with you, find other friends to discuss it with. When your idea is new and raw, discuss it with those you know will support you; you cannot afford to expose it to their criticism until it is mature enough to take it from others. Keep talking about it until you craft it into a repeatable catch phrase, which you can use at parties when someone asks you the dread question – 'So, what do you do?'

This is your purpose. Tell people about it. The more people you tell, the more collaborators you will find. When I started Authentic Business I told 4000 people in an e-mail. Now I have many, many collaborators, all of us inspired by visions similar enough that we can support each other.

All of the businesses that I work with also have a profound and positive purpose. They are as varied as we are as individuals because each one reflects the sum of the experiences of the person or people who came up with them. They are often subtle yet powerful calls to action and are used to inform decisions, motivate staff and engage customers, suppliers, investors and partners.

Marneta Viegas positively bubbles as she talks about her company Relax Kids and its profound purpose: 'Encouraging children to believe in themselves and giving parents space to breathe'.

This purpose is born from her own life experience where her parents taught her to meditate at the age of twelve. Marneta uses the benefits she has experienced from her meditation, along with her experience as a children's entertainer, to create the most beautiful inspiring and meditative CDs and books for kids of all ages.

The profound purpose for Henry Stewart and Happy is: 'helping people to be the best that they can be', initially through computer training, and subsequently through other sorts of tuition. Happy abide by the mantra 'Tell me and I will forget, show me and I will remember, involve me and I will understand'.

Many people feel that they have no idea what their purpose is, even if they have been searching for it for years and still don't know what it is. They often have a belief that somehow they don't have one.

And yet, very often, in the space of a conversation they are able to articulate it clearly. No one can tell you what your purpose is, only *you* know. Others may be able to hold a mirror up and reassure you, but knowing your own purpose comes from within.

COMMON PURPOSE

After working with authentic businesses for two and a half years I have found that their authentic purposes boil down to five main areas. The potential for authentic purposes is as varied as humanity – there will be many purposes that do not fit into these areas, so this list is offered for inspiration, not limitation. Which of these areas gives you the strongest emotional reaction?

(a) Climate change, sustainability and the environment

The Earth's climate is like our own health in macrocosm. Without our health we die. Similarly, without a life-sustaining climate, humanity ceases to exist no matter how clever or technically advanced we are. These stakes are so absolute, so fundamental to our existence, that our present climatic experiment is akin to sitting in a car with the exhaust pipe routed into it just to see what happens. It is vital (literally) that we turn the engine off. Any of the other solutions such as so-called carbon sinks or tree planting are nice ideas but we cannot allow them to distract us from the real answer. They are a bit like just opening the car window – they offer some respite and may buy some time but they do not solve the underlying problem.

We are in a crisis easily comparable to World War II – there is a clear and present threat to our very existence

This is the number one issue. I find it hard to comprehend how this issue is not the primary focus for politicians, the media and business. We are in a crisis easily comparable to World War II – there is a clear and present threat to our very existence.

During World War II, the entire population was mobilized to deal with the threat – people were encouraged to grow their own food, there was extensive rationing of most items including fuel, and all technical expertise and investment was routed into devising strategies and tools for overcoming the threat. What's more, the media backed the struggle 100%. The war effort was focused with slogans such as 'dig for victory', 'make do and mend' and 'waste not, want not'. Ironically, this focus on unity and common cause meant that, for many in Britain, the war was the happiest time of their lives, in spite of the lack of material goods and the threat of death and injury.

If we acted now, maybe we would not need rationing and some of the real hardships endured during World War II. So why do our news bulletins continue to focus on trivia? Why doesn't each bulletin end with a sustainability index or news of our daily reductions in carbon emissions, instead of the latest gambling scores from the city?

Coupled with climate issues are issues of the nature of the environment with which we surround ourselves. Builders, architects and designers who care about the feelings and energy we get from our surroundings are authentic businesses, especially if they care about the origins of the materials that are used as well.

Many authentic businesses understand the nature of the threat and are actively creating their businesses to deal with it and make profits at the same time. These businesses include Good Energy, Green Energy, Baywind, Ecotricity, Future Forests, Climate Care, Solar Century, Construction Resources, Alastair Sawday Publishing, architects Hetreed Ross and many others.

According to the survey conducted by *Be Unlimited* magazine, only 9% of their readership are signed up to a renewable energy supplier – this is crazy! It is so easy and so cheap that it is an absolute no-brainer – anyone who cares enough to recycle their bottles also cares enough to switch to a renewable energy supplier. You could switch before you read the rest of this chapter – go to www.good-energy.co.uk or www.greenenergy.uk.com and sign up. Within a couple of weeks you will be able to turn your lights on with a clear conscience.

Rebecca Renton founded *Be Unlimited* magazine after a career in senior management in IT companies had encouraged her own search to understand the connections between psychology, spirituality, philosophy and business. The purpose of the magazine is 'to provide a regular inspiration hit for people who have sat in too many meetings, on too many trains, had too little sleep or stared at the same walls for too long. To remind us all to dream, to believe and make our dreams a reality!'

(b) Social justice and poverty reduction

It is worth reprinting this statistic from the *UN Human Development Report 1998* at this point: the combined wealth of the richest 200 people in the world equals the combined annual income of the poorest 2.5 billion.

Of course we have terrorism and so-called illegal immigration – how could we not when we have created such astonishing differences? It is analogous to lightning – potential difference (voltage) in energy builds and builds, and eventually it has to dissipate explosively.

We talk glibly about free market economics but the system we have created is anything but free. Adam Smith must be spinning in his grave. We have created a system designed specifically to funnel riches from the poorest to the richest and to keep the poor poor. Our politicians wring their hands patronizingly and hand out

The combined wealth of the richest 200 people in the world equals the combined annual income of the poorest 2.5 billion

massively conditional 'aid' – do you really imagine that if we wanted to eliminate poverty we could not do it? Of course we could – the only reason that we do not is because it is not what is really wanted.

Again, authentic businesses are at the forefront of creating solutions to poverty, mainly through fair trade practices – food and drink companies such as Cafédirect, Green & Black's, Clipper Teas, Traidcraft, Suma Wholefoods, Plamil Foods and innocent, and clothing companies such as Howies, Hug and Footprint Clothing, are honouring the work and the lives of those who create their raw materials, and in many cases actively supporting their communities.

We can all help by focusing our spending on these and other fair trade companies and taking our spending away from companies who exploit others and condemn them to poverty.

(c) Biodiversity – life on Earth

Our ecosystem is called a system because each component plays a part. We are not remotely close to discovering all of the vital roles of the millions of insects, birds, fish, plants and billions of other creatures. Extinction of any species has consequences of which we have no comprehension. Loss of biodiversity is another experiment with our life support system – an experiment in which we have simply no idea what outcome we are creating for ourselves each time we adjust the balance.

We have created a fundamental conflict between supplying our needs for sustenance and the needs of virtually every other species on the planet

We have created a fundamental conflict between supplying our needs for sustenance and the needs of virtually every other species on the planet (apart from the few species who flourish on scavenging from our wastefulness).

This conflict is wholly unnecessary. We have the knowledge and the techniques to provide for all of humanity and allow for our cohabitants to exist.

- Biodynamic farming is the ideal of the farm as a self-contained, mixed farm providing its own seeds, fertility and feed for a wide range of different animals and a range of environments from ponds and hedges to orchards, woods and pasture. It is the art of the farmer to develop the right blend of animals, crops and environments to encourage bird and insect life, and to provide a harmonious and sustainable balance for each particular holding. In this sense each farm becomes an 'individuality' shaped by the interrelationship of the farmer and the land (source: www.anth. org.uk/biodynamic).

- Permaculture introduces design into agriculture in order to create permanent high-yielding agricultural ecosystems, so that humans can thrive on as little land as possible, thus leaving as much land as possible as wilderness, if necessary helping the wilderness re-establish itself (source: www.permaculture.org.uk).

Conversely, intensive farming produces about 1 calorie of energy for every 20 calories consumed in fuel and fertilizer and it takes on average 3–5 kilos of wild fish to produce 1 kilo of farmed salmon, according to *The Little Food Book* by Craig Sams.

Intensive food production not only seeks to destroy anything that it perceives as competition, it also often ends up destroying its raw materials, for example the depleted fish stocks and soils turning to desert all over the world. The depletion of soils creates an irresponsible drive to farm virgin land, such as in rainforests, where the productivity of the land is decimated for a few years of intensive agriculture, after which it is barren and dead. Habitat loss is the biggest cause of species extinction – how long can we afford to continue this experiment?

Organic farming, biodynamic farming and permaculture are all far more efficient in an absolute sense than intensive agriculture, where so-called 'externalities' mean that the true cost is seldom ever counted. It was us as taxpayers, rather than as consumers, who footed the bill for BSE and foot-and-mouth. If the true cost of species loss, soil depletion, disease and pollution were taken into account rather than being ignored or paid through centralized taxes, intensive agriculture would be a far from cheap alternative to organics.

Again, authentic businesses such as Abel & Cole, Authentic Bread, The Better Food Company, Doves Farm, Green & Black's, HiPP, Bread Matters, Yaoh and Organico lead the way in food production. It is also worth bearing in mind that cotton production uses more pesticide globally than food production – organic cotton (grown without pesticides) is used by Howies, Hug and Footprint Clothing.

(d) Energy and fossil fuel depletion

Although there is crossover with '(a) Climate change, sustainability and the environment' above, there are enough businesses focusing on providing the energy and reducing our consumption so that we can maintain our lifestyle to make this worth listing as an additional category.

Dr M. King Hubbert predicted in 1956 that oil extraction in the US would peak about 40 years after oil discoveries peaked in 1930. Oil extraction in the US duly peaked in 1971 and in spite of extensive exploration and massive spin it has been in decline ever since. For more information see www.hubbertpeak.com

Although the atmosphere will give up supporting us long before all of the fossil fuel reserves of oil, gas and coal are used up, it is worth bearing in mind that, worldwide, oil discoveries have been in decline since the early 1960s, and that oil production has to follow a similar curve, peaking about 40–50 years after discoveries.

In August 2004 the Texas oil baron and corporate raider T. Boone Pickens told the MSNBC TV business show *Kudlow & Cramer* that 'Never again will we pump more than 82 million barrels, as we are pumping 82 million barrels of oil a day at the moment.'

The news that Shell and Saudi Arabia have not been entirely accurate in their estimates of remaining oil reserves should lead us to consider that the days of cheap oil fuelling our economies might be numbered, and that it may be wise to start planning seriously for the post-oil era.

We in the northern hemisphere have grown rich and have fuelled our way to war and luxuries on the back of life from millions of years ago. Each gallon of oil consumes the equivalent of 80 tons of prehistoric life, or one full-grown tree. If you were to draw a straight line five miles long and put a small blip five millimetres long at one end, the five miles would represent the time it has taken for the fossil fuels to be deposited and the blip would represent our consumption of it – and we are now half way through the blip.

Of course in one way it does not matter. Oil production will peak and then prices will start to rise inexorably. I have great fun imagining all of those luxury cars, airliners, jet fighters and tanks sitting around with no fuel to power them, not to mention all of the plastics used in packaging

Each gallon of oil consumes the equivalent of 80 tons of prehistoric life, or one full-grown tree

and products that will be priced out of the market. However if we want to have any hope of maintaining our lifestyle we need to start coming up with some alternatives pretty soon. Again authentic businesses lead the way: Good Energy, Green Energy, Baywind, Ecotricity and Solar Century are all taking care of energy needs, and Hemp Plastic is working hard on replacing oil-based plastics with sustainable plant-based ones – starting with a hemp-based CD tray. OSCar, Drivelectric and Scoot Electric are all considering our future transport needs.

(e) Education, inspiration and authenticity

Of course this is a bit of a trick entry because authenticity is the key to all of the issues above and to everything else. Virtually all of the problems we face as a society are the consequence of human decisions. The reason that we take such poor decisions is largely because we lack the confidence or understanding to trust our true intuition. Those who make the breakthrough to authenticity and trust themselves find it much harder to make decisions that damage or exploit others.

If our society were one where everyone was entirely confident of their purpose and role then no one would feel the need to threaten, damage or exploit others. It amuses me that most science fiction films that contain any form of governance show a panel of wise elders who calmly dispense justice and decisions in perfect harmony and agreement with each other. What a contrast to our own parliaments, with egos, arguments and sometimes physical violence.

Those who make the breakthrough to authenticity and trust themselves find it much harder to make decisions that damage or exploit others

Just imagine a society governed without fear or ego, where the real issues were addressed and the population trusted and respected those who governed, not because of the propaganda but because they were genuinely trustworthy and respectable. Imagine a society where everyone can follow their authentic path and no one is coerced by a damaging education system or absurd housing prices into jobs that create fear and sickness. Imagine.

Imagination comes before belief and belief comes before reality.

Again, authentic businesses are leading the way in promoting global consciousness, working both with businesses, adults and children – Lift International, Vida, the Institute of Human Development, Positively MAD and The Angel Project are a very small number of examples.

If you believe in these issues and would like to see awareness of the issues and some of the solutions raised in our society, that is a good sign that you have the energy to found or work with an authentic business.

In addition to these five there is a sixth area, which is about helping others to live their lives in comfort and safety. This is a tricky one and slightly separate from the others because it depends so much on the way that it is done. A caring plumber who loves their work and protects their customers is authentic where another plumber who exploits customers is not. An insurance company will claim that it exists to offer peace of mind; an authentic insurance company will actually pay up with a minimum of fuss while too many others fight tooth and nail to avoid it.

DESIGNING A BUSINESS

Most businesses evolve more or less by accident until they are big enough to work out that what they have is not ideal, at which point it is usually expensive and complex to change. I am a strategist, and it is amazingly difficult to sell people strategy. Most people starting businesses think they don't need strategy or they can do it themselves.

The businesses they create are usually clumsily designed and borrow from obvious and usually inappropriate structural and operational models. Strategy is about understanding where you are and where you want to get to, and designing an elegant and flexible route between the two.

When creating a business it is useful to consciously design the structural, operational and business models which will help the business to achieve its purpose and generate a profit. When designing your authentic business, use your purpose to guide your decision making. With every decision ask yourself: is this helping me to achieve my purpose?

Strategy is about understanding where you are and where you want to get to, and designing an elegant and flexible route between the two

The business plan

When you seek advice on starting a business, the first thing that banks or other business advisors will ask for is your business plan. This is another piece of jargon designed to create the belief that you do not know enough and that you need their help to get into their exclusive club of people who do.

In reality, a business plan is a very simple document that articulates what the business will do, how it will do it, and a compelling rationale for why this will bring in more money than it spends. Part of the business plan is also a cash flow forecast, which predicts income and expenditure for one, three or five years. Like most predictions the cash flow forecast is a work of pure fiction.

In my days at Razorfish, shortly before Napster and peer-to-peer music downloading burst onto the scene, I remember meeting a woman who worked in the music business. I was explaining to her how digital technology and the Internet were going to completely change the nature of the music business. Her response was to tell me that she could not engage with this because she had just done her five-year budget based on incremental year-on-year sales growth! In the five years since that conversation the music industry has entered a spiral of decline driven by technologies such as peer-to-peer networks and home CD burning. Her five-year plan probably lasted less than a year before it became so seriously out of tune with the market that it had to be scrapped.

You will need to do a cash flow forecast (for the banks if no one else) and it is certainly a good discipline for ironing out any glitches in your strategy. Just do not be fooled into believing that the numbers won't evolve as your business does.

It is not within the scope of this book to explain how to write a business plan – most banks have perfectly useable templates to help you identify the questions that need to be answered. However, there are a few key authentic elements, such as your purpose and the values that will guide your decision making, which you can include in the plan.

Perhaps a far more useful document for the business, and one that could easily be used as the descriptive part of the business plan, is a constitution. For details on how to write a constitution see 'Drafting your LLP membership agreement or constitution' below (p. 53).

Branding and integrity

A 'brand' is defined by everything a company is: what it does, who it employs, what it believes, how it behaves, how it feels, how it looks, etc. The brand communicates with whoever is experiencing it, whether they are a client, a member of staff, an investor or a protestor.

An 'identity' encapsulates that brand and serves as shorthand for it, so that those experiencing the brand understand all of the subtleties and nuances of the brand – its meaning and purpose – all in a split second. Their response to the identity will depend on their perception of the brand, which could be negative or positive.

An identity is far more that just the logo, it includes the colours that are used, the tone of voice, the type of media, the packaging, the style of the facilities or equipment – in fact, everything that can be designed, chosen or created forms part of the identity.

Your impression of a brand is built up from every experience you have with that brand

Brand = identity + behaviour

Think about some of the great brands – what they mean to you is the brand personality. No one needs to spell it out to you – it has become embedded in your psyche through years of experience. Your impression of a brand is built up from every experience you have with that brand: how friends speak about it, media coverage, shop fronts, staff behaviour, the product itself and so on.

As an authentic business your brand and your identity needs to encapsulate your profound and positive purpose, so that customers, staff, suppliers, journalists and other stakeholders all experience the integrity of your brand. The identity that goes with that brand will encapsulate the whole experience of the brand and communicate it in a flash.

Cafédirect originally had a brand that reflected their roots in the charity sector. The brand was all about the producers, and product purchase was sold more or less as a donation to the producers, for which the buyer happened to get some 'free' coffee.

Under the leadership of chief executive Penny Newman, who cut her authentic teeth in the heyday of the Body Shop, their brand has been transformed to a highly credible and successful consumer brand that combines the strong lifestyle cues of a premium consumer product with its own powerful, ideological message.

The Cafédirect brand is strong because there is great integrity between communications and actions. Everything the company does demonstrates that they are passionate about their purpose and that they continue to hold it at the forefront of their thinking in everything they do. This integrity is what allows us to trust them. We have confidence that there will not be any revelation that they are exploiting workers or manipulating the product in some unethical way.

The opportunity for an authentic brand is to have a powerful identity that communicates their purpose, and to have that identity backed up with complete integrity within the business. Integrity in this context means that every member of staff and every action or decision is truly aligned with the purpose and the brand values.

We are often far more intuitive than we realize, and the more 'in touch' with our true selves we are, the more easily we understand our intuition. There are millions of subtle signals in language and/or action which we all pick up on. When we see someone speaking we can intuit whether they are being honest or not, their motivations and just how firmly they believe what they are saying. This intuition usually manifests itself as a slight feeling of discomfort with the dishonest speaker, and a reduced desire to hear them speak again.

Even if we are not consciously aware of our discomfort, it can be expressed in our body language. What can your own body language tell you about how you feel about your boss or other associates? Do you listen quietly with your hand near your mouth signalling that you will not interrupt? Or do you fidget uneasily, touching your ear or arranging your clothes, comforting yourself because you do not like what you are feeling?

The same is true of corporate identities; we are often able to pick up, from very subtle messaging in the colours, shapes and wording used in Web sites, brochures, packaging and so on, the level of integrity in a company or its products. Try it. Go into a supermarket or watch TV adverts and consciously consider the state of mind of the designers and producers of the material. Were they happy when they created it? Did they believe in the message? Did they care whether it succeeded or failed? Were they passionate about what they communicated? Were they inspired by the product and the outcomes it creates or were they just doing it for the money?

For an authentic business, the integrity of the product, the brand and the people who work on it usually shine through so that most people are able to pick it up unconsciously. With a little practice we can all pick it up consciously as well.

When brands lose integrity they quickly lose credibility and popularity. Brand integrity usually begins to fall apart from the top. When a company is taken over or the leadership of a company starts to panic because the business is not going to plan, new messages and behaviours are communicated to the stakeholders. The 'boss' communicates these messages, often unconsciously, and because of their source they are immediately 'acceptable'. The integrity of the brand starts to be diluted and a ripple of awareness of the dilution starts to spread out from the company in all sorts of subtle ways.

This is at its most stark when we look at a seriously damaged brand such as New Labour (at the time of writing – it is very difficult to identify examples of damaged brands where the story will be relevant in six months' or a year's time. The brand may disappear altogether or recover by the time this is read). One of the reasons that people find it increasingly difficult to trust Tony Blair as a nominally liberal and democratic leader is the way in which he has tied the fortunes of his country and party to a relationship with a US president who is neither liberal nor democratic. This has created a serious loss of integrity within the New Labour movement, which has damaged people's trust in Tony Blair, the Labour Party and politics in general.

Integrity is something that needs to be consciously created within an organization, either from the start or deliberately generated later on. The process is the same whether it is a new or existing business.

On Purpose

This is a workshop I use to help teams of up to about ten people to converge towards a single clear purpose. Ideally it is done at the initiation of the business, but it is more likely that it happens later on as part of an overall strategic review process. It may be useful as a check-in for a management team to realign and refocus on their core purpose.

It is vital for all of the leading players in the organization to understand and clarify their own unique purpose to the extent that they can communicate it. I believe that this is best achieved through a process of introspection, either alone or facilitated.

Once every member of the group can clearly and concisely articulate and communicate their purpose, the group can convene. This would ideally be in a workshop setting with a facilitator who can mediate and connect while maintaining focus on the agenda and driving through to a conclusion. The workshop is called 'On Purpose'.

You may choose a trained professional or a capable outsider as a facilitator. I find that having a facilitator for key meetings makes them far more likely to reach a positive conclusion in the time available. What a facilitator can do is to mediate between parties to help to find the common ground, help people connect with each other and their ideas, and help to focus the group on what needs to be achieved and move on from distracting discussions.

In this workshop each member of the group will articulate their purpose and their personal vision. All of the different purposes can then be laid out to form a map. The map is designed as a target and drawn on a flip chart (Fig. 2.1).

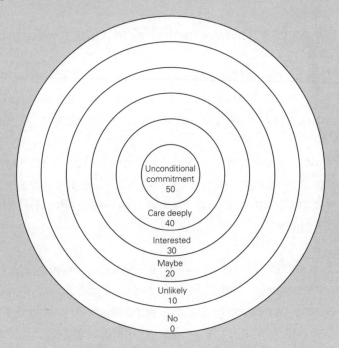

Fig. 2.1   The map of purposes

1 Each participant has a piece of paper with a results table on it.

Team member	Score
James	
Celia	

2 Each participant presents their purpose.

3 After each purpose is presented, team members score their commitment to it on their results table using the scores on the map.
   - 50 denotes that the scorer is unconditionally committed to this purpose.
   - 40 denotes that they care deeply about this purpose.
   - 30 denotes that they are interested in this purpose.
   - 20 denotes that they may be able to work with this purpose.
   - 10 denotes that they are unlikely to engage with this purpose.
   - 0 denotes that they cannot commit to this purpose.
     You do not score your own purpose – it is assumed that you would score it 'unconditional commitment'.

4 The scores are collated and the average score (total score divided by number of scorers) of each purpose is plotted in the appropriate place on the flip chart map with the initials of its presenter.

The first discussion is around the lowest scoring purposes. Anyone's purpose that scores an average of 10 or less needs to consider whether they have adequately articulated their purpose and whether the group has understood it fully. If the purpose was fully understood then thought needs to be given as to whether this group of people is really the one that they want to work with.

If anyone's deeply held purpose is this poorly supported by the other participants they will need to spend some quiet time considering their best course of action and with the support of the rest of the group can come to a decision about their continued participation.

Those whose purpose scores between 10 and 40 need to consider whether they would prefer to join in and work on creating a shared and aligned purpose, or whether they too prefer to separate and pursue their purpose elsewhere.

For all of the purposes scoring an average of 40 or more, the group need to consider how they want to align these purposes. They may be fairly easy to align and the participants are happy to engage in the process of crafting them into a single unified purpose. Or they may be more difficult to align, and the group might like to consider splitting to pursue the different purposes.

Those remaining then need to work together, probably with the support of the facilitator, to align behind a single unified purpose. This purpose should be simple, short and easy to understand.

One way of doing this is for the team to break out into pairs and for each pair to come up with an aligned purpose statement between them. Then two pairs need to join together and align their statements. Keep going, doubling the size of the groups until there are two groups, both of which have agreed their purpose. The facilitator can then take the two statements and work with the groups to merge them or decide what else to do with them.

For example: Good Energy exist to 'maintain a habitable world' and innocent exist to 'make a little bit of health available in daily life.'

At the end of this workshop you will emerge with great clarity about the focus of each individual and a clear picture of who can and, importantly, who cannot work together effectively. Hopefully you will also have a clearly articulated and easy-to-understand purpose, to which you are all unconditionally committed and with which you are going to proceed.

Unconditional commitment is the ultimate level of commitment. Once you understand your authentic purpose though, you will not be able to stop yourself from pursuing it; if you are unable to pursue it you are likely to feel very uncomfortable. With unconditional commitment we open ourselves up to the possibility of doing things that are truly amazing.

For your shared purpose to be realized you will all need to learn to live it. In order to learn to live your purpose, to truly be your purpose, the group will need to articulate some guiding principles and values that will help you and everyone else involved in the business to understand it and to make decisions. These principles can form the basis of a constitution for a Limited Liability Partnership or the articles of association of a Limited Company, and can then be used to underpin recruitment, induction and contracts of employment, marketing messages and practices, customer service, supplier choice and so on into every area of the business.

If all of this sounds horribly challenging and not remotely the sort of thing you feel you can put yourself or your colleagues through, just imagine the alternative. If you start or run a business with an unspoken lack of alignment, people will always be pulling in different directions. It is likely to end up in a messy and expensive divorce as the tension becomes too great. This cycle may be repeated over and over until alignment is eventually found by chance or by design.

Location

In designing your business, location is a critically important factor. Probably the most important consideration in determining the location is the availability of like-minded people who can collaborate with your project.

These days face-to-face communication with your collaborators is often more important than it is with your customers. Electronic communications mean that our virtual shopfront can offer us a national or global market independent of our location. The people you most need to interact with face-to-face are the people who are going to help you to make it happen, whether they are partners, staff or supporters.

Around the world there are growing pockets of ideologues – those who have escaped the rat race or who have never joined and who want to make a difference. In some places or environments it is easy for these people to feel isolated and very different from the mainstream. In other places it is easy to forget that the whole world is not authentic – yet.

You can identify the towns and areas that fit into the second category by a predominance of organic or health food shops and the existence of independent and ideological local media, and other businesses and retailers. I live in the Bath/

These days face-to-face communication with your collaborators is often more important than it is with your customers

Bristol area of the UK where we have *The Spark* – a local quarterly paper promoting ethical organizations. Triodos Bank, Yeo Valley Organics, Good Energy, The Better Food Company, Essential Trading, Alastair Sawday Publishing, Yaoh, The Green Stationery Company, the Soil Association, BORN, miniscoff and many more authentic businesses are also based in the Bath/Bristol area.

This creates a virtuous circle where like-minded people are attracted to the area and as they support these businesses, they attract more like-minded people in, and they start to influence local government, which attracts still more like-minded people and businesses.

The reason that this is important is that it is very easy for great ideas to be dismissed when they are new, because they are not established, and a supportive environment can protect them. If the people around you are unsupportive in those early stages then your confidence will waver and belief will turn to doubt. In a supportive environment the inevitable early wrinkles can be smoothed, the inevitable setbacks can be overcome, and the idea can blossom into an offer which can withstand the challenge of exposure to the wider world.

On a more practical level the availability of communications, both physical and electronic, makes a huge difference. Broadband and good accessible rail services have been vital to the founding of my businesses.

Structure and the LLP

Most existing authentic businesses are affected by a structure that is not necessarily the most appropriate for the style of business they wish to run. The default choice faced by most entrepreneurs in recent times when choosing a business structure has been between the limited liability company, a Public Limited Company (PLC), or possibly a not-for-profit company limited by guarantee.

For authentic businesses the problem with the first two is that they are legally obliged to put profit and returns to shareholders above all other considerations, except paying taxes and obeying the law. And the problem with that is that it creates a structural fault line between the owners of the business and the other stakeholders. This fault line can be circumnavigated to some extent through diligent and generous management but it cannot be erased or ignored.

Other structures do exist and during the 19th Century there was a great fashion for mutual and co-operative societies, which enjoyed a brief resurgence in the 1960s and 1970s when the hippy movement took up the cause. Co-ops however have their challenges – they can be difficult to manage, hard to set up and it can be tough to find investors. Having said that, there are some excellent and flourishing authentic co-ops around; Suma Wholefoods in Leeds, and Calverts Design and Print in London are two examples.

Mutuals were once fashionable as a way of providing money relatively cheaply for working people to own their own homes. But in the 1990s many of the largest mutuals demutualized in exchange for a quick hit of cash for the savers, who became shareholders.

Only in professional services has co-operation and mutuality taken a different course. In the mid-1990s partners in big accounting and legal firms realized that potential for professional liability claims left them open to unlimited losses and we can understand their concern in the wake of the Enron game of dominos which took accountants Arthur Andersen with it.

Partners in law and accountancy firms make more effective lobbyists than most: the UK government responded favourably by granting them the same limited liability protection offered to investors in PLCs and limited liability companies by creating the Limited Liability Partnership (LLP), which passed into law in 2001. LLPs have proved very popular with the professionals, with over 6000 set up in the first few years as many partnerships embrace the new limited liability option.

The LLP that was created is a remarkable thing, in that it is an almost completely blank sheet of corporate paper. The LLP allows authentic entrepreneurs to create highly aligned, multidimensional organizations with all manner of people and entities including staff, managers, investors, charities, NGOs, local authorities, other companies, banks and pretty much any 'body' as a partner.

The partners are also governed by their partnership agreement, which is effectively a contract of association. A partnership agreement can say anything that is within the law and, if such an agreement does not exist, it simply defaults to standard partnership law.

But perhaps the best feature of LLPs is that they are cheap and easy to create, which means you can have lots of them interwoven with each other. To set one up all you need to do is have two partners, fill in a two-page form downloaded from the Companies House Web site, and send it off with a cheque for £95.

The real opportunity for the authentic entrepreneur is in writing the partnership agreement or constitution. The partnership agreement can contractually specify the purpose, values, behaviours and activities of the business. It can also specify the kind of measures, such as the level of consensus required to change the constitution, that are put in place to protect the essential elements of the agreement from being changed.

In the LLP we can have absolute clarity of purpose and complete alignment between all of the different types of partner whether they are investors, suppliers or workers. We can have all partners motivated towards an explicit and specified end in a way which survives the departure of the original visionary founders, or even a takeover. In fact a well-written constitution might also contribute to making a hostile takeover far less likely because of protective measures built in to the constitution.

Drafting your LLP membership agreement or constitution

Here are some suggested headings and contents for your partnership agreement or for a constitution.

Purpose and values

- The purpose and values are fundamental to the existence and running of your authentic business.

- The purpose needs to be short, clear, useable and memorable.

- The values provide further guidelines of the context within which the purpose may be pursued. So if you have honesty as a value, you may not compromise on honesty in order to achieve the purpose – it would devalue the purpose to do so.

- All decisions within the business will be subject to evaluation against their contribution to the achievement of the purpose and their alignment with the values.

The nature of the business

This section describes how the business pursues its purpose, how it will sustain itself, and an outline of how will it be promoted and what will it sell.

Structure of business and relationships map

What types of partner are there and what are the relationships to each other? This could include a map such as the one used to design Authentic Capital (Fig. 2.2).

Executive partners run the business. Authentic Guides is a partner and carries out due diligence on investment prospects, recruits and supports clients. Business Partners have the job of growing their companies and the investments are made through another LLP set up with the Business Partner. Supplier Partners are sub-contractors who promote Authentic Capital, manage the partner information and ensure FSA compliance.

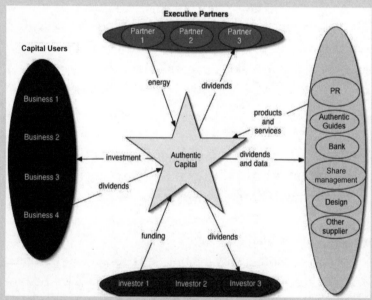

Fig. 2.2   The map used to design Authentic Capital

Origins

This section explains who the founders are and what their inspiration is. It is important to not only be explicit about the purpose of the business but also to be clear as to why the founder(s) felt that it was important to create it in the first place.

Governance – how the partnership will be managed

This section is essentially the management bible for the business, explaining how decisions will be made and how the joining and departure of partners will work. It should also cover any management issues that are specific to the business you are setting up as well as complaints and disciplinary procedures.

Operations – practice and methodologies

This section covers the detail of the operations of the business – how sales and marketing will be achieved, the nature of the financial management, how staff will be treated, etc.

Types of partner

This section expands on the map and outline of partnerships above. It will detail the roles and responsibilities for each type of partner if there is more than one type. It will also cover the investment, ownership and remuneration formulae for each type of partner.

Growth, recruitment, expansion

The constitution must also be forward looking in a practical sense and define ways in which new partners are recruited and how relationships and partnerships develop with other businesses.

Exit
This section will cover the route and protocol by which partners can resign or be asked to leave the partnership.

Writing your constitution

Most of us, as business people, are used to trusting lawyers to create contracts and other formal documents. The trouble with this is that most lawyers think in a defensive way and most contracts are written to defend the client (and the author) against potential risks. This is fine, except that the language and the tone are not generally conducive to trust and relationship building, which is what partnerships are specifically about.

In addition, your constitution needs to be an inspiring and living document, not one that is filed away and only brought out when there is trouble brewing. My preference is to draft the constitution collaboratively with the partners involved and then to have an authentic lawyer (they do exist – Gandhi and Mandela were both lawyers) review the draft and recommend any refinements.

Remember – you and your business will be living by your constitution, so be completely honest when you write it. If any of the sections leave you cold or make you feel uncomfortable then change them – and don't be afraid to go on changing and evolving your constitution, over months and years if necessary, until all partners are satisfied.

Unlike a conventional business plan your constitution will be used in every area of business on a daily basis. It is what new members of staff will read and sign up to as part of their contract of employment, it will be referred to when making important decisions and it will be used in making agreements with suppliers and customers.

FUNDING

Funding is the big thorny issue for authentic businesses. On the one hand, as soon as someone else has a stake in your business it is not your own; on the other, growth is all but impossible for many small businesses without funding.

There are examples of authentic businesses that have attracted various types of funding. Some of them have maintained their authenticity; others have had their authenticity diluted. As awareness of the benefits of authenticity in business spread, so it will become easier to secure authentic funding. Until then it is an issue for authentic entrepreneurs to face with great care.

Forecasting and business plans

In order to raise any money from more or less any source, you will need to be able to produce a cash flow forecast and business plan. This is a spreadsheet detailing projected income and spending over a one-, two-, three-, or even five-year period and, as has been said before, is a work of pure fiction. The bankers' faith in the forecast is based on the idea of incremental growth and the targets that businesses set themselves. However we exist in a chaotic system where there are so many millions of entirely unpredictable influences and effects on everything we do that meaningful prediction beyond a few minutes ahead is mere speculation.

Even if you are able to provide solid security (such as your home), you are likely to have to prepare a forecast in order to raise money. In spite of all that I have said, the cash flow forecast is a good discipline. It forces you to think of all of the potential income streams as well as all the possible costs and to do the sums to see if your business idea ends up with more or less money at the end of the year than it started with.

From my experience it is very hard to write a forecast that is not wildly optimistic. Once you have written your first draft, try halving the income and doubling the costs, or doubling the timescales, and see how it looks at the end of the year.

There are also some magic numbers in raising finance – one of the most important is 51%. 51% is the controlling interest in a business. If you sell more than 50% of your business (particularly to a single other entity) you are no longer in control, and the authenticity of the business you started is no longer in your hands.

From my experience it is very hard to write a forecast that is not wildly optimistic

Here are some different ways of raising money. You may use them in different ways and at different stages and times in your business development – and bear in mind that having more than enough leads to excess when you are working out what you think you need.

When you make initial calculations it is often tempting to set budgets for doing things in conventional and expensive ways. I find that with a little creativity it is nearly always possible to find a far cheaper way to do things or simply not to do them at that time. During the dot com boom, a surfeit of easily available money led to absurd excess, with consequent booms in luxury hotels, first class flights and fast cars. If money is available the budget will always expand to fill it and more; if money is not available you simply have to find other ways to achieve your aims. A lot of the work that we have done on setting up our authentic businesses has been done on a shoestring and with a positive cash flow. One of the consequences is that we have no external shareholders to answer to or debts to repay.

1   *Self-funding* – my personal favourite, even though I have never had a significant amount to actually invest. By default, most businesses are self-funded to start with while the idea is developed and the

plan is created. I like the clarity and the control of self-funding, and find that it creates a great discipline that helps you to focus on what is truly important for the development of the business and what is not. The initial founding of Authentic Business and Authentic Guides was funded through selling excess 'stuff' on eBay and through reciprocal deals agreed with supplier/customers where we exchanged services – for example to build the Web sites. Bear in mind that VAT is payable on barter deals if you are registered and that they may also be taxable.

Self-funding is only possible if the business you are planning is not capital intensive and can be cash flow positive (the money comes in before it goes out), or if you have enough ready cash to fund it already. These days it is also worth bearing in mind that you may have considerably more faith in your own endeavours than you have in pension companies and other conventional savings and investment schemes.

2   *Bank loan* – for small amounts of money your bank is not a bad place to go. Be aware that a bank's primary responsibility is to its own shareholders and they can be very tough on uncertain debts, but this can be a reasonable deal as long as you understand the bank's priorities. Unless you have an amazing track record, your bank will almost certainly ask for security, which generally means that they want you to sign over a part of your house in case you default on the loan.

There are also more authentic banking options than the high street banks, such as Triodos Bank in the Netherlands, Spain and UK, and the Co-operative Bank in the UK, both of which have ethical policies and seek to promote better ways of being.

3   *Private investors* – probably the mainstay of many small business start-ups is from investment by friends and/or relatives. They may be willing to just hand over the cash but it is still important to go through the discipline of the forecast to ensure that your plans are

realistic and also to have a written agreement (constitution) that details what happens under different circumstances. Watch out for any 'beneficial' shareholdings and ensure that any such rights and benefits are clearly set out and understood by all from the start.

4   *Share issues* – certainly once an authentic business gets to a sufficient scale it has the opportunity to raise finance through share issues to its own customer base. In 2004 Cafédirect raised £5 million and Good Energy £1 million through share issues exclusively to their own customer bases. For an authentic business the advantage of making the offering to your own customers is that they share your ideology and will be just as vociferous in demanding the ideological return as the financial one.

   Also in 2004 Google made their Initial Public Offering (IPO) and wrote cultural caveats into the share offer to protect their identity. They designed the shareholding structure so that the company would continue to be run by its founders, rather than by the short-term obsessions of institutional shareholders and Wall Street analysts. They also stated that the company motto would be 'do no evil'. It remains to be seen whether they can protect themselves and I hope that they do.

5   *Trade investor* – this is clearly not a likely funding source for a start-up, although it does happen, especially if you know the people. For an authentic business it throws up the immediate question of alignment. If any significant investor is not aligned with your purpose it is unlikely that the authenticity will remain if you are successful and the trade investor wants to cash in their investment.

   McDonald's currently have a 33% stake in sandwich chain Pret A Manger. Although I do not perceive Pret A Manger to be an authentic business, I feel they are considerably more authentic than McDonald's. Pret has been very successful so there has been little incentive for any interference from McDonald's, but what happens when McDonald's change their strategy and want to sell Pret? How much protection for the Pret brand is built in to that contract?

6   *Venture capital* – my experience of this has been extremely variable, ranging from virtual loan sharking on a big scale to highly supportive and valuable. Venture capitalists (VCs) are not usually interested unless you are talking about quite serious amounts of money, such as £500,000 upwards. Most, but not all, are also more interested in established businesses doing management buy-outs and that kind of thing rather than small businesses and start-ups. For me, venture capital is a serious game with its own rules, and I prefer to find other routes.

7   *Angel investors* – business angels are private investors generally with a big business or entrepreneurial background. Like VCs, angels vary enormously in their outlook. The main advantage of angels over VCs is that they are more likely to be able to provide real business support which may be important.

8   *Authentic Capital* – Authentic Capital is a new type of fund management company that will launch in 2005. Authentic Capital is an LLP and will have client companies as partners, investors, suppliers and executives as partners in the business. Authentic Capital will only work with authentic businesses and has Authentic Guides to offer hands-on support to businesses it funds. For more on its structure see Fig. 2.2 above.

PLANNING

I am, by nature, a strategist. I plan all the time. I am constantly thinking ahead, working out priorities, evaluating options and deciding how to do things. So I am astonished at how little planning I come across in the businesses I work with, and the larger ones are generally worse at it than the smaller ones.

Strategy or planning is actually very simple. It is about knowing where you are, knowing where you want to get to and creating a plan to get from one to the other.

The difference between planning and not planning is analogous to the difference between going for a walk and going on a journey. When you go for a walk, you are happy to be guided by the path and to just see where it goes – this kind of exploration has a valuable place in all of our lives. Going on a journey is different. When we go on a journey we need to decide on a destination (even if we change it later) and we need to plan a route identifying the key points along the way – especially the first ones.

Strategy or planning is ... about knowing where you are, knowing where you want to get to and creating a plan to get from one to the other

For a business, the same is true. If you intend to achieve your purpose you will need to have a plan. We need to know where we are and where we want to go. We need to know what will need to be done and in what order, and we will need to know who is going to do which jobs. Within the discipline of planning it is also important to ensure that there is the flexibility to allow for and embrace unexpected or unscheduled events, and adjust plans accordingly.

Traditionally a project manager who is told what the objective is by a manager does this job. The manager has had the objective handed down from the board of directors that took the decision. The project manager then maps out all of the tasks and allocates them to people or departments and then hands it back to the manager. The manager delegates all of the tasks and the project manager oversees the delivery. No wonder so many projects go wrong!

I run a 'project-planning workshop' where all participants in the project collaboratively decide what needs doing, and where individuals commit themselves to doing the jobs for which they have energy. Then a project manager can oversee delivery and remind people of their commitments.

I have run a great many of these workshops ranging from individuals to 35 people, for teams, departments and whole companies, and it seems to be an extremely easy, flexible and successful way of organizing things.

Here is how it works:

- *Preparation.* Some of the participants may want to present a summary on the current situation from specific points of view, such as finance, sales, general staff and so on, so that all participants are aware of where they are starting from.

- *Location.* I find the best results occur in something other than an office meeting room. Ideally there is very little furniture and the participants can sit in a circle on the floor. The room will need a large blank wall or, better still, a large window (sticky notes stick better to windows).

- *Equipment.* A flip chart, lots of sticky notes, paper and pens for everyone. Plenty of water and fruit is good to keep people's brains working well.

- *Participants.* Ideally only those who will be involved in the delivery of the project, plus a facilitator who may also be involved in the delivery.

Process

It is good to start with everyone settling in and feeling comfortable with the environment. If there are people who do not know each other (such as the facilitator) it is worth going around the room and having everyone introduce themselves.

The starting point is to define the objective and the timescale for achieving it – six months, a year, five years, etc. The facilitator will ask all participants to write their perception of the objective on a piece of paper. Once everyone has finished writing, all of the participants share their description and the facilitator makes notes on the flip chart. It is then up to the facilitator to chair the discussion and merge the descriptions until consensus is reached. This will only be possible if there is reasonable alignment in the group. If there is not then it may be worth doing the 'On Purpose' workshop described in the box on p. 44.

Once the objective is agreed, it is time to develop an understanding of the present situation, and the facilitator can invite a summary from those who wish to give one. After this the whole team will know the starting point and the destination and be ready to create the plan. The objective is posted on the wall.

Next we define the high-level tasks that need to be undertaken in order to achieve the objective. Writing on the flip chart, the facilitator will ask the participants to identify the high-level tasks. Here we are looking for things such as 'develop brand', 'produce catalogue' and so on.

If the plan is over more than one year then each year can be given a theme and the same process of identifying tasks can be undertaken for each year. Themes might follow an appropriate metaphor such as seeding, rooting, sprouting and branching if the project is to do with growing something new. The task sheet (or sheets with years marked on them) are then posted on the wall. The task sheet has the year and the theme written at the top and then all of the tasks as one- or two-word bullet points underneath.

The facilitator then focuses the group's attention on the first of the task sheets and hands out a pad of sticky notes to each participant. The group now goes through the list of tasks identifying each individual job that needs to be done to deliver on the task. Here we are looking for things such as 'appoint brand designer', 'articulate values', 'write copy for the catalogue', and so on.

By the end of this process you might have a total of 100 or 200 sticky notes. The facilitator now creates a matrix on the wall or window with more sticky notes. The names of each participant are arranged vertically on the left, and the months are arranged horizontally across the top (unless there are more than 12 people, when it is better to have the participants across the top).

The participants now put all of the sticky notes up on a spare wall in no particular order and then start to move them across to the matrix identifying the jobs for which they have energy and when they feel it should be done. A job allocated denotes responsibility for seeing that the job is done, not necessarily actually doing the job, which may be contracted out or delegated to someone not present. No participant is allowed to allocate a job to another without discussing it with them first and the sticky notes denote the start of the job, not its completion.

Once the matrix is complete and all the sticky notes have been placed, the participants must review their commitments and check that they are in the right order. They then take their own notes down, being careful to keep them in order, marking the beginning of each month with a freshly labelled sticky note, and finally their name on top. The facilitator can now collate all of the notes and replicate the matrix in a spreadsheet that can be shared with the whole group.

Any project plan is only as good as the project management, and one of the team needs to take responsibility for chasing people up and organizing regular project review meetings to check progress and make adjustments to the plan. At the end of the year, or when the activities on the plan run out, the whole process can be undertaken again (it is worth it even if it is a five-year plan) to organize for the next period.

RECRUITMENT

For an authentic business, who you hire is part of what defines the integrity of your business and the energy that it can channel into the pursuit of its purpose. Authentic businesses face a real dilemma when recruiting, whether to hire on ideology or to hire on craft skills, such as sales, marketing, accounts and so on. In practice, most authentic businesses hire on craft skills unless they are lucky enough to find people with both the relevant craft skills and the right ideology. Hiring on skills brings real risks if you cannot win your recruits over to the ideology.

Hiring on skills brings real risks if you cannot win your recruits over to the ideology

For some reason we have a more or less unquestioned tradition of hiring staff based on their past. It is pretty universal practice to ask for a CV as the first step in any recruitment process. This seems like a curious way to organize things when what you are actually hiring people for is their future! It is rare for a CV to be inspiring or exciting and school leavers and graduates are immediately at a disadvantage as they scratch around putting summer jobs onto their CV.

As an employer, what you are looking for is an alignment of objectives and purpose that will last at least for the duration of the intended employment period plus assurance that the candidate has the craft skills required for the job.

If you are looking for people to excel and be confident in their work you will need people who have an innate talent for their craft skill, rather than having it as an acquired skill that they have been taught. People are most likely to excel in something for which they have an innate talent.

Innate talents are those which are so easy for us to show that it is hard to remember when we didn't. They are things we do anyway, we barely notice we are doing them and believe that everyone else is doing them too. We find our innate talents fun and easy, and probably use them in our hobbies.

In my experience, employing people based on a manifesto that articulates their passion, purpose, talents and objectives is a far more relevant process than hiring people on their CV alone. What you are looking for is a clear statement of purpose that is aligned with the purpose of the business, plus an innate talent for the craft skills that you need.

Dilution

The risk of failing to engage staff with the purpose of the business is dilution. If a company's purpose becomes diluted, there is no focus to the energy and it starts to dissipate through gossip, politics and negativity. Your beautiful authentic business becomes just like any other and you end up spending your time managing a disparate and uninspired team.

Given that it is hard to find people with the right craft skills who also share your ideology in the present recruitment culture, and that hiring on skills ends up being the priority, an authentic business needs to take steps to protect itself from the inevitable dilution that will occur when the non-aligned staff outnumber the passionate ones.

A detailed staff manual (probably in electronic form) is a priority. The manual can contain all of the practical information such as how the phones work and how to make holiday arrangements, but it can also contain an inspiring history of the company that puts context around the purpose and stories that explain how and why the purpose is important. Once the first issue of the manual is written, then responsibility for its management can be handed over to the latest recruit who can add new information (for example, where the best sandwich shop is) and update existing information. If the job is given to anyone on a permanent basis, it will not happen.

A strong and inspiring induction process that introduces and engages recruits with the purpose is vital. This can be run in just half a day whenever there are new members of the team. One of the best ways to organize this is to have the last recruit run this session for the new one as teaching is very often the best way to learn. I use a four-step workshop for employee induction.

1 *Articulate.* The participants explain their own purpose and their understanding of the purpose of the business and it is captured on a flip chart by a facilitator.

2 *Align.* The participants discuss their own purpose and how it contributes to the purpose of the business.

3 *Engage.* The participants discuss the basis for the purpose of the business and understand how motivated they are by it.

4 *Authenticate.* The participants commit to the aligned purpose. Ideally this involves signing an employment contract that includes a commitment to the purpose of the business.

Before they go through the induction session, the new staff member will have read and probably contributed to the manual and will be able to articulate and understand the context of the purpose. Having been through the process they are now in a position to take the next recruit through it and further their own understanding.

Being an Authentic Business

3

LEADERSHIP AND MANAGEMENT

In this chapter I would like to challenge most of the current accepted thinking around leadership and management. Most of the ideas on leadership and management that we have grown up with are inappropriate for business or government today. I make this challenge not as a conclusion but in the spirit of posing a question. Our thoughts around leadership are based on thousands of years of conditioning. They are not the only way, they represent *one* way of doing things, and this chapter is intended to provoke thought and debate about other, potentially more suitable, alternatives for the kind of leadership we need today.

We have been conditioned to see leaders in the individual, the heroic and above all the hierarchical role. This conditioning extends from our image of God to our school teachers and leaves the impression that leadership is about being the individual at the top who takes responsibility for everyone and everything.

We have been conditioned to see leaders in the individual, the heroic and above all the hierarchical role

The problem with hierarchical leadership is that in most situations you do not have the most appropriate leader for the job. Two examples of leaders who are often cited as role models for business are Winston Churchill and Ernest Shackleton. There is no doubt that these two men were courageous individuals who performed spectacular feats of leadership, in defending a nation against a supremely aggressive enemy and in leading a crew to escape the Antarctic ice floes in the face of impossible remoteness and conditions. However, both cases were just about the only situation in which their type of leadership was relevant and neither of them was in business.

In both cases their leadership style could be coercive, rigid, manipulative, isolated and aloof. I do not believe that this sort of behaviour is consistent with authentic leadership. In both cases these leaders were also responding defensively and motivating their people largely from a place of fear: in the case of Shackleton his men feared an icy grave and, in the case of Churchill, it was fear of invasion. For them the fear was largely justified, but it is harder to justify the level of fear perceived by many managers in business today.

The role of a leader is to engage, not coerce; to set free, not control; to inspire, not manipulate; to be integrated, not isolated; to be connected, not aloof. This is especially true as populations become more educated and see through the deceit and sleight of hand that is so often used to control.

Hierarchical leadership is not even healthy for the leader. They bear far too much responsibility for things outside their control and outside their competence. The stress that hierarchical leadership puts on leaders, mentally and physically, creates scars that rarely heal.

Followership
The fundamental weakness of hierarchical leadership is followership. The stronger a hierarchical leader is, the greater the weakness they create in others. By taking responsibility for something, you take it away from someone else, and a person without responsibility reverts to

childhood neediness. The conditioning of our society is to follow and, faced with a strong hierarchical leader, most of us will settle back and let them take responsibility from us.

Just look at what we let our politicians and employers get away with because most of the time we are not prepared to take the responsibility to do something about it. Also, look at your significant relationships – do you take, or give up, responsibility?

Followership is the abdication of responsibility and an open door to exploitation, abuse and extremism

Followership is specifically taught and encouraged in school, religion, the military and business. In schools we are taught to do what we are told by teachers; the main monotheistic religions see God as a supreme being who rules the universe; the military is based on discipline and obedience to orders; and the military model has often been carried over into business. Followership is the abdication of responsibility and an open door to exploitation, abuse and extremism.

For the authentic leader, followership leads to unwanted and unwarranted responsibility. As an authentic leader you need leadership to be distributed so that everyone in your community takes full responsibility for their actions, consequences and requirements, and every member of the community takes responsibly for the co-creation of the vision. In this way energy can flow around the community to where it is most relevant and most needed in the moment.

If you would like to explore leadership in a more physical way, you could have a go at playing the Leadership Game.

The Leadership Game is a football match with three halves:

- In the first half it is every player for themselves.

- In the second half there are two teams, each has a manager (if there are enough people you can even have middle management). The managers and the middle managers decide what happens and no one is allowed to do anything without a specific instruction. The players must abdicate their responsibilities to the leaders. The managers will be instructing their players to score goals.

- In the third half there are two teams without any individual leader. All the players take responsibility for themselves and they coach and support one another, collaborating to achieve their goals.

The analogy of the football team is very pertinent. On the pitch, the captain does not run around telling players when to kick or pass. Leadership flows dynamically around the pitch to where it is most relevant: sometimes it will be the player with the ball; at other times it will be the player near the goal or the one marking another player. In a team, everyone takes responsibility for their role in achieving the stated purpose, and in communicating with and supporting their team-mates.

An authentic leader is part coach, part facilitator, part team-mate, part student. Their goal is for the whole team to be authentic leaders, with no sense of hierarchy, and with explicit and acknowledged areas of strength and weakness.

Management

In most organizations no matter what you do the only promotional goal is to be a manager. Of course there are exceptions, like university professors, but for most organizations, management is the route to promotion and better pay. The conditioning and the propaganda attach an aura of glamour around management so that it appears to be a desirable goal.

So whether you are a designer, an administrator, or a salesperson, your advancement apparently lies in managing others. In most cases people are promoted because of their ability in their craft skill. Managers want to be able to offer talented people something so they don't leave the company and their only option is to give them the responsibility of management which is, of course, what also happened to them. When this happens, it is actually rare for the individual's management abilities to be the deciding factor.

Some companies offer training, but even the best training struggles to overcome a lack of aptitude. It is little wonder that the most common reason given for dissatisfaction at work is a bad relationship with a manager. Ironically, it is not just the managed who are unhappy. The managers, no longer able to practice their craft skill and challenged by the role, are often unhappy, too.

Fundamentally, whatever the aspiration, the job of managers is usually one of getting other people to do what someone else wants them to do. Managers are often the pinch point between the distant directors or trustees and the workforce. They have the difficult job of communicating unpopular decisions that they may not agree with out to the workforce, and unwelcome news that they may not be responsible for up to the board.

Managers are often the pinch point between the distant directors or trustees and the workforce

Enlightened managers turn it into leadership and add in coaching and mentoring roles for themselves, which helps. Unfortunately it does not get them out of the 'piggy in the middle' role, being pulled and pushed from both sides with little real influence on events. Managers rarely have significant flexibility in terms of strategic direction and yet all too often they are left to carry the responsibility when things go wrong. Managers are the organizational fall guys.

Managers exist to patch a structural problem in the design of businesses. As an organization grows and succeeds, the original founders become unwilling and/or unable to lead the organization themselves. This may be because they are entrepreneurial and their skills lie elsewhere, or because they would rather spend time on the golf course. In most cases these organizations are designed as hierarchies and are unable to tolerate the removal or distancing of their head, so the solution most often applied is to insert a manager as a go between, rather than to redesign the business so that it does not need one.

Mostly, managers exist to maintain the illusion of control. Those people who lack the self-confidence to accept that, except for the smallest things and the shortest time frames, life is generally beyond control, comfort themselves with the illusion that they can control events and people. Accepting that life is beyond control allows us to move past the frustration and continual disappointment at our failure to control. Acceptance helps us understand that engagement is a better option. Engagement is a process of connecting with people where it is relevant and valuing their contributions. Once we accept that engagement is the way forward, we can focus our energy on engagement techniques such as inclusion, alignment and inspiration.

Inclusion means involving people in the task in question, where their contribution is relevant. Alignment is the need to check the purpose and the energy of the team members to ensure that plans are aligned with the purpose and people are doing work for which they have energy. Inspiration is the opportunity to ensure that team members are enthused with the overall aim as well as their own responsibilities.

If we can apply this thinking to the way in which we run our organization, and take out the management role, we open up the opportunity for team-led and self-managing organizations that are aligned in their purpose and motivation. We are currently working with this model in a number of our businesses, notably Authentic Guides, and following the example of some of the successful workers' co-operatives such as Suma Wholefoods, Calverts or the huge Mondragon in Spain.

Another way to manage – Suma Wholefoods

Suma is a truly radical, super-ethical workers' co-operative and a multi-million pound company with 120 employees, supplying 3000 customers across the UK and abroad. Suma distributes around 7000 product lines to independent retail shops, supermarkets, institutions, community groups and caterers. Suma manufacture their own products to their designs and have pioneered major new products and categories in the UK, including recycled paper toilet tissues, dairy-free margarines, organics and fair trade. They've also introduced leading environmentally friendly brands like Ecover to the UK. Here is what Suma say about themselves on their Web site:

Suma is, at heart, a political statement that workers can successfully manage their own businesses without an owner/manager elite.

Our philosophy
Suma is an ethical business. Our reputation is our greatest asset. Suma workers can uphold or damage that asset.
    Suma's mission statement is ...
To provide a high quality service to customers and a rewarding working environment for the members, within a sustainable, ethical, co-operative business structure.
To strive to promote a healthier lifestyle by supplying ethical, eco-friendly, vegetarian products.
We practise:
- *Equality of wages for all jobs*
- *Multi-skilling and job variety*
- *Personal development within the company*

- *Ethical business and employer*
- *100% employee-owned and managed*
- *Democratic decision making processes*
- *Equal opportunities*
- *Environment-friendly products*
- *Common ownership*
  (Common ownership means that while the present members control and use the assets of the business, they may not benefit from their liquidation.)

No boss?

We manage the business as far as possible by democratic consensus. The management style and method is therefore highly unusual for the UK but similar to other democratic worker co-ops such as those in the Mondragon federation in Spain.

The General Meeting (GM) of members is the boss. At the shareholders meeting, the GM (which meets six times a year) agrees strategies, business plans and major policy decisions. Any member can make proposals. GM decisions are mandatory on all workers.

The GM elects six of its number to be the Management Committee (MC) which meets weekly to implement the Business Plan and other GM decisions and to advise the GM with, for example, draft business plans for the coming years. MC members are our elected directors.

The MC appoints company officers: Personnel, Operations, Finance and Function Area Co-ordinators (FACs) to implement its decisions and to advise it. Company officers being the executive managers take part in the MC but have no vote. At Suma, the non-executive (elected) directors have the power not the executives. This avoids the executive running the business for its own self-interest.

All of these people are current members. If we lack particular skills we train suitable members to, for example, lead Strategic Planning exercises. The jobs are functions, not status positions. MC members only hold GM-delegated authority when they are meeting.

Company officers only hold authority, e.g. the power to institute disciplinary proceedings, within their remit. No one 'hides behind their suit' at Suma.

The MC monitors the implementation of the Business Plan by the Function Areas. Weekly Business Information covering finances, quality of service and labour productivity indicators are reported to the MC by company officers. The MC issues Action Points where variances from plan occur. These hold GM authority and cannot be ignored.

The MC reports back to GM which, occasionally, flexes its muscle to remind us all who is the boss!

Suma has avoided the Chief Executive bottleneck that restricts the development of most larger businesses. We do not have a single CEO who must somehow cope with an ever larger flow of information, increasingly remote from the production process. Any worker can speak to the MC or any officer or FAC. Any member can put a proposal to a GM. All Weekly Business Information and MC minutes are available to all workers (members are required to read them). All members and most workers use the internal e-mail communication system and lunchtimes freely to discuss the business.

There is complexity of information and decision making flows which lead to a conservative but highly sustainable corporate governance. This, again, is remarkably similar to Mondragon co-ops, and while it can be frustrating for goal-driven people, is undoubtedly part of the secret of our success.

The MC also monitors and acts as the sponsor for major projects such as our 2001 relocation to Elland, which we accomplished over a long weekend in only 75% of the planned time. Now we have settled into our new home, the MC is strategic planning to take Suma into the future. In a typical Suma way, this process started with a whole workforce visioning exercise. The consultant coped well with 100+ participants when such exercises more normally entail a board of directors in a nice hotel over a weekend.

Working at Suma

Working at Suma is quite unlike other businesses. Our workers must be more self-motivated and take more initiative. Suma departmental co-ordinators do not have an overseer role in the normal sense. Workers support each other to fulfil daily tasks and get home on time.

Working as an effective member of a co-operative, not just doing the daily tasks but taking part in the management of the business, is a new skill which all new members have to learn, whether they have been on the shop floor or management previously. The business can only succeed when all members share this responsibility.

We encourage our members to show 'individual initiative within collective responsibility.'

All Suma workers (member, employee or casual) are paid the same daily wage plus allowances and overtime or time in lieu to reduce hours imbalances. It's a good wage for manual warehouse workers and the extra reflects the collective management element of our jobs. Wage costs overall are industry average. We simply share it out fairly.

Other benefits are better than average. (Although the average is catching up.) Maternity leave is six months on full pay. Leave for partners of new mothers is one month on full pay. Members can have unpaid leave of up to 12 months. We don't have job sharing, we have job flexibility.

In return, we expect much more commitment. When the need arises, when customer orders are waiting, we are expected to work until the job is done!

Job variety is important. Drivers will drive for a maximum of three days and then work in the warehouse or office. Office people will do manual work for at least one day a week. Most members will have done a far wider range of jobs and taken on greater responsibilities within Suma than equivalents in other businesses. We encourage members to take up training and courses to bring in new skills.

Multiskilling is the new buzzword in management theory; Suma has been doing it for 25 years. It allows us to use labour and skills more efficiently to cope with the troughs and peaks of business. It enables Suma members to cope with high workloads. It keeps people fresher and enthusiastic for longer and it allows recuperation from stress. Many a Suma member has spent 6 months throwing sacks in the warehouse after leaving a front line, super responsible position and then re-entered the fray in a different job.

Does it work?
Suma has grown consistently since 1974, latterly in a fiercely competitive low-margin market by providing a better service to our customers and better jobs for our workers.

We continue to successfully control and develop the business and seek new and different customers. At Suma, changes are democratically agreed and supported by the membership, not imposed by management and paid for by the workforce.

Many companies say they want new recruits to be good team members. We mean it.

Of course these structures are not appropriate for all businesses, but then hierarchical structures are seldom the optimal solution and yet they are almost universally applied. There are plenty of other choices out there using established models such as co-operatives or inventing a structure that suits your specific purpose. The key is conscious design of appropriate business structures rather than simply applying the norm.

Authentic leadership

A more appropriate role model than Shackleton or Churchill for modern business leadership can be found in Gandhi. Gandhi was not prime minister or president and was not elected to power, and yet he led 700 million people to independence from the most powerful empire the world has ever seen.

Gandhi led through an absolute commitment to the truth, through inspiration and alignment. He was as courageous in facing up to bullying and intimidation as he was humble in his lifestyle. It was Gandhi's absolute authenticity and integrity that inspired so many people in India and, perhaps more surprisingly, in England.

In contrast to Churchill and Shackleton, Gandhi was proactively motivating his people positively towards their independence and was working in a spirit of love, the opposite of fear. The opportunity for authentic leaders is to lead by proactively motivating others towards a shared purpose, not reactively or defensively – even when under attack.

When David Hieatt at clothing company Howies received a letter from lawyers acting for Levi Strauss demanding that they stop selling their jeans and account for all the ones they had sold, he could justifiably have felt that they were under attack. Levi's claim was that Howies had infringed their copyright and that customers might confuse Howies jeans with Levi's jeans since both have a cloth tab on the back pocket with the name of the maker on it.

Howies' response, in keeping with their purpose of 'challenging the way people think about the world we live in' was to require customers to perform a colour blindness test and confirm that they could spell so that they could be sure that customers could tell the difference between Levi's and Howies jeans. They also made a point of telling the media who, loving a good David and Goliath story, spread the news around the world.

Eventually Levi's lawyers had had enough and asked Howies for a private meeting to stop the publicity. Howies readily agreed but asked that they book a large enough room for all of the media who wanted to come. Two years later Howies are still waiting to hear a date for the meeting.

For truly effective and positively world changing leadership there is much that we can learn from Gandhi and Howies about positive, proactive, authentic forms of leadership.

My research has identified these common attributes amongst the best authentic leaders which you can cultivate:

- *Self-knowledge.* Know your values, strengths, weaknesses and limitations so that you can focus your efforts to be effective without wasting energy.

- *Clear, positive purpose.* Clarity of purpose motivates you and inspires others.

- *Integrity.* Strength comes from integrity. You will not inspire anyone who does not trust you.

- *Truth.* Telling the truth is about having the courage to communicate what needs to be said to those who need to hear it.

- *Humility.* Ego will always get in the way of integrity.

- *Inner strength.* Take strength from self-knowledge and not from trinkets, status and sycophancy.

- *Intuition.* The emotional connection you have with your purpose will enable you to be guided by your intuition.

- *Connection.* You never know where your most profound lessons will come from; have the courage to connect with everyone.

- *Trust.* If you do not trust others you cannot expect them to trust you.

There are also some attributes that an authentic leader is without.

- *Fear.* Fear leads to controlling behaviour that will limit the possibilities of any enterprise (fear is different from caution – fear is generated by a lack of confidence to deal with what may lie ahead; caution is the act of taking care and minimizing risks).

- *Insecurity.* In order to trust others, we must first trust ourselves.

- *Ego.* Ego is the shield we have built up to protect our 'self' from the world – you cannot deeply connect with others through your ego.

My own greatest experience of leadership was when I started work at chbi which went on to become Razorfish – one of the Internet consultancies that flourished in the dot com boom. I was the sixteenth employee in at chbi, a company founded by Mark Curtis and Mike Beeston (the 'c' and the 'b').

Mark and Mike trusted me. I realize now that it was my first experience of an 'authority figure' trusting me and the difference it has made to my life is profound. That trust enabled me to explore and grow and to follow the path that I have. I am profoundly grateful to Mark and Mike for their love and trust.

A critical moment for me was when I went to Mike with an idea to create a strategy service for our clients. Up to that time we focused mainly on Web design and technology, and I was responsible for new business development. I told Mike that if we wanted to move further up the food chain with our clients we needed to have a strategic offering. I knew that this had significant implications for what was by then an office of 40 people in a company of 200 with offices in New York, Stockholm, Hamburg, Helsinki and London.

I was expecting Mike to ask for the business case. Instead he asked if I believed in it. I said that I did. Mike replied, 'well, you better go and do it then'. So I did. Two years later we had 100 strategists in 13 offices and 8 countries, and I was responsible for all of those in Europe.

My own experience of management and leadership probably started when I was racing cars at 21. We had a small team with very little money and we worked collaboratively to get the car ready to race.

A few years later I was asked to manage a small exhibition company; again there was very little cash and we relied heavily on our staff wanting to participate. Leadership had to be very participative and ensure that the whole experience was enjoyable enough for people to stay with us in spite of the challenging and inauthentic business we were in.

The next experience was managing a small sales team within a larger company. Here I had far less influence over other aspects of people's working lives and the role was a constant battle to keep the sales team, and myself, motivated.

Then came Razorfish. With a team of highly intelligent people you cannot possibly take any type of controlling role in the relationship; the role of leader is very much one of service. In this situation the leader's role is simply to provide all that is necessary to enable the team to perform at their best.

It was at Razorfish that I first started to work with authenticity, specifically in a course that we ran called Authentic Leadership. The principle of this was that all of the team members should be leaders so that they could provide leadership for our clients in the uncertain times of the dot com boom.

As the market disappeared, the business started to disintegrate and the leadership of the company were memorably described as having 'gone limbic' – meaning that they were using only the limbic part of their brain, the part used in 'fight or flight' mode. For those with responsibility for numbers of people this was a very difficult time and many people struggled to cope with the stress it created for them.

Post-Razorfish I have been developing my understanding of non-hierarchical authentic leadership and applying it in the work we do with the Authentic Partnership (see Chapter 4, p. 138).

SUPPLIERS

Modern business practice often uses suppliers as short-term profit margin enhancement opportunities. The basic model for big business is to drive out competition, both by lowering prices and by promoting the idea that low prices are a good thing. Think about the way your local supermarket has driven independent local shops out of business. Their ability to lower prices is achieved not by real efficiencies but by screwing down suppliers, and very often quality, with the ironic side effect that it not only drives out competition for the business, but also competition among its own suppliers.

Supermarkets are so 'good' at negotiating cheap prices that they have created significant consolidation in their supply chain. This means that, in some areas, they are getting to the point where they have seriously limited their choices of suppliers. It seems likely that the supermarkets' drive for the lowest possible supply prices will soon create a sellers' market for some products and commodities, where limited choice of suppliers will push prices up again.

Authentic businesses work with their suppliers, supporting them in the short term for mutual long-term gain. I see this again and again in the businesses I work with. One simple measure is that I have never had a bad debt with any of my authentic clients, and many of them even pay before the invoice is due. I never find myself chasing payment from authentic clients.

Businesses like Yeo Valley Organics, Doves Farm, Howies and Hug work with their suppliers in a 'fair trade' way. Yeo Valley went as far as setting up the Organic Milk Suppliers Co-operative; Doves Farm is a founding member of Ethical Trade, an initiative of the Soil Association to promote fair trade practices when dealing with UK-based suppliers. Howies and Hug both ensure that their clothes are made in 'happy' factories that contribute to their communities.

Authentic businesses work with their suppliers, supporting them in the short term for mutual long-term gain

Another sound business reason for supporting suppliers is that this enables them to support you. During the recession in 1989 Neal's Yard Remedies were, like many other businesses, having a hard time. Their suppliers helped them through by extending payment times. The suppliers did this because they trusted Neal's Yard and its founder, Romy Fraser. Romy had always made a point of paying a fair price and paying on time when business was good. When cash was tight, the trust remained, and the suppliers were prepared to wait.

By contrast, an inauthentic company I worked for years ago hired a new production manager because he claimed he could save the company £1 million. He came in, did some hard bargaining with the suppliers, and he did indeed save £1 million in a year. However the cost of that saving quickly became apparent. Suppliers who had previously pushed deadlines and gone the extra mile no longer would. New, cheaper suppliers made more mistakes, and quality was impaired. The million pounds had certainly been shaved off the supplier costs, but had simply shifted elsewhere into compensations paid for mistakes, recruitment costs to replace overworked staff, courier costs to mitigate late deliveries and so on. In the current 'rational' world of businesses seeking to maximize their wealth redistribution the apparent million pound saving seems to be the right thing to do.

Michael Marriage at Doves Farm speaks earnestly when he explains a situation where they had contracted a number of farmers to grow a fairly specialized type of grain. Some unfortunate weather meant that the crop was not suitable for the purpose intended and did not fulfil the specifications on the contract. Doves Farm would have been legally within their rights to reject the entire crop. As an authentic business Doves Farm valued their relationship with the suppliers more highly than that and went to considerable trouble to find another buyer for the crop. This sort of action creates a strong bond between supplier and buyer and creates a relationship where mutual care is taken, service is given, and results are good.

This is exactly the sort of intuitive decision making that occurs in authentic businesses, where the decision makers have an emotional connection with what they do and the opportunity exists to take a balanced decision, which looks to the long-term and wider consequences as well as the short-term and immediate effects.

For authentic businesses the ideal supplier relationship is one of true partnership, where interests are aligned and outcomes are shared. Whether you choose to do this by actually including suppliers as partners in the business or through a contract designed to create a partnership is optional. The main thing is to start with open discussions where purpose and objectives are discussed and can be aligned.

Supplier and buyer have the opportunity to create an arrangement where both can achieve their authentic purpose and share in the risk and reward of the enterprise. Of course risk-sharing contracts are not unique to authentic businesses. The difference is in the intent and the integrity of the negotiation. In a negotiation between authentic businesses both parties are positively and openly seeking to win/win/win (I win/you win/wider society wins) rather than negotiating with hidden agendas and win/lose intentions.

To practice win/win/win negotiation, you need to be clear about your own purpose and to be dealing with a supplier who shares that purpose. You will both benefit from being open about what you need from the arrangement as well as what you want. You may be prepared to compromise on what you want, but not on what you need. You will also benefit from thinking about the long term even if the specific contract is only a one-off.

STAFF AND PERSONAL DEVELOPMENT

Employing staff, by definition, creates a relationship with tension. Good companies mitigate this tension as much as they can with integrity and opportunity – they trust and are trusted by their staff, and support them in their own personal development; bad companies magnify the tension through poor management and greed. If you need to employ people, it is worth being aware of this tension so that you can take steps to mitigate it.

The tension is created by the recruitment process and through the potential transfer of responsibility for the individual's livelihood. In the recruitment process, a hierarchy is established where one party decides if another is good enough to join or not. Whether it is declared or not, the employer takes responsibility for the income and livelihood of the employee. This implicit transfer of responsibility creates an unhealthy level of dependency on the one hand and power on the other – power which is often used to control, coerce and intimidate the individual in subtle and not-so-subtle ways. Here I refer to the subtle pressures that see people working late when they would rather not, and the less subtle pressure when someone is asked to relocate to another city or country with the implicit threat that it will be 'bad for their career' if they decline.

The tension is no healthier when it is the other way around – where a business feels itself to be over-reliant on an individual and burdens them with unreasonable expectations and responsibilities. This is one of the factors that can lead to drug taking in professional sport, when an athlete feels an unhealthy level of responsibility for the performance of the team, for example.

Another example is that at the height of the UK post-war consensus in the 1960s and 1970s, unions attempted to reverse the tension through collective bargaining and striking. Although conditions did improve in many ways, this power too was open to abuse and damaged many businesses and industries. In the 1980s, the Thatcher government declined to invest in railways, which they saw as being held hostage by militant unions. Today we live, and in some cases die, with the legacy of years of chronic under-investment in the railways.

To avoid this tension we need to conceive different ways of engaging people to collaborate in the achievement of our objectives. Once again the key words are alignment and partnership, engaging equal participants around a common purpose. If, as businesses, we can be explicit about our purpose, we have the opportunity of engaging with others who share our purpose. This cannot be achieved in an environment of fear. All parties need to feel free to express their feelings and opinions so that the deal that is arranged is based in truth, and does not create tension for either party.

Although it will not seem practical from the mindset of control, the opportunity lies in creating an open, self-managing relationship geared towards a common goal. Instead of employees, you may be able to create a semi-freelance, flexible arrangement.

The prime criteria is to only work with people where their energy is aligned to the purpose of your business. Secondly, the relationship needs to be one of balanced interdependence. Pay is based on over-all results, individual commitment and energy. The monogamy of employment that leads to overdependence is replaced by the opportunity for people to make up income and fill in downtime with other employers or activities.

A flexible pool of collaborators that expands in times of intense activity and declines in times of scarcity can mitigate the tendency that many businesses have to chase commercial growth simply because of headcount creep.

... the opportunity lies in creating an open, self-managing relationship geared towards a common goal

These permanent and flexible employees are arranged in dynamic, self-managing teams tasked with delivering their aspect of the overall project in whatever way they see fit. Governance is achieved through excellent communication between teams, which support and challenge each other to deliver on their targets and objectives. All of the teams have representatives who meet each other regularly to co-ordinate the overall project.

Clearly, honesty and excellent communications are vital for this type of organizational structure to exist, both of which can be hard to find in our damaged society. This is probably one of the reasons why control-based forms of organization are so popular. However, with authentic businesses, it is possible to go far beyond the compromised structure we have become used to. I do not believe that dishonesty, greed, aggression and closed behaviour are part of human nature, but that they are a natural response to the unnatural environment we find ourselves in all too often. Ironically, the evidence for this often comes out in the worst situations, where people often seem to pull together selflessly in the face of disaster.

Personal development

Personal development is a double-edged sword for businesses that are not authentic. It has become fashionable to believe that staff should be confident and self-aware to maximize their potential contribution to the business. It is certainly true that people will achieve more with self-confidence and self-awareness. However, my experience of doing this work in inauthentic businesses is that when you run these wonderful sessions, the best people leave the company. What happens is that through the training session they are opened up to their potential and to different levels of expectation for their life. When they go back to work after the training session, the disconnection becomes clear and they find themselves with the confidence to do something about it.

For an authentic business, where the purpose of the business and the purpose of the individual are aligned, and where they are already treated with respect and integrity, personal development of team members is a massive opportunity.

No competitive sports team would consider existing without a coach to help its members develop their craft skills, their team playing and their potential. So why do so many businesses imagine that they can be successful without coaching for the team?

Craft skills, such as selling or presenting, are usually better catered for than team development or personal potential. Ironically, this is where the real opportunities for growth lie.

Team building fashions have evolved from the 'outward bound'-style events of the 1980s to more competitive activities in the 1990s. These are often good fun and, if done well, can create a sense of a team, but it is usually temporary and not necessarily with the right people. Another way of building teams and achieving significant and direct results is to organize work rather differently.

Instead of work being largely about individual effort with the occasional get-together, the potential exists to do it the other way around. For example, make Monday a day of team working (without phones or e-mail) – resolving issues, identifying opportunities, sharing learning and supporting each other together. Then spend the rest of the week carrying out the actions agreed. Working in this way, a business can integrate the development of personal potential and team-building with a better way of running day-to-day business.

MEETING IN OPEN SPACE

For years I have been dissatisfied with the format of the standard internal business meeting. Specifically I am talking about team meetings, board meetings and company meetings. All too often they are used as opportunities for showboating, politics and bitching. They are seldom used as a forum for creativity, solutions and progress.

For years I tried to find or invent a model for business meetings that was about enabling and energizing, practicality and progress. The answer came when I was invited to a meeting that was held in 'Open Space.'

Open Space is a way of organizing meetings devised by Harrison Owen. Owen was working as a conference organizer when he realized that the part of the conference that delegates found most useful was the coffee breaks. He determined to design a conference that was mostly coffee breaks. Open Space, as he called it, is now an established way of running meetings of all sizes and for most purposes. We use Open Space for many Authentic Guides meetings and it is very effective where you are seeking to develop any complex and multifaceted project.

Harrison Owen's own description of how to run an Open Space meeting in his book *Open Space Technology* refers to conferences. I have adjusted my description based on my own experience of running Open

Space meetings for a day or less with between 10 and 100 people. The Open Space format does not suit everyone; you are likely to struggle with it if a sense of control is important to you.

Requirements

The Open Space needs to be held in a room that will allow all participants to sit in a circle. For larger numbers of people you may want to have concentric circles. The introduction session can become unmanageable if there are too many people (over 100), although Open Space itself works well with thousands.

The venue will need several break-out spaces. In general you need the facility for the number of sessions to be equivalent to half the number of participants. So if you are expecting 40 people you will want to be able to offer 20 sessions which could be four time slots in five locations or five time slots in four locations. You will need to create a matrix of these locations and time slots on a wall or board in the main room with the time slots on one axis and locations on the other. You will need to decide how long the time slots should be to fit in with the time you have available and allowing for lunch and coffee breaks.

You will also need to provide paper and pens for people to record their sessions.

Introductions

Before the meeting starts, while waiting for everyone to arrive, I like to encourage people to talk to those they do not already know to aid the introduction process. The ideal start to an Open Space meeting is for everyone to sit in a circle and to introduce themselves to each other, explaining who they are, what they have to offer the group, and what they would like to get from the meeting. Even if everyone knows each other already, this check-in is useful to engage everyone with the meeting.

Context setting

Although it is not strictly part of Open Space, I have found it extremely useful to follow the introductions with some form of context setting, inspiration or focusing process. This could take the form of breaking out into smaller groups to look at things 'we' want to start, stop and encourage. It could take the form of a presentation, meditation, reading, or another relevant stimulus, depending on the overall objective of the meeting.

This is also the time when the four principles of Open Space are introduced:

- Whoever comes are the right people.

- Whatever happens is the only thing that could have.

- Whenever it starts is the right time.

- When it's over, it's over.

There is only one law: the law of two feet which says that 'if during the course of the gathering any person finds him or herself in a situation where they are neither learning nor contributing they must use their two feet and go to some more productive place.'

This law allows people to play different roles in the meeting such as the bumblebee and the butterfly. Bumblebees buzz between groups cross-pollinating ideas, and butterflies appear not to participate at all by sitting in the canteen or out in the sun. However, every so often someone will pass by and may engage them in conversation – and when that happens it is usually significant, according to Harrison Owen.

Agenda setting

Now we get down to the nitty-gritty. The agenda setting is the space where all of the participants have the opportunity to contribute what they feel is important to the agenda. Everyone is invited to convene one or more sessions with the implicit responsibility that they will ensure it is hosted and that notes are taken. They do not have to do this themselves if they do not want to, but they must make sure it is done.

Those who want to propose a session write a brief description on a sheet of paper and then announce the name and nature of the session to the whole group. They then place the sheet on the prepared matrix that shows the time slots and locations in which sessions will be held.

Once everyone who wants to has had the chance to offer a session there may be a little trading as session conveners agree to merge sessions that are similar. Then the participants can review the board and sign up for the sessions they want to participate in by writing their name on the relevant sheet of paper. Of course, this commitment does not hold them to participation in that session. It just gives others an indication of the popularity of a session.

Open Space

Once the agenda is set, the participants go into self-managing mode – it is usually worth telling them this, otherwise it is amazing how many people wait to be told that one session has finished and another has begun.

Participants can go to the session that they signed up for and keep managing themselves until the end of the last session. Sometimes it is also useful to bring people back to the group in the middle of the day for the opportunity to offer new sessions or revise existing ones.

Reporting back

Once the last session is completed the full group reconvenes in the circle to hear a report of each session. Each convener gives a brief summary of the events of their meeting and, if relevant, lists action points. They may also invite participants to opt in to further involvement in any project that has arisen.

Closing circle

To close the session down everyone has the opportunity to express any reflections on the day to the whole group.

The beauty of Open Space is that it is an entirely inclusive and participative approach to meetings and management. Participants are encouraged to focus where their energy lies. People who have energy for projects populate those that come out of the Open Space. What gets discussed are the things which are important to the people who are there on the day and nothing that the participants feel is important is missed out.

SALES AND MARKETING

One of the common characteristics of authentic businesses seems to be that they spend relatively little money on advertising. Even the larger authentic consumer brands like innocent, Yeo Valley Organics, Doves Farm and Neal's Yard seem to spend less on marketing than their inauthentic counterparts. Authentic businesses have the advantage of their purpose as a uniting message to communicate to their customers: a message that can appeal to consumer's hearts rather than their wallets and does not attempt to brainwash their heads.

Many authentic businesses rely heavily on word of mouth to promote their offer. This works well because customers tend to be highly aligned with the purpose of the business – you might even call them fans – and the integrity between the product and the purpose means that customers are very keen to tell others about the company.

Many authentic businesses rely heavily on word of mouth to promote their offer

In contrast to more mainstream marketing theory, which often uses low prices to appeal to the broadest possible audience, this is more about appealing strongly to a more focused audience and building up deep brand loyalty.

Howies key marketing tools are their catalogue and their 'believers'. The catalogue is an inspirational piece of brand communication and product marketing. If you haven't seen it, it's worth getting one just to see how well a brand can be communicated. The Howies catalogue has a conversion to sale rate of 20% compared with an average of 1–2% for clothing catalogues. The 'believers' are retailers who not only buy the products, but support the philosophy too.

Using your purpose as the key message

Businesses that can articulate their profound and positive purpose can make use of it as the mainstay of their marketing, and there may well be opportunities to develop specific campaigns around different aspects of the message.

Working with your core purpose, you can create different campaigns that will resonate with your target market. The Body Shop quickly built a very high profile through campaigns such as 'Against Animal Testing' that resonated with a significant group of consumers revolted by the exploitation of animals in the cosmetics industry and delivered on their overall purpose.

In a similar way, a business focused on reducing waste might campaign around reuse and recycling, or a business focused on renewable energy might campaign around reducing carbon emissions.

Triodos Bank, for example, exists to support ethical, environmental and cultural projects. Each year Triodos Bank publish their booklet *Inspiring Change*. The booklet contains a brief, inspiring story about every organization and project they lend money to. The booklet also conveys Triodos Bank's value of transparency and helps build a bond of trust with customers.

One of the fundamental advantages of authentic businesses is their opportunity to engage their consumers and customers in their purpose. Where other businesses resort to ego pampering or greed as their primary marketing message, an authentic business can truly connect with its customers.

The model is to take the overall purpose and to distil from it a consumer-friendly campaign. Doves Farm are in business to promote healthy eating, and they produce and distribute 100,000 copies of their own recipe book. The book explains the health benefits of organic eating and suggests ways of preparing healthy food, including using various types of flour – their staple product.

One of the fundamental advantages of authentic businesses is their opportunity to engage their consumers and customers in their purpose

Engaging supporters

When you do need to create a marketing strategy for your authentic business these are better created in collaboration than in isolation. Here is a design for a marketing workshop based on my experience of running them over the years. It takes about half a day and ideally it involves your team plus any marketing/communications agencies you may use.

Once you have made your introductions and the overall objectives of the project have been shared, the team can start by establishing criteria on a flip chart or similar. The sort of things you are looking for are:

- *Basic parameters*
    - Define the audience.
    - Can you fulfil demand generated?
    - Are there additional resources required to deliver the campaign?
    - Knowledge of the performance of existing marketing methods.

    The basic criteria are intended to help to focus the thinking on things that are doable and relevant.

- *Evaluation criteria*
    - How much does the message resonate with the audience?
    - How much does it deliver on your purpose?
    - How much does the campaign deliver on business needs?
    - How passionate does the team feel about the campaign?
    - How clear is the message?
    - How compelled to act does it make you feel?

    You will use the evaluation criteria to score your ideas later on, to focus them down to a short list.

With parameters and criteria agreed, the team can move on to brainstorm potential ideas for the campaign. The brainstorm is intended to generate a mass of ideas; at this stage, quality is not as important as quantity. The important rule of brainstorming is not to evaluate any ideas during the process as this limits people's willingness to explore. Be expansive and creative first; evaluate and narrow down later.

Warm up

Before you start the brainstorming it is important to stimulate the team in some relevant way. This may be a presentation of some sort, a discussion, a short film, a reading, or it may take the form of getting the team to work together in small groups to develop something that they then present back. If it is not a new business, it is worth including a review of experience with other marketing methods.

Brainstorming

There are all sorts of established methods of brainstorming you can experiment with. You can choose the one that works best with your team and style of business. Examples include:

- *Open.* A facilitator encourages the group to call out ideas and captures them in a list on a flip chart.

- *Discrete.* Every participant has a stack of sticky notes and a facilitator asks them to write ideas, and offers questions and challenges to stimulate.

- *Mind Map®.* A facilitator captures ideas in a Mind Map that shows relationships between ideas.

Evaluation

Now it is time to go back through the mass of ideas to take out duplicates and evaluate the remainder. Once any duplicates are removed, the team can review the remaining ideas and each member can score them out of ten against the criteria established at the beginning.

The first step is to narrow the ideas down to a shortlist of three or four key concepts. The team then breaks out in small groups to work up the shortlisted ideas into some kind of articulation or presentation, being conscious of the established evaluation criteria on which they will be judged.

The team can then reconvene to consider the various articulations. It is important to ensure that they are all presented to a roughly equal standard so that it is the quality of the idea, not the articulation, on which the concept is judged. It is also worth checking that the articulations are sufficiently different, and if any of the ideas can be merged.

Validation

It is now time to expand the evaluation group. This may be a case of bringing other members of the company in, dragging friends in or inviting real or potential customers.

You then go back through the evaluation scoring process to see which ideas are the most popular and achieve the highest score against the criteria given.

At the end of this process you will have one or two ideas clearly articulated that can be turned into a brief that explains the objective, the mechanisms and how performance will be measured. The next task is to work out how it will be delivered, to what extent it is an internal project and how much external help will be required.

Action

The next step is to put together a project team who will be responsible for making it happen, including external suppliers if necessary. From my own experience, better results are generally achieved by fully engaging with a group of independent, freelance suppliers than with an established agency. Although the agency will give the impression that it will require less of your time to get what you want, this is rarely true in the end. The freelancers will feel less need to rip up all of the work you have done previously in order to make their mark on the project.

Once you have identified your team, one way to get them started and optimize results is to co-locate them with a facilitator to manage the agenda for a few days. Preferably this will be somewhere away from the office so that they can focus on establishing themselves as a team and get stuck in to the project.

Being the brand

Simply being the brand is a vital part of the communication of your offer and of building relationships with people once the initial introduction is made. By this stage you will have a clear articulation of the brand, purpose and values of your business. You will also have a workforce who are fully aligned and living the brand.

The greatest opportunities lie where there is the maximum congruence in the business; the areas where the qualities of the brand are most obvious. All communications have embedded in them the energetic qualities with which they are created. Any discontinuity or lack of integrity about the business will be communicated, explicitly or implicitly. The more we can live our brand and walk our talk, the more compelling our message will be.

Alastair Sawday has green blood. He has been a Green Party candidate, published an environmental newsletter and is a director of the Soil Association, which accredits organic farms and products. Alastair founded Alastair Sawday Publishing in 1994 with the first of his *Special Places to Stay* books and has subsequently published the influential *Fragile Earth* series of books. For years Alastair had been cautious about his eco-ambitions at work, not wishing to push them on people. At their annual gathering in 2003 Alastair told the whole company of his dream that Alastair Sawday Publishing could be a 'beacon green business'.

The effect of this has been energizing and has galvanized the whole team. The company has relocated to converted barns now reused as offices. The new premises have been converted to the highest environmental standards, with high levels of insulation and natural ventilation, low-energy electrical appliances and automated switching wherever possible. The new office is also more easily accessible by bicycle than the previous one.

As well as their day jobs, every member of the company is also in one of three ideologically led teams.

- *The Green Team* – who actively focus on minimizing the environmental footprint of the company and measure their progress with an environmental audit. The Green Team are constantly looking for ways to reduce consumption of natural resources and minimize pollution generated by the business. This includes initiatives such as printing books on recycled paper and running cars on biodiesel (vegetable oil).

- *The Better Business Team* – who look at the ethical aspects of the business so that they can optimize the social impact of the company. The team work on creating their own best practice for paternity and maternity leave, and devise initiatives such as offering all staff six counselling sessions per year.

- *The Trust Team* – who look to the wider social impact of the business and work out how best to spend the business's own £5000 charity budget, as well as working with the Greater Bristol Foundation to raise more money for causes they believe in.

The results of this way of working and the integrity that it creates within the business are impressive. It has added a new dimension to the workplace and has further engaged all members of staff in their regular work in the business. It gives everyone greater meaning and satisfaction in their work. There is virtually zero staff turnover in a company of over 30 people.

The business enjoys a very low level of management input in its day-to-day running, there are very low levels of office politics and each employee has an average of 2 or 3 sick days per year, compared to a national average of 11. All of this is certainly aided by a management approach that is based on affection and respect for all members of staff and a recruitment approach that focuses on shared ideology and culture.

In a wider context the business sells 120,000 of its beautiful *Special Places to Stay* books per year and has hundreds of hotels and bed & breakfasts (B&Bs) on a waiting list to pay to be listed in the books. Alastair Sawday Publishing is one of the most profitable specialist publishing businesses in the UK and benefits from enormous support from readers and owners. It is very common for readers to recruit new B&Bs or hotels, for hotel and B&B owners to recruit readers and for readers and owners to recruit other readers and owners.

Alastair Sawday is supported every day by its customers and by many journalists who are fans in their private lives. Journalists often take opportunities to write about special places they have stayed and the guide books that helped them to find them. This combination means that Alastair Sawday Publishing achieve their sales on a marketing budget of only £50,000 per year.

Alastair Sawday Publishing have even been able to influence the owners of the 'special places' to participate in their own ideological campaigns such as the Fine Breakfast, where they have encouraged 250 out of 700 British B&Bs to sign up to providing organic and local breakfasts.

All of these benefits are available to any authentic businesses who are prepared to consciously work with their purpose and their integrity. The key facets are:

- *Integrity* – constant focus on creating a culture of integrity with purpose.

- *Inclusiveness* – engaging the whole team and even customers and suppliers with the purpose.

- *Imagination* – being creative about how you apply your purpose to all aspects of the business.

FINANCE AND ACCOUNTING

Sustainability isn't just about having a positive social and environmental impact. It is also about feeding yourself. In business terms, this means generating enough income to survive and achieve your objectives. At its most basic level, this means not spending more than you receive. However, this is too simplistic to be useful – it is far more common for businesses to fail due to cash flow difficulties than from a fundamental lack of profitability.

Understanding money

Money is love, money is energy and money is life-blood. Far too much of our conception of money is negative and associated with greed, selfishness and scarcity. We are liberated if we can shift our conception around money to seeing it more positively as an enabling tool which, used in the right way, transforms lives. It is attitudes and mindsets that are greedy and selfish, not money.

The idea that money is scarce is a myth. Banks create money. Of the money in circulation in the UK, 97% has been lent into existence by banks – only 3% has been actually minted by the government (source: *The Little Money Book* by David Boyle, a really excellent introduction to the reality of money in our society). Inflation is a measure of the speed with which banks are creating money. The way banks create money is simple: when you ask your bank for a mortgage or a secured loan the bank uses the security of your property to create cash, which they then lend to you and charge you interest for the privilege. The idea that banks lend money which comes in from savers is not the whole story.

Not only do banks ask small businesses to offer security for loans, they also charge them far more interest, because they are deemed to be more 'risky'. For a £929,000 loan a small business will be charged £299,000 in interest while a FTSE 100 firm will be charged £153,000. The small business will work 117 days for that, while a FTSE 100 firm will work 60 days for the same borrowing (source: Ivan Favennec).

Of the money in circulation in the UK, 97% has been lent into existence by banks – only 3% has been actually minted by the government

Banks understand the abundant nature of money, and we too can apply abundant thinking to our finances by understanding that if we do the right thing, the money and energy will follow. As with everything else, money still needs to be treated with respect, used with wisdom and managed with care.

Understanding finance

If you are feeling intimidated by this section because you don't think you understand financial issues, that is probably a very good reason for reading it carefully.

As someone who wants to maintain the authenticity of a business, it is vital that you are willing and able to understand the finances that underpin it. Most accountants and finance directors have absolute rationality and logic underpinning their decisions, recommendations and ideas. If they are not utterly committed to the authentic ideology of the business, and in touch with their authentic selves, their contributions are likely to be based on their financial focus rather than on the purpose of the business.

By being fully up-to-speed with your understanding of the finances of the business, you will be able to understand the financial arguments and come up with compelling ideas that will deliver on both the financial and ideological bottom line.

The fundamental rule of business financial management is to know where you are across key measures and to understand what to do about it if anything goes awry. Conventional management accounts are always retrospective and do very little to inform those responsible for the business where they should be focusing their effort for maximum benefit.

Financial plumbing

Ivan Favennec is an Authentic Guide and a numerical magician who turns money into water and water into money so that it is transparent to CEOs, chairmen, directors and business managers who would rather focus on business than accounts. When he showed me how it worked I was blown away by its potential to make running a small to medium-sized business way, way easier and more effective.

In 2002, Ivan calculated his Golden Ratios – the key metrics and ratios of the FTSE 100 companies, so that you can make direct and daily comparisons with the performance of your own business. These ratios are not perfect for every business, as all businesses are different. They are intended only as a baseline from which to judge what is most suitable for your business. For example, a service business is likely to have far lower levels of current assets than a retail business and this is entirely appropriate.

Ivan's Golden Ratios for comparison are as follows.

From the balance sheet
The balance sheet describes the value of the various different types of liabilities (what you owe) and assets (what you

own) of a business. It is called a balance sheet because overall, assets and liabilities should be equal to one another. The total funds put into a business and the total value of the things that a business owns should come to the same figure.

Total assets = fixed assets + current assets

Total liabilities = long-term liabilities + current liabilities
+ shareholder funds

Liabilities or debts (what you owe)
Businesses use a variety of methods to pay for their purchases of assets and perhaps to finance their start-up costs.

The three basic categories of debt and their Golden Ratios are:

- *Shareholders' funds – 46% of total assets.* The money owed to the shareholders (the owners) of the business – this represents the amount they have put into the business plus the accumulated historic profit they have not yet taken out.

- *Long-term liabilities – 22% of total assets.* All debts due after more than a year, such as bank loans and mortgages.

- *Current liabilities – 32% of total assets.* All debts due within a year, such as overdrafts and money owed to suppliers. Of course, most businesses are not exactly comparable to those in the FTSE 100, but this gives an approximate benchmark, and highlights the fundamental point that an imbalance between what you owe and what you own can lead to difficulties.
  For example, an excess of current liabilities (debt) can mean that when the creditors (the people you owe the money to)

need to be paid, there is not enough cash to pay them. An excess of long-term debt may mean you are paying too much in interest and that you are effectively working for the bank.

Assets (what you own)

A business uses the various forms of borrowing above to finance the purchase of assets, amongst other things.

The two basic asset categories and their Golden Ratios are:

- *Fixed assets – 59% of total assets.* Fixed assets need to be maintained for the running of the business, and are most likely to be property, but can include the brand, machinery and equipment.

- *Current assets – 41% of total assets.* Current assets flow in and out of the business on a daily basis – they are likely to be mainly stock, debtors (those who owe money to you) and cash in the bank. This split is about whether the business has an appropriate level of stock and debtors. Too much in the way of current assets may show that stock levels are too high and that borrowing could be reduced. Low levels of current assets might indicate that the assets are being underutilized.

From the profit and loss account

The profit and loss (P&L) account shows how the business has traded for the period. It shows how much has been spent and how much has been earned.

The three main headings for spending in the P&L account and their Golden Ratios are:

- *Cost of sales – 66% of sales turnover (total sales).* Costs that are directly linked to sales – such as cost of marketing, manufacturing or buying goods for resale.

- *Fixed overheads – 20% of sales turnover.* Money spent on maintaining the business infrastructure that is not related directly to sales, such as rent, utilities and monthly administrative costs.

- *Earnings before interest and tax (EBIT) – 14% of sales turnover.* The money that is left over after cost of sales and fixed overheads are deducted from total income. Clearly there is little harm in having higher earnings, but having fixed overheads that are too high may mean that your business is unable to respond easily and quickly to changes in the market.

Percentage returns

The figures that really clarify the health of a business are the percentages and ratios that show how the business is performing.

The main measures of this and their Golden Ratios are:

- *Capital employed (CE) – 68% of total liabilities.* CE is the combination of shareholder investment and long-term loans.

- *Return on capital employed (ROCE) – 20.91% of the capital employed by the business.* ROCE looks at the liabilities side (what you owe) and is calculated like this:

ROCE = EBIT ÷ CE

Return on capital employed gives you a clear picture of how efficiently you are using the financial resources that you have available to you. Authentic businesses, with their fundamental advantages in decision-making, motivation and support from outside the company, have the opportunity to be highly efficient in their use of financial resources.

So, with this Golden Ratio, £100 invested as loans and shares would see a return of £20.91 on top of your initial investment at the end of a year, before interest and taxes had been paid.

A ROCE that is too low may indicate an inefficient use of resources and that you could evaluate capital spending and assets for their contribution. Assets that are performing less well may need some additional attention.

- *Return on total assets (ROTA) – 14.22% of total assets.* ROTA looks at the assets side (what you own) and is calculated like this:

ROTA = EBIT ÷ total assets

Return on total assets helps you to understand how efficiently the business is running as a whole. The higher the figure, the more efficiently the business is converting total assets into profit.

Break-even
Break-even for a business is critical. The break-even point is the one where you have met all your fixed and variable operating costs and can start making profits.

The break-even point can be calculated by multiplying overheads by sales and dividing the result by gross profit:

(Overheads × total sales) ÷ gross profit

Gross profit = sales − cost of sales

Overheads = cost of sales + fixed overheads

This will give you your break-even point. If you then divide that figure by total sales and multiply by 100 you will have your break-even percentage.

Ivan likes to graphically illustrate what the break-even percentage actually means by showing you what day in the year you will start making a profit from (see Table 3.1).

Table 3.1 Number of days left to make a profit in the year (starting 1st January)

Break-even %	Break-even date	Break-even days left in the year
60%	7 August	(146 days left …)
70%	12 September	(110 days left …)
75%	30 September	(90 days left …)
80%	19 October	(73 days left …)
85%	6 October	(55 days left …)
90%	25 November	(36 days left …)
95%	13 December	(18 days left …)

These include Bank Holidays, Saturdays and Sundays!

Debt

Except for public companies, where lack of debt can put a company at risk of hostile takeover, debt is an unproductive cost for a business, and sets back your break-even point.

There are, of course, times when debt is necessary in funding growth or funding sales, but debt carries costs as well as risks; the greater the risk perceived by the lenders, the higher the cost of the debt. For an authentic business existing in an inauthentic business world, the maximum degree of autonomy and flexibility is desirable. The more you owe, the more you pay in interest, and the more risk there is of creditors seeking elements of control of the business.

The horror stories of the late 1980s where banks called in debts at short notice and sold off assets for a fraction of their value may seem a long time ago, but a repeat is only a downturn away. Banks are heavily committed to their borrowers. According to the Bank of England, consumer credit in the UK topped £1 trillion in July 2004. Banks have good reasons to be very nervous when there is large-scale defaulting on debts, and their reaction is to secure whatever they can as quickly as possible. Paradoxically they are always likely to call in small debts first, partly because it is easier, and partly because with larger debts it may be perceived to be worth waiting for an upturn.

Debts are also expensive, and significant interest-bearing debts reduce the amount you have available to spend on or invest in your purpose. As explained in 'Funding' (see p. 57), there are alternatives to debt, and LLPs may be an effective way for you to fund your business and secure alignment between funding and purpose. By going into partnership with your funders you can link repayment to performance so that you are not locked into unaffordable costs.

EXIT STRATEGIES AND PARTNERSHIPS

You may not yet feel ready to think about what happens after you leave the company you have helped to shape, but there are good reasons to think about it sooner rather than later. Specifically because, as an authentic entrepreneur, you are likely to feel a need to ensure that your lovingly created business and brand does not find itself turned away from the purpose for which you formed it in the first place.

Entrepreneurs

Entrepreneurs are notoriously bad at running businesses and there is not much mystery as to why. Entrepreneurs have skills of vision, creativity and risk taking, and are bored by day-to-day management. An entrepreneur responsible for a stabilized business may well seek to destabilize it just to get their entrepreneurial fix.

Once a business becomes established, it moves from the creative building phase to a consolidation phase where the needs of the business are different. As a business matures it needs honing skills to get better at what it does, and it needs organizational skills to optimize the use of resources in an ongoing way.

Part of authenticity is knowing your strengths and weaknesses and, if you recognize yourself to be entrepreneurial, it is worth working out what you are going to do to effect a smooth transition after start-up mode.

It may also be that you started the business because of a craft skill that you possess other than management, and that both you and the business are better off with your focus on the craft skill and someone else brought in to manage.

Support

Once the business is up and running, there is an opportunity to bring in a partner to complement your skills with the additional expertise needed for running an ongoing business. Of course, when bringing a partner into an authentic business, the issues of alignment and suitability are even more crucial. Many businesses have been brought to their knees through the appointment of an inappropriate person to an influential position.

It is important to take time over the selection process. You are looking for someone with whom you will have a close relationship, probably the next closest to that with your significant other. When I think of successful partnerships I have known, they actually transcend individual businesses and often go on to work together on other businesses and projects. And the way not to have to hurry the process is to start thinking about it well in advance.

You need to find a partner who you will trust absolutely, who you would be happy to give half of the business to, if it were yours to give, because you know that having them in the business will make such a difference. A partner should be someone who you will be happy to work with day in, day out for years, and someone whose skills complement your own without too much overlap.

Finding such a person will take time. There are probably not very many out there. So once you know who you are looking for, put the need out there, tell people and have them recommend other people. One of the difficulties you are likely to face is that the normal roles adopted in these situations are that of 'seller' and 'buyer'. You can neutralize this role-play by not participating and being completely open and honest.

There are three elements you are looking for: personal, ideological and skills.

- *Personal.* When you find someone, you need far more than an interview to evaluate them adequately and, if you are to work together long-term, your significant others will need to engage with them as well. Take a family weekend away and see how you feel about each other on Monday. If the very idea fills you with horror then you may not have the right partner. In my experience partners who work well together love each other, and they and their families are very happy to spend time together.

- *Ideological.* Try using the model for the 'On Purpose' workshop outlined above (p. 44), including both parties writing out their manifesto. Use the On Purpose workshop to understand how aligned your purpose and ideologies are.

- *Skills.* This is where personality profiling tools can be useful. I have tried a few (Belbin, Myers-Briggs and others) and my favourite is the Enneagram, from which Myers-Briggs is derived. It seems to be more insightful than others I have tried and will give you greater clarity around roles and how your skills fit with each other.

SUMMARY

An organization built on shared values and ideals with distributed leadership instead of hierarchy is a more robust, responsive, resilient, flexible and intelligent organization than one built on the authority of an individual leader.

An organization built on shared values and ideals with distributed leadership instead of hierarchy is a more robust, responsive, resilient, flexible and intelligent organization than one built on the authority of an individual leader

Being authentic does not necessarily make a business the most efficient at redistributing wealth from the population and the environment to a few senior executives and shareholders. What it does offer is greater value in more dimensions to more living creatures, including the participants in the business and, for many people today, that is what is more important.

Case Studies and Resources

4

My intention in this section is to demonstrate that authentic businesses are fundamentally better businesses than others that focus their energy on redistributing wealth. I have interviewed five different authentic businesses and Ivan Favennec has been kind enough to assess the financial performance of some of them and draw comparisons with FTSE 100 companies.

Clearly, any comparisons have limited value as FTSE 100 companies are entirely different beasts to the – generally small – authentic businesses. A far better comparison would be with similarly sized inauthentic peers. However, it is extremely difficult to make this comparison because in most cases they do not exist. In fact, it seems that many authentic businesses simply could not exist on the scale that they do without their authenticity – as the demise, unprofitability, or acquisition of many of their inauthentic counterparts demonstrates.

The businesses I interviewed were all small. The largest – Neal's Yard Remedies – employs 200 people. Others include an energy company, a 320-acre farm, a bank and a health & beauty company. These are all sectors that have come to be dominated by large multinationals with very few successful independent players. The businesses interviewed all flourish because they offer more to their customers, staff and owners than the tangible value of the transaction – the value of authenticity.

Authenticity is lost through the dilution of purpose that can occur when staff are employed more for aptitude than for attitude and through investors who demand a focus on profit over purpose

It is not easy to identify large authentic businesses and among large businesses there are some that are more authentic than others. However, size itself is not an obstacle to authenticity. Authenticity is lost through the dilution of purpose that can occur when staff are employed more for aptitude than for attitude and through investors who demand a focus on profit over purpose.

It is clear from all of the conversations that I have had and the research that I have done that the businesses interviewed gain very significant and specific financial benefits from their authenticity:

1   Much lower marketing costs – it appears that authentic businesses spend relatively little on promotions and marketing, and largely this is because of the support they get from their customer base. Every marketer knows that the best form of marketing is referral and authentic businesses benefit from the strong positive relationships they have with their customers.

2   Much lower HR costs – staff turnover and absence are very low in authentic businesses: up to 90% below the national average on both counts. In addition, most authentic businesses have significant numbers of people asking for jobs with them, which can reduce recruitment costs.

3   Reduced demands on management time – most of the businesses interviewed found that their staff required relatively low levels of management because of their motivation and commitment to the purpose.

For many large businesses, the core model for growth is to continually reduce prices to drive market consolidation – in other words, to put competitors out of business. This can be seen most clearly in retailing, where supermarkets and chain stores have all but wiped out independent retailing and homogenized every high street. The most vulnerable to this strategy are independent shops, which have gone out of business in their droves, while larger competitors merge with others and lower their own prices.

The authentic differentiation effect can be seen in all of the sectors where I have interviewed authentic businesses – energy, publishing, farming and health & beauty. It appears that the competitive advantage of authentic business is not just that these businesses are more profitable than their peers, but that in most cases it is the only way to survive as a small or medium-sized business facing destructive competition. The message appears to be that if you are running or want to run a small or medium-sized business in a sector dominated by large corporations you had better be authentic – it is not just a competitive advantage, it is the only way to stay in business in the long term.

GOOD ENERGY – ENERGY FOR LIFE

What do you do if you have a degree in atmospheric physics, another in environmental economics and a burning desire to ensure that we can continue to have a habitable world? The answer if you are Juliet Davenport is that you set up a renewable energy company.

Good Energy ○
100% renewable electricity

What do you then do if your original parent company disappears and you need to refinance the business without risking selling out ideologically? The answer again if you are Juliet Davenport is that you sell shares to 600 of your customers, raise £640,000, win yourself 600 evangelists for the company, and buy a wind farm.

Good Energy exists to ensure that we can maintain the lifestyle that we have become accustomed to without destroying the planet

Juliet Davenport is the Chief Executive of Good Energy (formerly unit[e]), and she is so overflowing with energy you could be forgiven for thinking that she was plugged in to the wind farm herself.

Good Energy exists to ensure that we can maintain the lifestyle that we have become accustomed to without destroying the planet. Juliet sees a stark choice facing us as a society – sustainable behaviour or catastrophic environmental collapse.

If we are able to convert to sustainable behaviour, critically in energy production, and convert now, we do have some chance of maintaining our lifestyle. If we fail to convert the choice will be taken away, nature will be unable to support us any longer and life will change dramatically.

Good Energy supply renewable energy mainly from wind energy, with some small-scale hydroelectric power and solar power, to consumers and businesses in the UK. They believe passionately in distributed rather than centralized energy generation, seeing a future where towns, villages, and communities have a stake in their own local generation from whatever source happens to make sense. Where there are rivers, small scale hydroelectric power can make sense; we are talking weirs and mill wheels rather than dams and turbines, and small-scale wind farms and individual wind turbines in windy areas.

Good Energy have put real commitment into this with their Home Generation offer where they will buy energy from home and small business scale generation schemes. Where most energy companies make this uneconomic for small generators by insisting on expensive and proprietary metering schemes, Good Energy will take the supplier's own meter reading and pay for supplies based on that.

As a private or business customer you can contact Good Energy now and change your supplier to only renewable power. Obviously no one can guarantee where your individual electrons come from (unless you have your own wind turbine), but Good Energy will ensure that your consumption of electricity is matched by their production. The one way that you can ensure the growth of renewable energy production and supply now is to transfer your purchasing power to renewable energy, and Good Energy make doing that very easy.

Good Energy plan to grow demand for renewable power to the point where the case is proven, both politically and commercially, thereby encouraging government energy security strategy, environmental strategy and commercial investment to be directed towards renewables. Good Energy currently supply 10,000 customers in the UK, 25% of which are business customers. Their plan is to supply 500,000 domestic customers by September 2008.

The established wisdom is that a conventional energy company needs to have five million customers and to have vertical integration in generation and supply to survive in such a cut-throat market. This seemed to be borne out by the collapse of other independents such as Maverick Energy, Independent Energy and Atlantic Electricity and Gas. What makes the difference for Good Energy is their authentic focus on 100% renewable energy, which enables them to be profitable already with only 10,000 customers, of whom 65% pay cost-effectively by direct debit.

The other independents, in a totally commodity-based market (who can tell the difference between electrons?), had no form of differentiation except price. It was a game they were always going to lose against the deep-pocketed major suppliers who could always cut prices further.

Good Energy in contrast benefits from highly cost-effective marketing where ideologically aligned customers are only too happy to promote their energy choice. They are also able to team up with aligned organizations such as Friends of the Earth, the Liberal Democrats and Tearfund, and indeed Authentic Business, to help to spread the word. There are also many journalists who feel strongly about renewable energy and are happy to tell the Good Energy story.

Good Energy are based in ecologically designed offices and the passion for a sustainable alternative to fossil fuels is shared. The whole team exude energy for solutions and new ideas and are utterly committed to the success of the company. This translates into further cost savings as Good Energy benefits from very low numbers of staff sick days and a low staff turnover. This commitment extends to the customers – not just the ones who became shareholders, but all customers – who form a real community with the company and give great feedback on their performance as well as the tactics of other energy companies.

Good Energy's plan is to grow this community both because the increased sales increase demand for renewable energy, and because the more customers they have and represent, the more political clout Good Energy has in influencing government policy.

Part of the problem with our whole energy market is that revenue is based on unit sales. So as far as most energy companies are concerned the less efficient you are with your energy consumption, the better for them, as you will buy more energy. Energy efficiency is actually disincentivized for energy companies, most of which aim, like other exploitation-based companies, to generate profits and transfer wealth from the natural world to their shareholders.

In contrast, Good Energy have shareholders who have bought into the importance of their aim of maintaining a habitable planet, and who understand that they will get a double return on their investment (both profit and ecological) through Good Energy's success. With this in mind, Good Energy are planning to offer an energy efficiency product to their customers in 2005 that will actually help them to reduce consumption. The strategy being that, while renewable energy still commands a premium over fossil energy and subsidized nuclear power, it makes sense to offer an economic incentive to customers by helping them to reduce their overall bill through reduced consumption.

Good Energy are also keen to find a way of offering an ecological gas product soon as well, as combined electricity and gas services are very popular with customers.

Good Energy have an interesting way of making big decisions through what it calls its Gaia meetings. Gaia is essentially the persona of the purpose of maintaining a habitable planet. At board and management meetings decisions are referenced against the Gaia ahead of commercial considerations. The Gaia is very influential in the way that the business is run.

DOVES FARM – FARMING THE SEEDS OF CHANGE

After 350 years of practice, you would expect the Marriages to know a thing or two about farming. Coming from a long line of farmers, Michael Marriage took over his father's farm in Wiltshire around 1977 and promptly started to convert to organic farming methods in 1978. Michael had previously worked for Oxfam sup-
porting agricultural development in Africa and had seen how poorly conceived aid programmes, giving high-tech tractors and chemical farming to subsistence farmers, had failed to serve them.

It was early days for organic food in the UK in 1978. The Marriages found that although consumers wanted organic flour products, there was no ready intermediary market for their organic grain. So they went out and bought a small milling machine and started to mill, pack and distribute their own high-quality flours direct to health food shops. Michael and his wife Clare would harvest the grain from the field, mill it in their barn, package it themselves and then drive around the country in an old van and deliver it to the health food shops who loved it.

This self-reliance and vertical integration is highly evident in the business today where they now manufacture their own range of Doves Farm branded high-quality grain-based products. The range includes biscuits, snacks and breakfast cereals, and is still underpinned by their range of flours. The food is all organic and studiously takes account of varying dietary needs to fulfil the Doves Farm purpose of producing foods of a high standard for people who care about the quality and healthiness of the food they eat and the world we live in.

In the mid-1980s Doves Farm learned a valuable lesson at the hands of the big supermarkets when one big chain took two of their flours on. The Doves Farm flours sold very well, so well that the supermarket in question decided to make it an own-label product so that they would have more 'flexibility' in negotiating with suppliers, and asked one of their existing non-organic suppliers to make it. The own-brand organic flour flopped in stores and the whole experiment with organic flour was dropped. Doves Farm are now extremely cautious around supplying any own-label products, recognizing that without the brand they become an interchangeable commodity supplier, and that this is a weakness that has allowed supermarkets to exploit farmers.

According to Michael, flour is an unusual product. It is one of the few things you can buy in a supermarket which is only an ingredient and has to be cooked and combined with other ingredients to make anything useful. This makes flour buyers a conservative bunch who, once they have found a flour they like and that works with their recipes, are not interested in experimenting with other flours. This leads to tremendous brand loyalty even over generations and a huge resistance to producers or retailers tampering with the product, and hence great resistance to a product they feel is unpredictable.

Doves Farm have extended from their core flour products and in the late 1980s started to make their own biscuits and then breakfast cereals. They also experimented with goats and had one of the largest herds in the UK producing goats' milk and goats' milk ice cream. The experiment lasted for three years before they conceded that cereals were what they knew and what they would continue to focus on.

Doves Farm have always been explicit about why they farm the way they do – their feeling of responsibility for nutrition and for the environment. They clearly articulate this purpose both on their packaging and on their Web site. The purpose is also clear from the way that they do business and the quality of their finished product, and it is their purpose that helps them to come up with ideas and decide on which new products to go for.

One of their core marketing tools is the *Doves Farm Recipe Book*, which they give away through box schemes all over the country. Doves Farm finds that customers really appreciate the honesty with which they perceive the company to operate and this leads to a high degree of trust and customer loyalty. The evidence for this comes in the 50 or so letters and e-mails that Doves Farm get every day from appreciative customers. One of the biggest thrills, which is shared with all of the workers, is when someone writes in with a story about how their children's behaviour has changed as a result of changes in diet, including eating food from Doves Farm.

> *Doves Farm have always been explicit about why they farm the way they do – their feeling of responsibility for nutrition and for the environment*

Having built up this loyal following, Doves Farm have a very strong brand that gives them significantly more bargaining power with the supermarkets. Such brand strength can either be built up through big TV spending or through integrity. Doves Farm have built up their brand with minimal marketing budget and big doses of excellent product and good practice.

This integrity extends to Doves Farm's relationships with their suppliers. In most cases Doves Farm have worked with the same suppliers for a long time and over that time they have built up great loyalty and commitment to each other. This commitment extends to really helping each other out when the opportunity arises and a high level of care in all dealings and goods supplied.

Another tangible benefit of the Doves Farm ethos is that they have lower levels of sick days than comparable companies. This is a common benefit enjoyed by authentic businesses but in the case of Doves Farm it may have a different cause: Michael Marriage believes that it may be due to the lack of exposure to the many concerning additives that are routinely added by other food manufacturers. Staff are also trained in the nutritional and other benefits of organic food and receive a company newsletter every eight weeks.

Doves Farm are also working to change market perceptions more generally through their work with the Soil Association to establish 'Ethical Trade' as a quality mark that assures customers that suppliers, animals and the environment have not been exploited in the production of the food.

Doves Farm have established themselves as a successful company and a strong and independent brand in a sector notorious for crippling competition and exploitation driven down through supermarkets to farmers to the land itself. Doves Farm are an inspiring example of how farmers can build up a business that is not subject to the whims and profiteering of big supermarkets. Crucially, their authenticity enables them to prosper in relatively small-scale farming (they only have 320 acres) – a sector more usually known for its poverty than its profits.

NEAL'S YARD REMEDIES – REMEDIES FOR THE FUTURE

I have met many business leaders, both authentic and otherwise. After a while you get used to them being a certain way. Even the authentic ones generally conform to certain patterns, although their thinking is very different. So when you meet a business leader who does not conform to the usual pattern it is very refreshing.

Romy Fraser, founder, very active chair and 70% owner of Neal's Yard Remedies, is quite disarming. Our interview starts with Romy gently tidying her office around me, washing a couple of glasses, offering me a drink and telling me, with humility rather than irony, that she is not really a business person. Romy's humility itself is quite ironic as she is probably one of the most influential business-women in the UK, and it is hard to imagine many other business leaders being quite so modest.

Romy explains that when she started Neal's Yard she was actually a teacher working in progressive schools and that forming the company was really to give her a vehicle to talk to people about how to take responsibility for their health and to make good-quality homeopathic remedies available.

Now, 23 years later, Neal's Yard Remedies have 200 staff; 23 shops in the UK (14 of which are company-owned, 9 of which are franchised); a distributor in Japan with 5 shops; and a further 185 accounts with franchise holders and department store concessions. Neal's Yard Remedies still exists to pursue the same purpose, to provide ways for people to find out how to be healthy in a way that allows them to take responsibility for their own health. And their product range has extended from homeopathic remedies to all sorts of health and beauty products, courses and books.

Neal's Yard Remedies still exists to pursue the same purpose, to provide ways for people to find out how to be healthy in a way that allows them to take responsibility for their own health

The business has grown organically since 1981, when Romy borrowed £18,000 from the bank to start the business. Romy is happy that she has been able to make a living and a difference at the same time although she believes that present legislation would make it impossible to start a similar company today in the same way. Lobbying for restrictive legislation, for example around health and safety, is a technique that big business uses to limit the threat of competition. The legislation is expensive to implement and affects small businesses disproportionately more than it actually improves health or safety.

As the logo suggests, Neal's Yard Remedies started with their first shop in Covent Garden, London, and their first factory was in a builder's yard. The quality of the product was evident from the start, as buyers from famous stores around the world came looking for exclusive deals to sell the remedies. These were resisted and the initial franchises were offered to existing staff.

Romy says simply that homeopathy depends on the quality of the remedy and then suggests we go on a tour of the business. As she shows me around I realize that this is a remarkably vertically integrated business which takes responsibility for everything, including inventing and formulating their products; growing their own raw materials; manufacturing their own macerates and products; designing their packaging, marketing and other materials; storing, packing and dispatching products; writing and publishing their own books; running courses and their own retail stores. The vertical integration is driven not by the usual business motives, but by the need for the finished product to be of the highest quality.

As we walk around the design studio, the warehouse, the research lab, the packaging room and the dispatch area, Romy engages every one of her staff with a warm welcome, an introduction to me and often a caring question about the staff member or someone in their family. Romy seems to know everyone and there seems to be a genuine affection that goes both ways.

As we talk, Romy explains three of the principles which are practised in the business:

1   It is possible to support young people's development into responsible adults by helping them to understand choices. Neal's Yard employ many young people from the local area and bring them into a very warm and supportive working community.

2   The way to create value is to transform raw materials into something more useful – the sort of alchemy that Neal's Yard Remedies perform by taking raw materials from their own herb gardens in Dorset and trusted suppliers, and turning them into tinctures, creams, remedies and other products.

3   Part of our role in society is to pass on what we know without price barriers. Neal's Yard Remedies run courses and publish books on all aspects of personal responsibility for health and complimentary health practices and keep the prices as low as they can.

Romy is passionately interested in how good business has a responsibility to change the world we live in for the better. In living up to this responsibility Neal's Yard have explored and experimented with different idealistic techniques and models. They tried paying people according to their needs, but found that others found this hard to accept and had to create a fair wage policy. They have sought to create a transparent business where staff and customers can find out anything about the finances and how the business is run. They have worked hard to minimize their environmental impact and carry out social audits into their impact on people and the community.

Romy cannot see how or why anyone would want to run a business without values and purpose and although, like any company, it has not been without its challenges, it is the only possible way for her to do business. Romy says she is almost embarrassed by the level of goodwill and support from customers, staff and suppliers.

This level of goodwill and support saved the company when they had a hard time in 1989. Suppliers gave additional credit that enabled the company to keep going, one supplier even saying they just trusted Romy when she said that she would pay when she could and then waiting patiently for the money to come in. This difficult time did challenge their commitment to their principles, but they stuck by them and pulled through.

Another example of the level of goodwill is illustrated by an employee who left and went on to successfully pursue a different career. For five years she worked in corporate life earning a substantial salary. After those five years she came to see Romy to say that she had had enough of that and now wanted a 'real' job again and came back to Neal's Yard Remedies.

Neal's Yard Remedies trade in the ruthlessly competitive health and beauty sector, where general practice is to misinform and exploit. Neal's Yard Remedies is a beautiful business with a warm heart and wonderful, honest products. The business has been hugely influential in the worlds of homeopathy and natural healthcare, and they still have the humility to honour their roots, value everyone, and learn every day.

TRIODOS BANK – BANKING ON PASSION

For those who know, Triodos Bank is the UK's most ethical bank and for those of us seeking supply chains entirely consistent with our values and principles, Triodos are the only choice. Founded in The Netherlands in 1980, Triodos have been in the UK since 1995.

Triodos ⊛ Bank
Make your money make a difference

With just 55 staff, they are not in a position to offer full consumer retail banking, but they do offer business banking to organizations which offer positive social, environmental or cultural benefits. They also offer a range of retail savings accounts with transparent reporting of where the money is invested. The money is made available again only to organizations offering positive social, environmental or cultural benefits, usually as loans, but Triodos Bank are nothing if not creative in looking for ways to fund projects they believe in.

Triodos Bank have their UK offices in a beautifully converted detached town house, high on the hill above the Avon gorge in Clifton, just north of Bristol. Having had some personal experience of bank head offices in the past this, is most un-bank-like. The immediate differences are in the personal way in which you are treated as a visitor, and the lack of suits.

Triodos Bank started as an experiment to prove that money could be used in a positive way. The fact that in 2004 they added a Spanish operation to complement their Netherlands, Belgium and UK offices, and that they return a healthy profit by lending to, and working exclusively with, positive contributors to social, environmental or cultural issues, and with deposits driven largely by values rather than the absolutely highest savings rates, would seem to suggest that the case has been proven. Their ongoing challenge is to continue to support positive projects and businesses, and help them to realize their success.

Inevitably in such a principled organization, there have to be selection criteria to ensure that the values are not compromised by working with organizations that do not support the principles. Most organizations facing this kind of challenge (FTSE4Good for example) use negative screening criteria – not working with weapons companies for example. At Triodos Bank a committee meets each Monday to positively screen applications for their social, environmental or cultural benefit whether they are applying for a loan or a business account.

This committee system works well (I know – I have been through it), because all of the people involved are passionate and deeply knowledgeable about the areas they work in. The ethical criteria are the primary considerations, and the commercial details of an application are not even considered unless it passes the ethical test.

Triodos also publish a remarkable 'Inspiring Change' project list each year that communicates in inspirational detail all of the organizations and projects Triodos have lent to in the previous year, from large international campaigning groups such as Greenpeace, to influential businesses such as Cafédirect and Yeo Valley Organics, to smaller local enterprises meeting local needs. In each case loan managers, who are highly likely to be experienced in the applicant's field, will get to know the organization and understand their authentic passion and commitment to the task before loans are agreed. A far cry from the clinical box-ticking and credit-referencing approach relied upon by most lending institutions for all but their biggest clients.

Triodos are so passionate about the causes they work with that they will look for the most appropriate fund-raising vehicle for the project, offering venture funding, share and bond issues, as well as loans where appropriate. They have also developed a system of 'communities of guarantors' to help charities which might not on their own be able to offer sufficient security for a loan. The 'community of guarantors' brings together a group of supporters of the charity to provide the security and spread the burden.

I met with PR and Communications Manager James Niven. One of the advantages of working authentically that James highlights is that when you are liberated from the consuming primacy of the profit motive, you are free to look for more innovative solutions. This is not to say that Triodos do not seek to make a profit – they do, but because their primary motivation is to support and enable socially, environmentally or culturally positive projects, they look for ways to do that first and know that by pursuing that aim they can offer competitive services and make a profit as well.

One of the advantages of working authentically … is that when you are liberated from the consuming primacy of the profit motive, you are free to look for more innovative solutions

Another of the key advantages of authenticity which Triodos Bank enjoy is support from customers. The positive screening process ensures that Triodos and all of their customers are pursuing the same objectives of social, environmental and cultural benefit. This enables them to form true partnerships with truly shared goals and achieve win/win/win relationships. These types of partnership are unavailable to exploitation-based businesses who have to compete for profit with all of their customers and suppliers, where most relationships are win/lose.

Not only that, but Triodos are very much at the centre of a community of savers and organizations committed to positive change. This community gets together at the Triodos annual meeting in the spring where 500–600 people turn up to hear about and discuss the work of the bank. What is true externally is also true internally and, with co-workers authentically committed to the same mission, James describes

Triodos as 'a pretty amazing place to work'. Monday mornings are for co-worker meetings across all of the company offices, providing a space for everyone to have a say in company activities and even 'in-principle' loan decisions. This sense of engagement, participation and mission can make the regular day-to-day stresses and strains far easier to cope with by putting them into context.

In addition to the criteria of supporting social, environmental and ethical projects, Triodos also lives values – humanity, innovation, transparency. Their humanity is evident in the way that they talk to and about their clients.

As with most authentic businesses with shareholders, the risk of ultimately being forced to sell out ideologically is something which needs to be handled with care. Triodos Bank have been careful to build structural protection into their ownership to shield them from buyers who might admire their balance sheet more than their ethics. All shares are held in a special trust known as an SAAT under Dutch law where they are registered. The trust issues shareholders with depository receipts for Triodos Bank Shares. Around 6500 investors hold these receipts. Almost 44% of the priority receipts are held by financial institutions, and the balance is held by private individuals, with no one holder allowed more than 7.5% of issued capital.

Voting rights at the AGM are exercised by the SAAT trust, whose board members are appointed by the general assembly of receipt holders. The voting rights of each depository receipt holder are limited to a maximum of 1000 votes.

Triodos has an ambition to be Europe's sustainable bank. Given the care that they have taken to protect themselves, and the care with which they choose who they lend to and invest in, perhaps they are already there. Given that we probably have to have a banking system of some sort, I will be very comfortable if Triodos Bank can grow and be successful enough to influence the rest of the banking industry to follow in their ethical and sustainable footsteps.

HAPPY – PLACE TO BE

Henry Stewart has a philosophy that everyone, without exception, is born good, energetic, capable, intelligent and loving. If people are not like that, it is because they  have been hurt along the way. Henry believes that people work best when they feel good about themselves, when they can celebrate mistakes and when they believe the best of each other. This philosophy is based in the theory and practice of re-evaluation counselling or co-counselling from the work of Harvey Jackins, who was its founder and principal theorist. Re-evaluation counselling is a process whereby people of all ages and of all backgrounds can learn how to exchange effective help with each other in order to free themselves from the effects of past distressing experiences.

Henry applied his philosophy and beliefs to his work. In 1991, Henry started Happy Computers because he felt that seeing people unhappy and not fulfilling their potential in dead-end environments was such a waste. Since its early days in a shared flat in Hackney, Happy Computers has grown to be one of the best-respected independent IT training companies in the UK, and one of the top 50 in terms of size. Apart from being obvious in every interaction you have with Happy Computers, the passion and motivation is evident in the awards for the best customer service in the UK (Henry is completely passionate about customer service), being selected as one of the best places to work in the UK, and the multiple awards for IT training.

Happy are now extending this philosophy wider and have set up Happy People under the Happy umbrella to enable people to create great places to work. Henry asks 'What would your organization be like if everyone was trusted? What do you need to do to get there? How would it be if management was about helping people feel good about themselves and building an environment of trust?'

Henry's main interest lies in doing things that enable people to reach their potential and he would love to do this work with local authorities and government departments. 'Imagine what could be achieved if those people felt valued and trusted,' he says. Henry does not see computer training as being about teaching people how to mail merge, as much as it is about giving them confidence so that they can be effective. Happy have pioneered a mode of training based on involvement and enablement and are guided by the age old maxim; tell me and I will forget, show me and I will remember, involve me and I will understand.

This theory is applied not just to customers – around 20,000 of whom come every year from businesses and charities – but it is also applied very thoroughly to the working environment at Happy as they seek a principled way of doing effective business. The results are that Happy is a great place to work where people feel highly valued even though they are not the highest paid in the industry. Happy People is about extending what Happy have been practising in their own offices to others and creating emotionally literate environments where people value each other's feelings, and building confidence and capability in the companies they train.

One of the ways in which Happy have achieved such success in their own workplace has been by reducing the sense of hierarchy, and separating the functional role of management from the nurturing and coaching role. At Happy they have one set of people to take care of the strategic planning, target setting and organizational management, and another set to take care of the coaching, nurturing and personal development. Each person has a manager to support them personally, and it is perfectly possible to keep your current job and change your manager. These managers set the principles and communicate the targets and then get out of the way, apart from offering support and mentoring where necessary. It makes for quite a complex structure but it certainly is effective.

One example of the way that this works is that a team – the administration team for example – will be given the responsibility for ensuring that the administration is done. How they do it and who does what is something that the team work out for themselves and can adjust to suit changing circumstances.

Interestingly, as a training company, Happy are confident to employ people based on attitude rather than aptitude. Having tried it, they know that it is easier to train people in craft skills than it is to persuade them to engage with the purpose if they do not already hold it dear. This practice protects the authenticity of Happy from the dilution that can occur through hiring people who are not aligned with the purpose of the business.

Happy are a wonderfully inspiring example of how a regular limited company can organize itself in a purpose-led, staff and customer focused way and grow, succeed and profit in the process

The company is totally transparent and all salaries are shared knowledge. There is a balance in the demands that the company places on people to ensure that everyone has 'me time', including the opportunity to spend one paid day per month working on a community project. If someone is not performing, there is a genuine concern for the person and how they can be helped to re-engage in their work. Inevitably, Happy recycle, buy fair trade, use renewable energy and have been paying a carbon tax since 1990.

Strategically, Happy never follow trends and always think and define their own route. With 35 staff, the direction of the company is no longer defined principally by Henry. Key votes have gone against Henry andm as Chief Executive, he has to accept the group decision.

"It's a good idea to accept the decisions – because they are normally right," he comments.

"Other people in this company do things much better than I do – the training, the people management, the attention to detail," he continues. "We have some fantastic people. What I think I did well as the company grew was to set down key principles and then give people freedom to innovate and work within them."

If there is a conflict between short-term profit and customer service then service will always come first. Happy now have an investor who supports their philosophy and this has strengthened the business and added more discipline around the need for profit.

Happy are a wonderfully inspiring example of how a regular limited company can organize itself in a purpose-led, staff and customer focused way and grow, succeed and profit in the process. One of the crucial ingredients has been Henry's self-confidence which enabled him to let go of the illusion of control and encourage others to step up to their potential. The results are both evident and heart-warming.

Appendix

The Authentic Partnership is made up of five key enterprise communities which connect with and support one another. Importantly, because all these businesses are connected into the ecosystem of the federation, they support one another, helping each element to flourish.

Authentic Guides was the first to be launched in April 2004 and the other businesses will be variously launched or further promoted, starting in the winter of 2004 with a road show. The road show will visit a different city each month for a three-hour session exploring the philosophy of authentic business, introducing the elements of the Authentic Partnership and inspiring business people and journalists with the commercial potential of authenticity. Our intention is that this road show is ongoing with one event per month for the foreseeable future as the central core of our communications. The road show will be sponsored by other authentic businesses who will be able to engage with and offer support to our mainly small business audience (see Fig. 1).

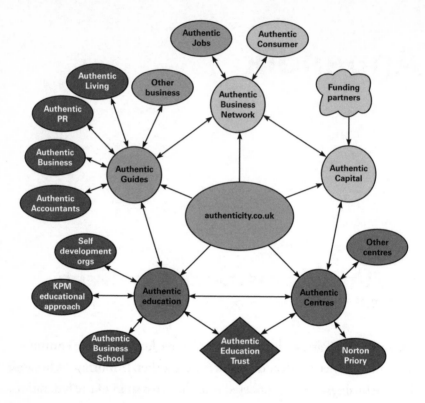

Fig. 1 The Authentic Federation

Authentic Guides

Founded in April 2004, Authentic Guides is a community of business service professionals, ranging from accountants and lawyers to healers and coaches. It exists to change the way that business is done to a way which is better for business, better for the people in the business and better for life on Earth.

Authentic Guides offers a wide range of support to authentic businesses and support for those businesses seeking to become more authentic. Potential clients can find suitable guides to work with them at the Web site www.authenticguides.com and can look them up by skill, location or name.

Authentic Guides is designed to grow rapidly into a community of thousands all around the world. This is achieved by taking out the usual barriers that would prevent it from growing.

Many businesses talk about having a very flat structure and then still have a boss and a layer of middle management. Authentic Guides has no hierarchy. The first evidence of this is that anyone who goes through the induction process and signs up to the constitution can join.

Often when I introduce Authentic Guides, people are concerned that there is no 'quality control' over who gets to be Guides, and that this might potentially lead to damage to the brand. Perhaps the first point is that this kind of 'quality control' is what most companies do, and it appears to offer very little protection against hiring the wrong people for them. Secondly, our experience so far is that the people who come along to the Induction and Inspiration sessions, so far, have all been outstanding. I remember back to the days when I was hiring furiously for Razorfish, and wish that I had had access to the kind of talent that we have joining the Guides every month.

Thirdly, we do have built-in 'quality control', in that most guides are self-employed, and would not last long if they were not competent or engaged. Guides are encouraged to put client feedback on their Web page so that other clients can see how they perform. All Guides have at least one co-coaching relationship with another Guide to help them to develop, and each year every Guide goes through a re-accreditation process.

In order to be re-accredited, a Guide must identify three other Guides who they would like to reaccredit them. The three must then evaluate the Guide against a set of criteria in the constitution. If the three decide not to reaccredit the Guide, the Guide may find another three to go through the process again. There is no specific limit to the number of times a Guide can go through this process.

Any two Guides with suitable preparation can run their own induction and inspiration sessions. After running five of their own sessions, they can start training other Guides to run induction and inspiration sessions. When Guides run an induction session, they keep all of the payments made by the participants, and all of the subscription revenue from those who join goes to Authentic Guides itself. Authentic Guides is not intended to make a profit, and spends all of the subscription income on marketing, both to attract more Guides and to attract clients to Guides.

Structurally, Authentic Guides is cellular, with every Guide belonging to at least two cells – their local cell and their craft cell. The local cell is about mutual support, collaboration on projects, and local new business development, as well as supporting their local Authentic Business Network cell (see below). The craft cell is about developing the authenticity and the methodologies of your craft, so for accountants for example, it is about developing authentic accountancy practices. Authentic Guides is an LLP with all Guides having the option to be partners in the business.

Of vital importance to the running of Authentic Guides is a 'Free Press'. Authentic Guides has an editor who creates, collects and collates stories from the Guides to form a newsletter available both internally and externally. Any Guide, supplier or client can contribute to this newsletter and it provides an important part of the self-management mechanism for the community as a whole.

Authentic Guides are closely connected to other elements of the Authentic Partnership. Authentic Guides will carry out the due diligence on potential investment prospects for Authentic Capital, as well as working with the businesses that Authentic Capital invests in to help them to flourish. Authentic Guides will organize and participate in their local cell of the Authentic Business Network facilitating connections between authentic businesses. Authentic Guides will also provide the curriculum for the Authentic Business School. In addition to this, many of the people working directly for businesses within the Authentic Partnership will be recruited from Authentic Guides.

Authentic Business Network

During the launch of *Authentic: How to Make a Living By Being Yourself* in November 2003, six authentic business leaders gathered together to share their experience of running an authentic business.

This was tremendously powerful. Collectively these businesses demonstrated that there is a definite movement towards authenticity and business with a positive purpose within the UK's culture. This brought an abundance of fresh opportunities to authentic businesses and the Authentic Business Network was born.

The Authentic Business Network is designed to connect authentic businesses together so that they can learn from as well as support and inspire each other whilst creating the opportunity to take collective action to encourage the progress of conscious business into the mainstream business culture.

Structured as an LLP, founder members are also partners with a say in the running of the network. The network is designed to bring maximum opportunities and take action as well as creating all of the usual networking benefits.

Members belong both to their local cell and to their purpose cell.

The purpose cells are based on the five common purposes described above:

1   Climate change, sustainability and the environment.

2   Social justice and poverty reduction.

3   Biodiversity – life on earth.

4   Energy and fossil fuel depletion.

5   Education, inspiration and authenticity.

In the purpose cells the businesses can collaborate with one another in the pursuit of their purpose. In this way two quite different businesses with a passion for the environment can support each other's purpose. For example Alastair Sawday Publishing and Good Energy might find a way to cross sell to each other's customers in a way that benefits both businesses and helps the pursuit of their common purpose. In addition the network can help authentic businesses to trade with one another, offering each other further support.

Membership will fall into local or national categories. Local members are those who are primarily concerned with a physically local market such as a health food shop. National members are those who seek customers from all over the UK. And the Authentic Business Network will grow to other countries as the culture for positive business grows internationally.

Specific opportunities for members include:

- A collective PR campaign that will raise the visibility of conscious business culture and the innovative authentic businesses pioneering this movement in the UK, with consumers, politicians, business schools, business and media.

- Quarterly inspiration and learning workshops with sessions given by pioneers from authentic businesses in their different areas of expertise, coupled with sessions from groundbreaking visionaries in different areas of business e.g. personal development, purpose, finance.

- Regular sessions, organized by the local Authentic Guides cell, for authentic businesses to gather to discuss the issues that many businesses face and learn about how other authentic businesses have dealt with the same issues.

As the network develops we will be working to add further services such as:

- *Authentic Jobs*. Authentic Jobs will do two things. It will be an outsourced HR and recruitment function for authentic businesses that helps them to find staff who both share the ideology and have the relevant craft skills for the job. Authentic Jobs will also be a career management service for ideological people, helping them find work with meaning.

  One of the challenges that authentic businesses have is that they are often too small to offer the kind of career progression that the people they would like to recruit are looking for. Authentic Jobs will help to ease this situation by helping people to transfer between authentic businesses. When a transfer is arranged the receiving company will pay a transfer fee to the departing company. Working with Authentic Guides, Authentic Jobs will offer collective training sessions to local Authentic Business Network members.

- *Authentic Life*. *Authentic Life* will be a consumer magazine that writes about authentic products and companies to promote buying from authentic businesses as a way to both get the best products and to influence the way that business is done. Authentic Business Network members will be a source for news and features. We are working with the fair trade magazine *New Consumer* to create *Authentic Life*.

Authentic Capital

Finding funding from an ideologically appropriate source is another big issue for authentic businesses. The danger is that if those funding the business are not as interested in its purpose as they are in the financial returns, the business will ultimately be forced to sell out ideologically. As pressure to keep shareholders satisfied constantly grows, corners have to be cut and values diluted. When this happens, all that is special about the business disappears, and it becomes simply another enterprise seeking to redistribute wealth with nothing to differentiate it from the next one.

Authentic Capital exists to provide authentically raised funding to support the growth of authentic businesses so that they are protected from having to sell out ideologically.

Authentic Capital will be structured as a LLP with four basic types of partner as shown in Fig. 2.2 (p. 55).

- Executive Partners are those running Authentic Capital on a day-to-day basis and being responsible for the investment and management of the funds on behalf of the other partners.

- Capital Users are those businesses in which Authentic Capital invests. They are also partners in Authentic Capital.

- Service Partners are the businesses who supply services to Authentic Capital, such as banks and Authentic Guides. All Service Partners have the option of being paid in cash or by way of being partners and receiving a dividend.

- Capital Providers are those who invest money in the fund and will primarily be drawn from other authentic businesses and customers of authentic businesses.

All partners are rewarded according to results and their input. Executive and Service Partners have a nominal value for their input based on published rates or prices. Their investment in Authentic Capital is calculated as the amount by which they discount their rates. Returns are calculated on the basis of the amount invested.

Authentic Guides provide due diligence and advisory services on behalf of the Executive Partners to help to assess the basis for any investments to be made. The principle of Authentic Capital will generally be to make investments conditional on the business acting on the recommendations by the Guides. A sound, established business with excellent working practices may have a quarterly meeting with a Guide representing Authentic Capital. A business felt to have more significant challenges may have far greater input from Authentic Guides, helping with marketing, strategy, finance, training and so on.

The primary difference between this and conventional capital providers is the innovative use of a LLP that allows a true confluence of interests and sharing of risk and reward between capital providers and capital users.

The objective is to create a highly ideologically aligned, supportive and efficient investment environment that sees high growth in client partner businesses with the minimum of administrative or management costs from Authentic Capital itself, hence aiming to provide good returns to the investors while maintaining authenticity.

Authentic Centres
Our intellect is very powerful. We often overuse it to make our major business decisions, and indeed our major life decisions.

There are, of course, other places we can look to help reach the right answer and way. We can listen to our heart and we can listen to our soul. We can listen to our love and we can listen to our intuition.

Authentic Centres is a network of retreats to provide a space where we can quieten our intellect for a moment and let these other vital aspects of our humanness be heard.

The core purpose of Authentic Centres is to allow people to reconnect with their own natural intuition, love and spirit so that they can make their own true, authentic choices.

The centres are non-denominational and will offer activities which will promote greater consciousness, including meditation, silence, reflection, deep thought and connection.

Authentic Centres will provide venues for the leading personal development courses and teachers from around the world. They will provide places where we can learn and grow as sentient beings. The vision of Authentic Centres is a network of beautiful, inspiring venues, managed and run by caring people, that will provide a wonderful space to withdraw from the distractions of daily life and experience a time of peace and serenity.

In short, Authentic Centres will communicate the infinite potential of the human spirit, simply by their existence.

The members of the Authentic Partnership will be able to use the centres for development either as individuals or as groups. The space will encourage engagement with the spirit to help the mind to think differently.

It always amazes me that workshops which are intended to generate new ideas, come up with new ways of working or thinking, or create new products, are held in the board room or at the Ramada, Hilton, Copthorne or other standard business hotel.

How can we expect people to think differently when everything else around them is the same? If you want a team to believe that the meeting is important, what do you think it says about your commitment to that meeting when you tell them that it is at the same old type of venue?

> *The significant problems we face cannot be solved at the same level of thinking we were at when we created them.*
> *(Albert Einstein)*

To create new ideas or to make changes happen we need to hold the ambiguity of feeling both confident in ourselves, and challenged in our spirit, which leads to energy for change. When we plan a session looking for breakthroughs and change, we need to create the conditions where both confidence and challenge exist side by side. Sadly, many meeting rooms in offices or hotels promote neither, and often end up only creating lethargy in the participants.

Authentic Centres will have presence and beauty. Their very existence will challenge people to go beyond their previous thinking and limitations.

Authentic Education

At present, our education system in the West is largely designed to create conformity rather than to celebrate and develop the individual. The system was designed for a different era during the industrial revolution and the age of empire, when what was required was a population who would work in factories and fight in trenches. It was designed to create a population who would do what they were told.

Society, expectations, and even the demands of employers are quite different today, and yet the education system has only shifted marginally from its original intention. Surely the primary task of an education system is to prepare children for adulthood?

Authentic Education is being created to help prepare children for adulthood and to repair adults from childhood. Authentic Education will search for the best ways to achieve this. It will bring together the organizations who offer these opportunities so that they can support and learn from each other. Authentic Education members will range from complete school set-ups to single day courses for adults. All organizations will be welcomed as long as they are aligned with the purpose of Authentic Education.

Authentic Education will include organizations such as the new UK school based on the KPM Approach to Children. This is being set up by The Angel Project to complement the existing KPM schools in India and the US.

The KPM Approach seamlessly integrates the major educational movements of the 20th Century and goes beyond them:

1   The Holistic Movement – a focus on the emotional and social aspects.

2   The Humanistic Movement – in order for someone to want to learn from you, trust is essential.

3   Progressive Education – Learning by doing (Montessori principle).

The non-denominational KPM Approach is based upon:

- Mutual trust relationships between child and teacher.

- Flexible classroom setup, using demonstrations and events that students can walk in and out of freely.

- Teachers simply as resources of knowledge for the child so there is no separation in teacher and student relationship.

- Children encouraged to co-operate rather than compete, with no categorization according to 'abilities'.

This has resulted in:

- Integrated learning experiences (where children learn all the time).

- Unselfconscious immersion (deep learning when children are doing what they want to do).

- Students valued unconditionally by teachers (which means the students are not afraid of giving wrong answers) – if children behave inappropriately, teachers gently explore the causes and guide them, ensuring the children always feel secure that their fundamental relationship with the teacher is never endangered.

- Life-enhancing experiences (unleashing knowledge, imagination, feelings, etc.).

The Authentic Business School will also be a member of Authentic Education. In the Authentic Business School, Authentic Guides will offer modules in a 'pick and mix' curriculum that will amount to a preparation for authentic entrepreneurs. This book will form the basis for the module I will be offering on Authentic Business.

The best of the self-development courses will also be a key part of Authentic Education – for instance, the Hoffman Process, which has been found to be highly effective as both an educational and a healing programme. Participants speak of new-found energy by overcoming depression, anger and grief, developing better communication skills, and finding a deeper spiritual connection.

Authentic Education will be closely connected to the Authentic Education Trust which will raise money both to fund the search for new ways to prepare and repair, and to fund and manage a scheme to subsidize participation in the courses offered by members of Authentic Education.

RESOURCES

Name	Resource	Details
Abel & Cole	www.abel-cole.co.uk	Fresh organic fruit and vegetable delivery
Alastair Sawday Publishing	www.sawdays.co.uk	Travel guides and environmental books
Angel Project	www.theangelproject.org	Bringing the KPM school to the UK
Authentic Bread	www.authenticbread.co.uk	Passionate about bread
Authentic Business	www.authenticbusiness.co.uk	Authentic Business Web site, including the newsletter by, for and about authentic businesses
Authentic Business Network	www.authenticbusinessnetwork.com	Connecting authentic businesses together to learn and grow
Authentic Capital	www.authenticcapital.com	Authentic investment vehicle launching in 2005

Name	Resource	Details
Authentic Centres	www.authenticcentres.co.uk	Space for the growth of humanity
Authentic Education	www.authenticeducation.co.uk	Preparing children for adulthood, and repairing adults from childhood
Authentic Federation	www.authenticity.co.uk	The authentic hub
Authentic Guides	www.authenticguides.com	Community for authentic business service professionals
Authentic PR	www.authenticpr.co.uk	Communication with integrity
Baywind	www.baywind.co.uk	Green energy co-operative
Be Unlimited	www.be-unlimited.co.uk	Magazine providing brain food for life
The Better Food Company	www.betterfood.co.uk	Organic supermarket thinking differently about food
BORN	www.borndirect.com	Baby equipment retail
Bread Matters	www.breadmatters.com	Organic bread-making and baking courses
Cafédirect	www.cafedirect.co.uk	Fair trade hot drinks company
Calverts Design and Print	www.calverts.coop	Print and design co-operative
Climate Care	www.climatecare.org	Repairing the damage individuals cause to the climate
Clipper Teas	www.clipper-teas.com	Teas, coffees and infusions without exploitation of people or planet
Companies House	www.companieshouse.co.uk	Information and guidance on corporate structures

Name	Resource	Details
Construction Resources	www.constructionresources.com	Ecological builders' merchant
Co-operative Bank	www.co-operativebank.co.uk	Ethically guided banking
Directive95	www.directive95.com	Dedicated to eradicating junk mail
Doves Farm	www.dovesfarm.co.uk	Organic, ethical farming and foods
Drivelectric	www.drivelectric.com	Electric vehicle specialists
Ecotricity	www.ecotricity.co.uk	Green electricity for home or business
Enneagram	*The Enneagram Made Easy* by Renee Baron and Elizabeth Wagele	An excellent introduction to the Enneagram
	The Enneagram in Love and Work by Helen Palmer	More advanced and detailed information about the Enneagram
Environmental Media Services	www.ems.org	Providing facts and contacts on environmental issues to journalists
Essential Trading	www.essential-trading.co.uk	Co-op supplying vegan, vegetarian and organic wholefood
Farmers' Markets – National Association	www.farmersmarkets.net	Information about farmers' markets in the UK and where and when to find them.
Footprint Clothing	www.footprint-clothing.co.uk	Ethical and environmental responsibility with high quality fashion
FTSE4Good	www.ftse.com/ftse4good	Performance measure for companies meeting globally recognized corporate responsibility standards

Name	Resource	Details
Future Forests	www.futureforests.com	Helps neutralize the contribution individuals or businesses make to global warming
Good Energy	www.good-energy.co.uk	Renewable energy company
Green & Black's	www.greenandblacks.com	Organic fair trade chocolate
Green Energy	www.greenenergy.uk.com	Green energy company part-owned by customers
The Green Stationery Company	www.greenstat.co.uk	Recycled paper and green office products supplier
Happy	www.happy.co.uk	Computer and people training
Hemp Plastic	www.hempplastic.com	Environmental and viable alternatives to petrochemical based plastics
Hetreed Ross	www.hetreedross.com	Bath-based architect with expertise in environmental design
HiPP	www.hipp.co.uk	Organic baby food
Hoffman Process	www.hoffmaninstitute.co.uk	Eight-day residential programme to help resolve issues around self-esteem, relationships, forgiveness and other core issues of life
Howies	www.howies.co.uk	Clothing company challenging the way we think about the world
Hug	www.hug.co.uk	Clothing company making fair trade fashionable

Name	Resource	Details
innocent	www.innocentdrinks.co.uk	Drinks company promoting accessible health
The Institute of Human Development	www.ihd.co.uk	Awakening people to humanity and how life on this planet can work for everyone
Jeff Gates – Shared Capitalism	www.sharedcapitalism.org	Creating a more equitable and sustainable form of free enterprise
The Kaos Pilots	www.kaospilot.dk	Danish business school for social entrepreneurs
KPM School	www.avef.org	Teaching method used in India, US and now UK
Lift International	www.liftinternational.com	Inspiring people to greater levels of effectiveness and success
miniscoff	www.miniscoff.co.uk	Organic home-baked meals for children
Mondragon	www.mondragon.mcc.es	Spanish co-operative conglomerate
Natural Capital (Paul Hawken)	www.naturalcapital.org	Researching principles and practice leading to social justice and environmental restoration
Neal's Yard Remedies	www.nealsyardremedies.com	Authentic health and beauty
New Consumer	www.newconsumer.org	Fair trade magazine
OMSCO	www.omsco.co.uk	The Organic Milk Suppliers Co-operative
Open Capital	www.opencapital.net	LLP and capitalism reform
Open Space (Harrison Owen)	www.openspaceworld.org	Open Space official Web site

		Details
	.uk	Natural food produced naturally
	siness.co.uk/archive/	Open Source fuel cell car development project
	.co.uk	Producing quality vegan gluten- and GM-free food
	ad.co.uk	Taking life planning skills into primary schools
(Harvey Jackins)		Teaching people how to exchange effective therapeutic help with each other
Relax Kids	www.relaxkids.com	Inspiring meditations for kids
Scoot Electric	www.scootelectric.co.uk	Electric scooters
The Soil Association	www.soilassociation.org.uk	Organic food, organic farming and sustainable forestry
Solar Century	www.solarcentury.co.uk	Solar photovoltaics (electricity directly from light)
The Spark	www.thespark.co.uk	Local Bath/Bristol quarterly paper promoting ethical organizations
Suma Wholefoods	www.suma.co.uk	Wholefoods co-operative
Traidcraft	www.traidcraft.co.uk	Fighting poverty through trade
Triodos Bank	www.triodos.co.uk	Ethical banking
Upstarts Awards	www.upstarts.org.uk	Supporting social enterprises and entrepreneurship in the UK

Name	Resource	Details
Vida	www.vida.tv	Holistic approach enabling optimum life performance and balance
Yaoh	www.yaoh.co.uk	UK organic vegan hemp products
Yeo Valley Organics	www.yeovalley.co.uk	Promoting organic farming and products

Index

of making a will, and many of them who do know postpone the chore unduly. The layman should be informed about wills, the great savings that can be effected by making a will, discretion available to him in disposing of his estate by making a proper will, and the unique independent administration of estates in Texas.

People often are involved in various business relations, such as partnerships, limited partnerships, and corporations, but without understanding the meaning of these relationships. They may become partners without realizing that the relationship exists. Everyone should be aware of workmen's compensation insurance, arbitration of disputes, assignment for creditors, limitation of personal actions (or the time in which to sue on personal obligations), the statute of frauds, abatement of nuisances, damage suits, and the fact that a man can lose his personal property by lending it to a neighbor and not demanding its timely return.

Every Texas citizen should know what to do when sued, and the civil court trial procedure should be of interest to him. The average person is a law-abiding citizen. Nevertheless he should be somewhat acquainted with the criminal laws of the state as set forth in the Penal Code and other laws where every punishable offense is defined and its punishment fixed. He should be interested in the general scope of criminal laws of the state and the Code of Criminal Procedure which charts the administration of the criminal laws, defines the rights of accused persons, and dictates the course of action the courts must follow to attain justice. He needs to know what to do if accused of crime, and he is more at ease in the court room if he has a general understanding of trial procedure in a criminal case.

It is hoped that this book will be pleasant reading for the layman and that it will bring him to a better understanding of the laws that govern his daily life, and also that it will appeal to students in general but especially those who contemplate entering the practice of law. It should serve in some small measure as a kind of preview of what is to come. If it serves these ends the author will feel rewarded for his efforts.

1. The Law and the Family

Husband and Wife

Celebration of Marriage

Marriage ceremonies may be performed by ordained ministers and priests; Jewish rabbis; authorized officers of religious organizations; justices of the peace; and judges of any courts in the state, including federal judges, except judges of municipal courts.

Who Shall Not Marry

Males under sixteen years of age and females under fourteen years of age are forbidden to marry by Texas law.

License

The law requires persons who want to marry to obtain a marriage license from the county clerk, which is directed to all authorized persons to perform the marriage ceremony, and is sufficient authority to perform the marriage. However, before the clerk issues the license, he is required to demand and receive from the man a certificate from a reputable licensed physician showing he is free from all venereal diseases.

Both the man and the woman must present the clerk with a certificate from a qualified physician licensed to practice

1

medicine and surgery in Texas, or in any state or territory of the United States where the applicants reside but who wish to marry in Texas, which certifies that the applicant has been given a thorough examination. The certificate also states the examination included a standard serologic test for syphilis, and that the test must not be given more than fifteen days prior to the issuance of the marriage license. The certificate must be accompanied by a report from the head of the laboratory making the standard serologic test, or from some other person authorized to make the report, and addressed to a physician (the one who will sign the certificate to the county clerk), but the report will not show the test results. The physician will not issue his certificate if the test shows positively that the person has syphilis.

An unmarried male, eighteen years of age or older, and an unmarried female, eighteen years of age or older, who are not otherwise disqualified may contract and consent to marriage. Those individuals younger than the above-mentioned are not authorized to marry without the parents' or guardian's consent. If a minor does not have a parent or guardian, the county clerk is forbidden to issue a marriage license to him unless he or she obtains the county judge's consent.

However, if a couple desiring to marry, or one of them, is under age there are certain requirements that must be met before the license may be issued. They must (a) come to the county clerk's office and apply for a marriage license; (b) give sworn statements of their addresses; (c) give proof of names and ages with birth certificates, or a current motor vehicle operator's license, or a chauffeur's or commercial operator's license, or a current visa or passport; (d) they must give sworn statements that they are not otherwise disqualified to enter into the marriage relationship; and (e) swear they are not related to each other within the prohibited degrees of kinship. If the county clerk is satisfied that the application is true and sufficient, he may issue a marriage license provided the application remains on file for not less than three days before the license is issued.

The county judge, at his discretion, may waive the three-day requirement, and the requirement for the parents' or guardian's consent, but no marriage of a male under sixteen years of age or a female under fourteen years of age can be authorized by the parents, guardian, or the county judge.

Void Marriages

The law forbids marriages within certain close kinships by blood and provides a two to ten year penitentiary sentence for violation.

A person may not marry:

1. an ancestor or descendant, by blood or adoption;

2. a brother or sister, of the whole or half blood or by adoption;

3. a parent's brother or sister, of the whole or half blood.

A marriage entered into in violation of these provisions is void.

A marriage is void if either party was previously married and the prior marriage is not dissolved. However, the marriage becomes valid when the prior marriage is dissolved if since the dissolution of the prior marriage the parties have lived together as husband and wife and represented themselves to others as being married.

Certain Void Marriages Validated. Marriages entered into prior to January 1, 1970, between people who are kin to each other by blood or marriage but which marriages would not be within the close kinship mentioned in 1, 2, and 3 above are validated by acts of the legislature in 1969.

Interracial Marriages. It is no longer a violation of the law for people of different races to marry in Texas or to live together as husband and wife if married elsewhere.

The law considers a marriage relationship as a partnership but sometimes persons intending to marry want a premarital contract in order to have the separate rights of one or both of them established. Such contracts were more important before January 1, 1968, when married women were fully emancipated. Married women can now transfer the title or mortgage their separate property or the part of the community property they control and manage without their husbands' agreement. Women can make binding agreements with their husbands regarding separate and community property, a privilege they did not have before. For this reason, premarital contracts probably will become obsolete, but if such a contract is desired, it should be prepared by a competent attorney.

Contracts defining property rights between the husband and wife with respect to land (real property) and its attachment should be recorded in the county clerk's office in the county or counties where the property is located.

Personal or movable property is often transferred across county lines within the state, and any contracts dealing with the interest in or right of each spouse to that property should be recorded in the secretary of state's office in Austin; now the only place where personal property contracts are kept.

The wife's separate acknowledgment on a contract, deed, mortgage, etc., is no longer required by law. Her acknowledgment form and a notary public's certification evidencing her acknowledgment are now the same as her husband's or any unmarried person's.

The Common Law Marriage

Despite all the provisions of the statutes, if a man and a woman live together as husband and wife, and publicly present themselves as man and wife without obtaining a marriage license and going through a legal marriage ceremony, they nevertheless are considered in law to be husband and wife. Their children are legitimate and capable of inheriting from the father, as well as from the mother just as if the parents had complied with all of the law's requirements for a legal marriage.

The husband and wife in a common law marriage have the same rights under the homestead law and the same exemptions from forced sale as those who comply with the formalities and consummate a legal marriage. There is now a provision in the law for registration of a common law marriage in the county of the couple's residence.

Dissolution of the Marriage by Annulment or Divorce

Annulment

It is presumed each party to a marriage is potent and without other impediment that would render the marriage void. In a case where one of the spouses finds the other has such a disability, then the marriage relation can be dissolved or annulled by a suit in a district court. The suit alleges that the disability existed before marriage and that the fact was unknown to the plaintiff (the one bringing the suit) at the time of the marriage.

The cause for annulment must exist at the time of marriage, and annulment is based upon the assumption that there never was a valid marriage, and therefore, it should be declared void. One induced to marry by false representation of material facts has the right of annulment, and marriages may be dissolved on proof of fraud, duress, or mental incapacity of one or the other party. Irregularities in the marriage license application, the lack of proper witnesses, or other technical deficiencies are not causes for annulment.

Persons under eighteen years of age are required by law to obtain their parents' consent to marry if the parents are living. If one parent is dead, then the consent of the survivor is needed. If both parents are dead, and there is a guardian, his consent must be obtained, and if there is no guardian, then the county judge's consent is needed. If a female minor over fourteen years of age or a male minor over sixteen years of age does marry without such consent, this does not give the parent, guardian, or county judge the right to have the marriage dissolved or annulled. The law favors a continuation of a marriage once it is consummated.

Divorce

A suit for divorce presumes a marriage is valid but asks that the relationship be dissolved for post-nuptial causes.

"A divorce may be decreed in the following cases in favor of either spouse when:

"1. The other is guilty of excesses, cruel treatment, or outrages against the complaining spouse, if such ill-treatment is of such nature as to render their living together insupportable.

"2. The other shall have voluntarily left the complaining spouse for three years with intention of abandonment.

"3. The other shall have committed adultery.

"4. The spouses have lived apart without cohabitation for as long as three years.

"5. The other shall have been convicted, after marriage, of a felony and imprisoned in this or a sister state or in a federal penitentiary; provided a suit for divorce shall not be sustained because of the conviction of the other spouse for felony until twelve months after final judgment of conviction, and not then if the convict shall have been pardoned; and provided that the husband has not been convicted on the testimony of the wife, nor the wife on the testimony of the husband.

"6. When a spouse, at the time the action is commenced, has been confined in a mental hospital, state mental hospital, or private mental hospital—in this or another state for at least three years, and it appears that the spouse's mental disorder is of a degree and nature that he is not likely to adjust, or that if he adjusts, it is probable that he will suffer relapse." *Article 4629 Vernon's Annotated Civil Statutes.*

"7. A divorce may be decreed without regard to fault if the marriage has become insupportable because of discord or conflict of personalities that destroys the legitimate ends of the marriage relationship and prevents any reasonable expectation of reconciliation." *Regular Session, 1969 New Laws Page 2960.*

These are the only grounds provided by Texas law for divorce. The spouse bringing suit for divorce may allege one or more of these grounds in the petition, but only one ground is sufficient if proved satisfactorily in court.

Time Element in Divorce Suits

One who brings a suit for divorce in this state must have been a bona fide resident of the State of Texas for six months and of the county in which the suit is brought for the ninety days preceding the filing of the suit. A trial cannot be held until sixty days have expired from the date the suit was filed.

Testimony of the Husband or Wife

In divorce suits and proceedings, the husband and wife may testify against each other. However, a divorce will not be granted if there is collusion between them.

Debts Created after Suit

While the husband has management, control, and disposition of general community property during marriage, he cannot pledge, mortgage, or dispose of community assets after a suit is filed for divorce if he does it with intent to defraud the wife. At any time during a suit for divorce, the wife can request that an inventory of the community property in the husband's possession be made; she can also obtain an injunction restraining him from disposing of it.

Alimony

If the wife in a divorce suit, whether she is plaintiff or defendant, does not have a sufficient income to support herself, she can petition the court for an order requiring the husband to pay her, or allow her sums of money out of the community assets for her support, but only during pendency of the suit. Texas law does not provide for any alimony after a divorce is granted.

Division of Property

The court granting a divorce decree must order a division of the community estate between the parties, giving due regard for each person's rights, and for their children. It is the judge who decrees a division of the property, even though the trial may have been by jury; the jury's decision in this respect being only advisory.

Change of Name

In a decree for divorce or annulment, the court, for good cause shown, may change the name of either party specifically requesting the change. However this is within the court's discretion, and a change in name will not be granted if there are children to be affected adversely. A change of name does not release a person from any liability incurred in a previous name or defeat any right which the person held in a previous name.

Children

A divorce does not affect the legitimacy of a couple's children. The court has power in all divorce suits to give the mother or the father custody of the children, having due regard for the parent's prudence and ability and the children's age and sex. The court will be most concerned for the children's welfare. The divorce petition will state whether there are children of the marriage under eighteen years of age, and if so, the name, age, and sex of each are shown. The court exercises jurisdiction over these children and their custody, and issues all proper or necessary orders and injunctions.

The court may order either the father or the mother or both to make periodical payments, usually monthly or weekly, for support of the minor child or children. The required payment, unless changed by a subsequent order of the court, will continue for each child until the child reaches the age of eighteen years after which the court cannot require further support. Upon motion of either parent or on the court's own motion the order for support can be changed from time to time by the court according to the circumstances of the child or children and the ability of the parents to pay. The court order may require that the payments be made directly to the parent having custody of the child or children or that the funds be delivered to the court clerk for transmittal to the parent having custody. In this way the clerk can keep a record of the payments.

Difficulty arises when the parent having custody of the child or children moves out of the state. The order of the court for support may require that the parent having custody not remove the children from the county or state without permission of the court. If this order is violated, the parent having custody of the children and violating the order will lose the aid of the court in collecting the support payments. More difficulty arises when the parent ordered to make support payments leaves the state, generally the father, and the mother finds that the cost of pursuing him exceeds the expected benefits to be gained for the children. Of course, the parent who leaves the state has a right to move to another state, but is nevertheless in contempt of court if he fails to make the ordered support payments. The mother who has custody of the children and is entitled to receive the support payments may follow him into the state of his new residence and bring suit against him there to enforce the order of the Texas court; or she can have him placed under orders of the court in the place of his residence to make payments the court may consider just and fair. A "drifter" can be sent to jail for failure to make support payments—not for the debt or obligation he owes, but because he is in violation of a court order.

Separate and Community Property of Spouses

"All property owned or claimed by either spouse before marriage and that acquired during marriage by gift, devise or descent and the increase of property thus acquired is a spouse's separate property. Each spouse shall have sole management, control and disposition of his or her separate property. The separate property of a spouse is not subject to liabilities of the other spouse unless both spouses are liable by other rules of law. All property acquired by either spouse during marriage, other than separate property, is community property." *Article 4613 Vernon's Annotated Statutes.*

This law was enacted in 1967, and was effective January 1, 1968.

A large part of property owned by married couples in Texas is community property since most newly married men and women do not generally own much property. Therefore, if they begin with no property and through their efforts after marriage accumulate property, it is community–owned equally by the spouses. Community property falls into two classes: (a) special community, and (b) general community.

Special community is the part of the community property that the wife can dispose of, manage, or control, and general community is the part of the community property that the husband can dispose of, manage, or control. While personal earnings of both spouses become community property, the wife's personal earnings are special community, and the husband's personal earnings are general community. If a spouse is injured and damages are paid, these damages are the injured spouse's separate property, except money awarded for loss of the injured spouse's earning capacity which is community property. It is special community and under the wife's control if she is the injured one, and general community and under the husband's control if he is the injured one.

Since marriage status in Texas law is considered a partnership, it could be supposed that any property belonging to either spouse could be reached by either spouse's creditors. This marriage partnership, however, may have several property classes:

1.   husband's separate property,
2.   wife's separate property, and
3.   community property.

Community property may be of three types: (a) that under the husband's control (general community); (b) that under the wife's control (special community); and (c) a combination of the two under their joint control. Much may depend upon the duty to support.

Duty to Support

> "Each spouse has the duty to support his or her children; the husband has the duty to support the wife; and the wife has the duty to support the husband when he is unable to support himself. A spouse who fails to discharge a duty of support is liable to any person who provides necessities to those to whom support is owed." *Article 4614, Vernon's Annotated Civil Statutes.*

If a wife goes to the grocery store and buys groceries or to the dry goods store and buys clothing for herself and children, because these are necessities, the husband must pay the bills. If the husband is unable to pay, then the wife is liable for those debts. If the husband is in necessitous circumstances, the necessities furnished him may be charged to the wife. If a suit is brought and judgment is taken under these circumstances, the court can direct what property is to be sold first to pay the indebtedness and what will be sold next out of the several classes of property that the spouses have.

If special community property and general community property become mixed, then that mixed community property is under the joint control, management, and disposition of the spouses. In such cases, one purchasing mixed community property should require both spouses to sign the instrument of conveyance, whether it is a deed to land or a bill of sale of personal property.

Either spouse's separate property which becomes intermingled with community property so that it cannot be separated, becomes community property. However, the spouses can transfer the title of property to each other making it the separate property of the recipient, and this can be done without the district court's approval, even though the property transferred from one to the other may not be equally valuable.

Sale of the Homestead

If the homestead is the separate property of one of the spouses, or is community property, both spouses must join together to transfer the title or mortgage it, if they are living together and both remain capable of transacting business. If the homestead is the separate property of one of the spouses and the other spouse has been judicially declared incompetent, then the homestead may be sold, conveyed, or encumbered without the incompetent spouse's consent. If the homestead is the separate property of a spouse and the other spouse is: (a) incompetent, whether decreed so or not; (b) or the other spouse disappears and his or her whereabouts remain unknown to the owner; (c) or the other spouse permanently abandons the homestead and; (d) the spouses are permanently separated, then after the expiration of sixty days, the owner may file a sworn petition in the district court describing the homestead and the facts that make it desirable to sell or mortgage the property. After required notices are given and a hearing has taken place, the court may authorize the owner to sell or mortgage the homestead without the other spouse's consent.

If the homestead is the spouse's community property and one spouse has been decreed incompetent by a court having jurisdiction, then the competent spouse may sell or mortgage the homestead without the other spouse. If the homestead is the community property of the spouses and one of the spouses is: incompetent, whether or not decreed so; or if a spouse disappears and his or her whereabouts remain unknown to the other spouse; or if one spouse permanently abandons the homestead and the other spouse; or if one spouse permanently abandons the homestead and the spouses are permanently separated, then after sixty days, the competent spouse, the remaining spouse, the abandoned spouse, or the spouse who has not abandoned the homestead in case of a permanent separation, may file a sworn petition in the district court describing the property and stating the facts which make it desirable for the spouse filing the petition to sell, transfer, or mortgage the homestead without the joinder of the other spouse. After the required notices and a hearing, the court may issue an order permitting the petitioning spouse to sell, transfer, or mortgage the homestead. The court can enter other orders and place restraints it considers desirable or equitable upon the petitioning spouse, since it is the duty of the court at the same time to protect the interest of the absent spouse.

Presumption as to Community Property

> "All property possessed by either spouse during or on dissolution of marriage is presumed to be community property."
> *Article 4619, Vernon's Annotated Civil Statutes.*

The presumption is rebuttable, however, and can be overcome if facts are presented to prove that the property or a portion of it is separate property. Texas law favors community property; that is the basis for the presumption. This means only that the property's status will be considered community if there is no proof or evidence to show that it has a different status.

The Homestead

The Texas Homestead Act is based upon that political philosophy that once a man has acquired a home, he and his family should not be deprived of it by forced sale, regardless of how indiscreet, foolish, or reckless he may have been in managing his financial affairs. If a man has a shelter for his family and himself, his situation is not hopeless. Previous generations became sensitive to their fellow men who suffered from starvation and despair after they were driven from their homes by creditors. They must have viewed the homestead law the next logical step after the constitutional provision that no person should be imprisoned for debt.

In their wisdom, the Texas Legislature adopted measures to protect a person against himself. A man cannot mortgage his homestead except for repairs, improvements or additions to it, as long as he has a wife living with him in the home. Banks and mortgage companies will not lend money on a homestead except for its improvement because loans for any other purpose could not be enforced. While this deprives the owner of a homestead of its use as collateral for loans, this is part of the protection for him and his family against himself. In effect, the law says the home is a sacred place for a family which creditors cannot confiscate unless a door is left open—a lien for purchase money, a lien for improvements, or a tax lien. Close these doors and no creditor can enter.

Our Texas Homestead Act was inspired by exemptions from forced sale contained in Spanish and Mexican laws, but the law itself is a Texas creation. The first homestead exemption was enacted by the third congress of the Republic of Texas on January 26, 1839.

Article 16, Section 50, of the Texas Constitution provides that a family's homestead shall be protected from forced sale for the payment of all debts except the money used to purchase the homestead, or a part of the purchase money, the taxes due on the homestead, or for work and materials used in constructing improvements. In the latter case, the lien will be valid only when the work and materials are contracted for in writing, with the wife's consent given the same way it is required in making a sale and conveyance of the homestead. It also provides that the owner, if a married man, shall not sell the homestead without the wife's consent. She must join him in the sale to make it valid. Mortgages, deeds of trust, and other liens on the homestead can never be valid, except for the purchase money, or improvements made to the homestead, and for taxes due on the homestead. Even if the husband and the wife may join together in attempting to create a mortgage on the homestead, if it is not for the money to purchase the homestead, or for improvements on the homestead, it is not valid. Of course, the taxes against the homestead create a lien against it, but this does not represent a voluntary mortgage given by the owners.

What Comprises the Homestead

The homestead of a family in the country may consist of any number of acres up to two hundred acres with the improvements, and the land may be in one or more parcels. A man and his family may live upon any size tract up to two hundred acres and the homestead would be exempt from forced sale. If he lives upon a thousand-acre tract and calls it his home, he could have the exemptions on only two hundred acres holding the residence. He can choose the particular two hundred acres, so long as the land he chooses has the residence on it.

The homestead in a city, town, or village consists of a lot or lots not exceeding a value of $5,000 at the time they were designated as a homestead, without regarding the value of the improvements.

So, once the homestead has been established, either in the city or in the country, there are only three kinds of liens that can be foreclosed against it: (a) the lien given to secure the payment of the purchase money, or part of it; (b) the lien given to secure payment for improvements, and this includes additions to the residence and its appurtenances, repairs, painting, etc., and a lien for such purposes must have the wife's consent, and the writing must have been executed before the work is commenced; and (c) the tax lien for taxes against the homestead.

The following are also exempt from forced sale:

1. All household and kitchen furniture
2. Any lot or lots in a cemetery held for the purpose of sepulture

3. All implements of husbandry

4. All tools, apparatus and books belonging to any trade or profession

5. The family library and all family portraits and pictures

6. Five milk cows and their calves

7. Two mules

8. Two horses and one wagon

9. One carriage or buggy

10. One gun

11. Twenty hogs

12. Twenty head of sheep

13. All saddles, bridles, and necessary harness for the use of the family

14. All provisions and forage on hand for home consumption

15. All current wages for personal services

16. All wearing apparel

17. Twenty head of goats

18. Fifty head of chickens

19. Thirty head of turkeys

20. Thirty head of ducks

21. Thirty head of geese

22. Thirty head of guinea

23. One dog

24. The cash surrender value of any life insurance policy which has been in force for more than two years.

Obviously this law must have been enacted during the "horse and buggy days." The present law providing the exemptions, originally passed in 1874, did not contain any of the last nine items in the list. The last item was added by a statute passed in 1929, and the eight items preceding it were added in 1935.

The legislature was agrarian-minded when it designated the exempt items since most of these items are not ordinarily owned by urban people. More recently, farmers often do not have mules, wagons, or buggies but, the courts have followed a policy of liberal substitution where trucks and pick-ups are substituted for wagons, automobiles for carriages, and truck-trailers have been exempted as part of the hauling equipment or apparatus. Diamond rings have been held as part of the wearing apparel and consequently exempted. The federal courts follow the Texas statutes in Texas trials in bankruptcy proceedings in this state, and they allow the same exemptions and substitutions that the state courts do in estate and foreclosure proceedings.

The homestead exemption favors the family. If there is no family, the exemption is not effective. As long as there is a head of the house (man or woman) and one or more dependents occupying the home, even though they may live temporarily in other places and even rent the home temporarily, the exemptions are their protection against forced sale for debt or in bankruptcy proceedings. But there must be a family relation in that the head of the house has a legal obligation and moral duty to contribute to the dependent's support. If the head of the house establishes a home for the family and the family then disbands, as in the case where the wife dies and the children in the family grow up, marry, and leave home, and he continues to use the home as his abode, then the exemption still remains as his protection. Conversely, if a man or woman singly acquires a house and lives in it as a home and takes in a minor child who is not related and does not adopt the child, then however long the two live together, the family relation does not exist and the homestead exemptions would not be effective.

After the marriage is dissolved by the death of one spouse, or by divorce, when the survivor is the owner of the homestead, he or she can mortgage it even though minor children may remain in the home as dependents of the survivor, and the mortgage can be foreclosed. The protection against forced sale of a homestead in this instance is a personal right that can be given up after the marriage is dissolved, or one spouse becomes insane, but not while both the husband and the wife remain sane and live together in the homestead.

The Business Homestead

The head of a house who has a profession or business can have a business homestead, which may be part of the residence or separate from it. The business homestead is likewise exempted from forced sale. The premises claimed as a business homestead must be reasonably suited to the transaction of the business or profession. Therefore, one may have a rural homestead where he and his wife and children live, and simultaneously have a business homestead in town. Conversely, he may have an urban homestead where he and his wife and children live, and also have a rural business homestead (a broom factory or a brick kiln for example).

Along with the business homestead, the equipment and machines necessary for carrying on the business or profession of the head of the family are exempt from forced sale. Moreover, the head of the house may carry on more than one profession or business in the business homestead, and the appurtenances of each would be exempt. The head of the house cannot have two different businesses or professions in two different places and claim both places as business homesteads. He can have the exemptions for only one business homestead.

The Tools of a Trade

The tools of a man's trade are exempt from forced sale for his debts, such as:

1. A barber's tools and the barber chair in his barber shop
2. A carpenter's tools

3. The tools and equipment in a blacksmith shop
4. The brushes, easels, paints, etc., belonging to an artist or a house painter
5. A physician's equipment, instruments, and books
6. The library, office furniture, typewriter, etc., in a lawyer's office

These few are mentioned as an illustration. Tools of any lawful trade when they are used by the owner are exempt. Even though the owner may cease using his trade tools temporarily, such as when he goes on vacation, this does not change the exempt status of the tools.

It is this state's policy that a man must be protected in the ownership and use of his home and in his means of making a living for himself and his family.

Guardians and Adoption

Often, guardians must be appointed to take care of other persons or to manage their estates, as in the case of:

1. Orphans who are in need of personal care or who own, or may be entitled to receive, an estate.

2. Minors who are dependent because of neglect of their parents, or because of illness, or insanity of their parents, or children who may own, or may be entitled to receive, an estate.

3. Habitual drunkards who are unable to care for themselves or who own, or may be entitled to receive, an estate.

4. Persons of unsound mind who are in need of personal care or who may own, or may be entitled to receive, an estate.

5. Any of the above-named classes of persons or others who are deemed incapable of managing their own affairs because of some disability and who are entitled to receive

money from some agency of the federal government.

In all such situations, the law provides for appointment of a guardian by the county judge, who is also the probate judge, in the county where the person or persons may reside, and a guardian may be appointed for the person or for the estate of any such person. The judge may require whatever bond of the guardian that he considers necessary to protect the estate.

In some of the state's more populous counties, there is a probate judge in addition to the county judge. The county judge is concerned with the county's fiscal or business matters, while the probate judge is concerned with guardianships, probate of wills, etc.

Guardians of Minors

Natural Guardian

"If the parents live together, the father is the natural guardian of the persons of the minor children of the marriage. If one parent is dead, the survivor is the natural guardian of the persons of the minor children. The natural guardian is entitled to be appointed guardian of their estates. The rights of parents who do not live together are equal; the guardianship of their minor children shall be assigned to one or the other, the interest of the children alone being considered." *Article 109 Texas Probate Code*

Guardian of Orphans

If the last surviving parent has appointed no guardian, the nearest ascendant in the direct line of the minor is entitled to guardianship of both the minor and the estate.

If there are more than one ascendant in the same degree in the direct line, they are equally entitled. The guardianship shall be given to the one or the other, according to circumstances, with only the orphan's interest considered.

If the orphan has no ascendant in the direct line, the guardianship shall be given to the nearest relative. If there are two or more of the same degree, the guardianship is given to one or the other, according to circumstances, with only the orphan's best interest considered.

If there is no relative of the minor qualified to take the guardianship, or if there is no person entitled to the guardianship, the court shall appoint a qualified person to be the guardian.

Guardians of Persons Other than Minors

If a person is an incompetent, or one for whom it is necessary that a guardian be appointed to receive funds due from any governmental source, these rules shall govern:

If the person has a spouse who is not disqualified, that spouse is entitled to the guardianship in preference to any other person.

If there be no qualified spouse, the person's nearest of kin who is not disqualified, or in a case where the spouse or kin refuses to serve or act as guardian, then any other qualified person is entitled to the guardianship.

Where two or more persons are equally entitled, the guardianship shall be given to one or the other according to the circumstances, with only the ward's best interest considered.

Persons Disqualified to Serve as Guardians

The following persons shall not be appointed guardians: minors; persons whose conduct is notoriously bad; incompetents; or those who are parties, or whose father or mother is a party to a lawsuit which determines the welfare of the person for whom, or for whose estate, a guardian is to be appointed.

Also included are those who are indebted to the person for whom or for whose estate a guardian is to be appointed, unless they pay the debt prior to the appointment, or who are asserting any claim to any property, real or personal, adverse to the person for whom, or for whose estate, the appointment is sought; those who are unable to read and write the English language; aliens disqualified by law; and those who because of inexperience or lack of education, or for other good reason, are shown to be incapable of properly and prudently managing and controlling the ward or his estate.

Adoption

Often, it is desirable that minor children be adopted by persons who are able and willing to care for them. Some of the circumstances, but not all, that present a need for adoption of children are: (a) catastrophe causing the death of both parents, (b) both parents deserting their children, (c) the parents are drunkards and incapable of taking care of the children, (d) or a child born out of wedlock to a mother who is unable to care for it or perhaps does not desire to keep it and care for it. In this instance, quite often the father cannot be found, or he may be a minor, or for other reasons cannot be made to take parental responsibility for the child.

It is a fact, too, that there are more homes open to orphaned or dependent children than there are children available to place in them.

An adoption proceeding is started by filing a petition by the adult person or persons who desire to adopt a child or children (a) in the district court; (b) in the county where the petitioner or petitioners reside; or (c) in the county where the child or children to be adopted reside; (d) or if the child or children are placed with a child-placing institution of this state, the petition may be filed in the county where that institution is located. The petition must state the circumstances of the person or persons seeking to adopt and the circumstances of the child or children who are to be adopted. If a married person is the petitioner, then the petitioner's spouse must also sign the petition, otherwise it will not be considered unless the petitioner is married to the natural father or mother of the child or children to be adopted. Then it is not necessary that the natural father or mother join in the petition.

After the petition has been filed, the court clerk will mail a certified copy to the executive director of the State Department of Public Welfare. The executive director or the court will then require a report for the court's information showing all of the pertinent facts about the petitioners and the child or children to be adopted. Of course, the court must be satisfied that the child or children are so unfortunately situated that the proposed adoption is desirable and that the petitioners are suitable persons for the adoption.

The court awards the temporary care and custody of a child to the petitioner, but an adoption is not permitted under the law until after the child has lived in the petitioner's home for six months. The reason for such a rule is obvious. Before the child is awarded to the petitioner, the court will set a hearing for the case, and the petitioner will be questioned in the presence of the judge at the hearing. The hearing must not be held less than forty days or more than sixty days after the clerk mails a copy of the petition to the executive director of the State Department of Public Welfare. If the child to be adopted is fourteen years of age or older, then the child's written consent to the adoption and his presence at the hearing are required.

If the child to be adopted has parents living, then their written consent to the adoption is also necessary, except in the following cases:

If the parent or parents have abandoned the child for a period of two years and during that time have not contributed materially to the child's support, the consent of the parent or parents shall not be required.

If the parental rights of the natural parent or parents have been terminated by a juvenile court order or other court of competent jurisdiction, the consent of such parent or parents shall not be required.

If the child was born out of lawful wedlock, then the consent of the father shall not be necessary, and the consent of the natural mother, regardless of her age, shall suffice.

If the child has been placed by its natural parents with a child placing institution licensed by the State Department of Public Welfare to place children for adoption, it shall suffice if the living parents have consented in writing that the child may be placed for adoption without specifying the names of those by whom the child shall be adopted.

After a child has been adopted in accordance with the law, the court may take away from the adoptive parents the custody of the adopted child and award the custody to the child's natural parents, or to either of them, or to some other person, upon proof of the bad moral character of the adoptive parents, or parent, or upon proof of abuse, neglect, or ill treatment of the adopted child by the adoptive parent.

No Caucasion can be adopted by a Negro, nor can a Negro be adopted by a Caucasion.

In view of the trend in decisions by the U.S. Supreme Court, it seems probable that this section will be held invalid when and if it is tested before that court. Repealed in 1969.

Status of Adopted Child

When a minor child is adopted, it becomes the child of the adoptive parents just as if it had been born to them. The adoptive parents owe it the same duties that they owe to their natural child, and they are obligated by law to furnish the adopted child food, clothing, a home, schooling, and such other attentions as they are required by law to give to their natural child. The adoptive parents are entitled to the child's services and the money that it may earn while a minor, and they are entitled to its company and to have control over it.

The adopted child can inherit property from its adoptive parents and the adoptive parents can inherit from the adoptive child upon its death. The natural parents who give the child up for adoption by others lose the right to inherit from the child, but the adopted child does not by its adoption lose the right to inherit from its natural parents. However, people who adopt a child can dispose of their property by will and in it they can provide that none of their property shall pass to the adopted child, even as they can provide in the will that none of their property shall pass to their natural child. It is mentioned above that the adoptive parents can inherit from the adopted child. Nevertheless, when the adopted child is capable of making a will, he can by its terms, provide that none of his property be inherited by the adoptive parents.

Family Code

Through recent years the Legislature has given much attention to a "Family Code" which, as presently enacted, covers the whole scope of family relations commencing with the formation of a family by the marriage of a man and a woman, setting forth detailed and specific rules to be followed in establishing the marriage relationship. While the code sets forth these rules, at the same time, in order to provide stability for those entering into the marriage relationship in good faith, the code sweeps aside for them the formalities normally required and provides, among other things, that fraud, mistake or illegality in obtaining a marriage license shall not affect the legality of the marriage once it has been consummated, and even provides that if by mistake the marriage ceremony is conducted by an unauthorized person the marriage, if otherwise valid, shall not be voided by that irregularity.

The code contains the laws pertaining to annulment and divorce and those setting forth the legal duties of husband and wife toward each other and to their children and the rights of parents to discipline their children and the duties of parents toward their children after the marriage has ended by divorce, and it provides a much more effective means of reaching the parent who abandons his or her children and moves out of this state than we have had before enactment of the code.

Under provision of the code, when a suit is filed for divorce, the court clerk gives notice that the judge may require counseling and gives to the attorney filing the original petition for divorce an availability of couseling notice which directs the plaintiff where the aid of counseling can be had. Those approved by the court to do this important work of giving advice, also try to determine whether there is a reasonable chance of reconciliation.

The family code contains the laws governing property rights as between the spouses and defines the right of each with respect to the different classes of property that each may control.

It contains many new enactments by the legislature on the parent-child relation, and provides "juvenile courts" for deciding the rights of juveniles who may be in difficulty with their parents and for their return to this state in cases where they have run away from home and have gone to another state. Under its provision the governor of our state can enter into a compact, the "Uniform Interstate Compact on Juveniles" with other states under terms of which the states mutually agree to cooperate in the handling of juveniles when a child has left his home state and gone into another state. These laws set up a whole new branch of jurisprudence, too extensive to be treated further here, giving the child the right to appeal the decision of the juvenile court under some circumstances.

It is here recommended that parents having the unfortunate problem of a child who will not be an acceptable child citizen in the home or who runs away from home, obtain and study the "Family Code" in that part that deals with the juvenile.

2. Wills and Estates of Decedents

Under Texas law, if a person owning property dies without making a valid will, it becomes the county judge's or probate judge's duty, when it is called to his attention, to see that the estate is properly administered and that the property belonging to the deceased goes to his lawfully-designated heirs. This procedure is costly to the estate resulting in necessary and extensive proceedings and piling up expenses that consume a high percentage of the estate's assets, and it does not compare favorably with the independent administration under a properly executed will.

In such a situation, the court will appoint an administrator, who must give bond with the bond's cost being chargeable against the estate. The administrator is allowed a fee for his services and the fee, or fees, are payable out of the estate. The administrator must have legal assistance, and the attorney's fees are also payable out of the estate. If any property of the estate is to be sold, or if money is to be borrowed to defray expenses, or almost any other transaction is to be made, a petition must be filed with the court and notices must be given. Next, there must be a hearing on the petition where proof must be given to the court that the proposed action in the petition is necessary or beneficial to the estate. If the court is convinced, an order will be issued authorizing the administrator to do what he has requested of the court. A report must then be made to the court showing what was done after its order, and then the court issues an order approving what has been done.

Wills

Under the Texas laws, a person who is capable of making a will may dispose of his estate by a duly executed will, which becomes effective upon its probate after that person's death. A will is a declaration by a person, usually in writing, directing how he would have his estate disposed of after his death. Wills fall into three classifications:

1. A will written entirely in the handwriting of the person making it, and it does not require any signing by witnesses.

2. A will that is typed or printed, usually prepared by an attorney, for execution by the one making the will, and this kind requires two witnesses, but there may be more, who shall sign in the presence of the testator (the one making the will) and in the presence of each other.

3. A will that is made without a writing as in the situation where a person is near death and calls witnesses to hear him state how he wishes his estate disposed of after his death. If the estate of the testator in this case exceeds $30, then there must be three witnesses who hear the testator speak the words that compose the will. To qualify as a witness to a will, one must be of sound mind and over 14 years of age.

Who May Make A Will

"Every person who has attained the age of eighteen years, or who is or has been lawfully married, or who is a member of the armed forces of the United States or of the auxiliaries thereof or of the maritime service at the time the will is made, being of sound mind, shall have the right and power to make a last will and testament, under the rules and limitations prescribed by law." *Article 57 Texas Probate Code*

Advantages Of A Will

A will can serve many good purposes. One who owns any property should make his will at an early date, always aware that he can revoke or change the will at any subsequent time when he is still of sound mind. He can make a new one, or add to the old one by codicil if he prefers. By making a will, a person can choose the individual or individuals who are to manage his affairs after his death, can give his property to the persons or institutions of his own choosing, can extend or shorten the time which may otherwise be used in completing the business of the estate, and he can control to a considerable degree the expense of carrying out the will's terms.

As mentioned previously, one type of will is that written wholly in the testator's handwriting. However, one thing that should be kept in mind by one desiring to make a will, is that it should be complete and prepared so that it will be accepted for probate to accomplish the purposes which impelled the testator to make it. It is a good idea to have legal assistance in preparing and executing the will. As one's possessions increase, and more particularly, as his business interests become more diversified and complicated, he would do well to have the assistance of a tax expert as well. This is especially true when the property owned is in more than one state, or where the testator desires to establish trust estates for minors or others who are to have income from his estate during its management by someone he appoints as "independent executor." These advisors are also helpful where the estate is encumbered by debt or other obligations that can be discharged through proper management over a period of time.

The Independent Administration

Almost all wills prepared by Texas lawyers provide for independent administrations. Such wills not only dispose of the testator's estate and all of his property, but also appoint an independent executor or independent executrix, without bond. These wills provide that, after the will is admitted to probate and an inventory and appraisement and a list of claims have been filed, the cause be dropped from the court docket. This limits the court's functions by removing the estate from the court's supervision and placing the estate in the hands of the person, bank, or trust company named in the will to take charge of the estate and carry out the will's terms.

Of course, the will must be probated, and that means that it must be proven to the probate judge's satisfaction (who is the county judge except in counties with a large population where there are one or more probate judges in addition to the county judge) that the will is the last, true, and valid will of the person making it. Roughly, the preliminary procedure to place a will in probate is:

1. The executor named in the will obtains possession of it and places it with an attorney for probate.

2. The attorney draws up a petition to the court stating that the testator is dead and that the court has jurisdiction of the cause, alleging the necessary facts; such as that the testator left a valid will, which is attached to the petition; that in it the testator appointed an independent executor without bond, etc.; and requesting that the will be admitted to probate.

3. The court clerk issues the necessary notices and gives them to the county sheriff or a constable for posting.

4. The officer posts the notices as required by law and reports to the court indicating how he has published the notices.

5. After the necessary time lapse, which is at least ten full days after the posting date, the attorney goes into court with one or more of the persons who signed as witnesses on the will, and generally the independent executor appointed in the will accompanies him, and the attorney offers the necessary proof to the court to show that it is a valid last will that he is offering for probate.

The proof that the court will require is: That the one who made the will (the testator or testatrix) is dead and that four years have not elapsed since his death and prior to the date of filing the application; That the court has jurisdiction and venue over the estate; That citation has been served and returned in the manner and for the length of time required by the probate code; That the person who made the will was at the time he made it qualified to do so; That the testator executed the will with the formalities and solemnities and under the circumstances required by law to make it a valid will; That the will has not been revoked by the testator; and That the person making the application is the person named in the will as independent executor (or independent executrix) and that that person is not disqualified to receive letters testamentary.

If all of this proof is made at the hearing to the court's satisfaction, the court will enter an order prepared by the attorney and presented to the court for signature admitting the will to probate. Letters testamentary will be issued to the person appointed in the will as soon as that person has signed the oath required by law, and the court, in the same order, will appoint one or more appraisers to evaluate the estate and make a list of claims.

As a matter of practice, the independent executor, with the attorney's help, will prepare the inventory of the estate and evaluate the several separate pieces of property. They will also make a list of claims or debts against the estate and a list of claims in favor of the estate and will sign it and give it to the appraisers for consideration, and any changes they think should be made, and for their signatures. When this appraisement and list of claims have been duly signed and filed with the court clerk, the attorney will ascertain from it, based upon the estate's value whether there are taxes on the estate that must be paid to the State of Texas and to the federal government. The attorney will prepare and file the necessary reports, showing the taxes due, if any, and the reports must be signed by the person appointed in the will as independent executor (or executrix).

After these procedures are completed, the court will drop the case from the court docket. The independent executor (or executrix), after signing the oath, is entitled to take over the estate to manage and control it. Of course, the estate is still charged with the debts that may have been created against it, and creditors have a year in which to file their claims with the executor so that they will be properly classed and put in line for payment out of the estate's funds. A creditor who fails to file his claim within that time will have consideration only if assets are left over after discharging those claims that were filed on time.

The will may be written so that it is clear that the independent executor's function is to complete the affairs of the estate and deliver the estate to those who are shown in the will to be entitled to it. Quite often a man will make his will and appoint his wife as independent executrix, giving all of his property to her. Conversely, a wife frequently will make her will and appoint her husband as independent executor and give all of her property to him. In these cases the one appointed and receiving the property will attempt to complete the proceedings as soon as possible and then own the property in his or her own name.

On the other hand, a person's business and his estate may prevent such quick action. He may choose to place his estate with a trustee or trustees with authority to manage and control it. The trustee can invest and reinvest the estate's funds so that an income is made over a period of time. The trustee can be instructed to pay or deliver the income to persons named in the will, and with further provisions that at the end of a certain time, or upon the occurrence of a specified event, the assets of the estate are to be distributed to persons named in the will. Moreover, a person having a considerable estate may have the purpose of saving taxes or postponing taxes upon his estate or a portion of it, and through careful planning with the aid of his attorney and his tax adviser much can be accomplished. In some instances, it is advantageous to set up trusts and put them in effect while the person making them is still living. He can manage these trusts during his lifetime and in his will, appoint a trustee to carry on after his death. This arrangement can sometimes save substantial taxes or result in the postponement of taxes.

The Unwritten Or Nuncupative Will

The unwritten or nuncupative will provided for under the law is the least used and the most unsatisfactory will form.

> "No nuncupative will shall be established unless it be made in the time of the last sickness of the deceased, at his home or where he has resided for ten days or more, next preceding the date of such will, except where the deceased is taken sick away from his home and dies before he returns to such home; nor when the value exceeds thirty dollars, unless it be proved by three credible witnesses that the testator called on a person to take notice or bear testimony that such is his will, or words of like import." *Article 65, Texas Probate Code.*

The court will be cautious, and properly so, in admitting an unwritten will to probate, since there is always room for doubt and uncertainty, and also because the law makes added requirements for proof of such a will as follows:

> "No nuncupative will shall be proved within fourteen days after the death of the testator, or until those who would have been entitled by inheritance, had there been no will, have been summoned to contest the same, if they desire to do so," and;

> "After six months have elapsed from the time of speaking the alleged testamentary words, no testimony shall be received to prove a nuncupative will, unless the testimony or the substance thereof shall have been committed to writing within six days after making the will," and;

> "When the value of the estate exceeds thirty dollars, a nuncupative will must be proved by three credible witnesses that the testator called on a person to take notice or bear testimony that such is his will or words of like import." *Article 86, Texas Probate Code.*

What To Do With A Will After It Is Made

A will, after it is executed, should be kept in a safe place where the person named as executor or executrix can find it so that it can be presented for probate, since a will must be probated to be effective. A safe deposit box in a bank is a common place for keeping wills. A person named in a will as executor or executrix can, after the testator's death upon proper application to the probate court, obtain an order to the bank where the will is kept to open the box and make an inventory of the box's contents. If the will is found, the bank must deliver it to the court or to the person named in the order, so that it may be submitted for probate. After the will has been admitted to probate and the executor has qualified, the executor can present the bank his letters testamentary issued by the court clerk and take charge of the box's contents.

A will may be deposited with the county clerk for safe keeping for a three dollar fee, but the deposit and the fee have no legal significance. The one depositing the will with the county clerk is merely indicating that he thinks the clerk's office is a safer place for his will than any one place on his own premises, or in his bank deposit box.

Self-Proved Wills

There is a method of making a will and providing its proof at the same time, or at a subsequent time, so that the subscribing witnesses do not have to appear in court at the time it is to be admitted and filed. Legal assistance from an attorney is needed in this procedure. This is often done when it is felt that the witnesses may not be available for giving testimony when the testator dies.

If the one making a will uses witnesses considerably older than himself, those he could reasonably expect to outlive, it may later be found that his witnesses are no longer available to prove this will. On the other hand, if he uses young people as witnesses who have not yet settled down in his neighborhood, they may move away, possibly to a foreign state or country, and it would be costly or impossible to get them to return to give testimony at the time of the testator's death. While there is a method of proving a will by taking the witnesses' deposition, this is costly and time consuming. For these, and other reasons, the law has provided for the "self-proven" will.

While the self proven will carries its own proof of execution, it, as any other will, must be probated to become effective after the death of the testator, and it is necessary to present to the court proof of the death of the testator and the date and place of death to establish the jurisdiction and venue of the court in which the will is offered for probate.

Change By Codicil

It is inherent that wills can be changed at any time while the testator is living and still of sound mind. A person making a will today can make another one tomorrow, next week, next month, next year, or years later, but it is the last one that is effective upon the testator's death, and its probate. A person may be satisfied with the will he has made, except for one or more things he has decided that he would like to include in it or things he forgot to put in it when the will was executed. The change may be made by destroying the old will and making a new one, or it may be made by a codicil, which is an addition. Since the codicil will become a part of the will, it must be made under the same rules that govern the making of wills. When it is made, and attached to the will, it becomes effective with the probate of the will after the testator's death, the same as if it had originally been written into the body of the will.

Change in Will Caused by Divorce

If a person makes a will and later is divorced, the provisions of the will concerning the divorced spouse are ineffective. For example, a man and his wife each make wills and each makes the other a beneficiary or legatee of a portion of his estate. The husband appoints the wife as his independent executrix and the wife appoints the husband as her independent executor, and each appoints the other as guardian of his or her minor children. After such a will is made, if a divorce is granted, these provisions of the will are not effective.

Passage of Estate of Testator to Descendants of his Legatees

If one making a valid will devises or bequeaths to his or her child or children or other descendants, an estate or any kind of interest in an estate and the devisees should die before the testator and leave children or descendants who do survive the testator, the devise or legacy will go to the children in the same manner as if the devisees had survived the testator and died intestate. This rule does not apply to those who are not children or other descendants of the testator. The child or other descendant of the original heir who is not a child or descendant of the testator will not receive the devise or legacy. For example: A man died leaving a will in which he made a bequest to his son; but the son died before the father, and this son left a will in which he made his adopted son his beneficiary. This adopted son, not being a descendant of the grandfather, will not receive the legacy from the adoptive grandfather. Or, if the testator named as one of his devisees a person who is not related to him and that unrelated devisee dies before the testator, the children of that unrelated devisee will not be entitled to the legacy.

The Right of Election

Sometimes a person making a will wants to dispose of property that is not his own. It most often happens in the case of community property, and it generally is the husband who makes such a will. He may honestly feel that he knows best how to provide for his wife, or he may not know that he cannot dispose of his wife's part of the community property without her consent, or he may not understand the law governing community property.

Suppose a man and his wife have considerable community property consisting of land with a home on it, livestock, cash in bank, stocks and bonds, etc., all of which is community property, and the man dies. His will provides that the wife shall have the use of the home and its furnishings, as long as she does not remarry, together with a monthly sum of money to be paid to her from the money in the bank as long as she remains single, and then he gives to each child part of the land which is valuable and divides up the stocks and bonds among his children and two or three of his sisters.

Now the wife owns one-half of all the two possess at the time of his death, and she has certain other rights as the survivor in community, such as the right to live in and use the home as long as she lives, his half of it as well as her half of it. She might consult her attorney as to her rights and decide that she will elect to repudiate the will and claim her community rights. Thereby, she will keep the home for her own use and will have certain benefits out of the community assets and a fee simple ownership of one-half of all of the other property. By this election, she will defeat a large part of the will, but she has a perfect right to do so.

However, it is not the wife alone who has the right of election. In any case where one making a will seeks to dispose of property not his or her own while at the same time making that other person, whose property is to be disposed of, a beneficiary under the will, then an election is available to that person.

This principle of the law is easy to understand by a simple illustration. Al says to Bill, "I am going to give you my black horse, and I am going to take your Shetland pony and give it to Carl." Now, obviously Al cannot dispose of Bill's pony without his consent, but Bill cannot accept the black horse and keep the pony. If he is going to receive the gift he must comply with the condition imposed with it.

Bill has the right of election. He can accept the black horse and give up the pony, or he can keep the pony and refuse the black horse.

Or suppose that John Doe, who is a widower with three children, marries Mary Roe and they have one child, John Doe, Jr. Neither the husband nor the wife has any appreciable property before their marriage, but through the years they amass a considerable community estate. Mary dies intestate and later John dies leaving a will in which he treats all of the property as if it belonged to him and he provides that it shall be divided equally among his four children.

Now, John Doe, Jr., being the only lawful heir of his deceased mother, Mary, who owned one-half of all of the community property, has the right of election. He may elect to receive under the will and give up his right of inheritance from his mother. But if he is well advised, he will repudiate the will and claim by inheritance from his mother, which he has a right to do.

Descent and Distribution

In Texas, a person may dispose of his property as he chooses. Of course, while he is living, he can sell it or give it to whomever he chooses. By making a will he can choose those who will have his property after his death, but if he fails to make a valid will, the law directs the handling of his estate upon his death. If a man dies without leaving a valid will he dies "intestate," and the laws of descent and distribution deal with this kind of estate. It is not enough that the husband tells the wife, or the wife tells the husband, "In event of my death, all of my estate is to belong to you," or "This part of my estate is to be yours and that part of my estate is to belong to the children."

Such a statement does not transfer the title nor give the person to whom it is made any right of claim to the estate after the death of the one making the statement. It does not benefit any who are mentioned as intended beneficiaries. If a person intends to make a will, but fails to do so, his expressed intention, however often it may have been repeated, is powerless after his death.

We shall now consider the provisions of the law with respect to estates of decedents who do not make wills or that part of a person's estate not disposed of by will, since sometimes a person makes a will and fails to dispose of all of his estate. In this case, that part of his estate not disposed of by

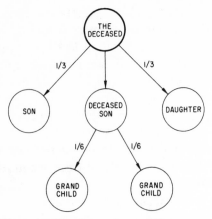

(Figure 2.1) The distribution of separate property when the deceased is not survived by a husband or wife and dies intestate (leaves no will). The property will first go to the deceased's children and their descendants.

the will is ruled according to the laws of descent and distribution.

Persons Who Inherit from an Intestate

1. *If the Intestate Leaves No Husband or Wife.* Where a person owning property dies intestate, leaving no husband or wife, his property passes and is inherited by his kindred in the following course: (a) to his children and their descendants (Figure 2.1); (b) if he has no children and there are no descendants of his children, then to his father and mother (Figure 2.2), in equal portions; but if only the father or mother survives the intestate (Figures 2.3 and 2.4), then one-half of the estate passes to that parent who is living, and the other one-half passes to the brothers and sisters of the deceased (the intestate), and to their descendants; but if there are no brothers nor sisters nor their descendants, then the whole estate is inherited by the surviving father or mother; (c) if there is neither a father nor a mother surviving,

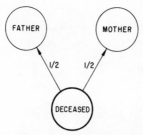

(Figure 2.2) Then, if there are no children or their descendants, the deceased's parents inherit equal shares of the separate property.

(Figure 2.3) If only one parent survives and the deceased parent is not survived by any descendants, the whole goes to the surviving parent.

and there are brothers and sisters (Figure 2.5), and their descendants, then the whole estate passes to these brothers and sisters and their descendants (if a brother or sister is deceased leaving surviving children, the part that would have passed to that brother or sister is inherited by that one's children); (d) if the deceased has none of the kindred mentioned above (Figures 2.6, 2.7, and 2.8), then his estate is divided into two equal portions, one of which passes to the paternal kindred (those on the father's side) and the other to the maternal kindred (those on the mother's side) in the following course:

to the grandfather and grandmother in equal portions, but if only one of these is living, then this portion of the

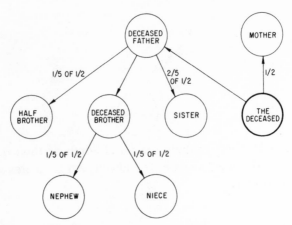

(Figure 2.4) **If only one parent survives, but the deceased parent has living heirs, then 1/2 of the estate goes to the surviving parent and the other 1/2 goes to the heirs of the deceased parent.**

estate is again divided into two equal portions, one of which passes to the grandparent who is living, and the other passes to the descendant or descendants of the deceased grandparent. If the deceased grandparent has no descendants, then the portion of the estate that would have passed to that grandparent passes to the other grandparent who does survive; if there is no grandfather or grandmother surviving, then the estate passes to their descendants, "and so on without end, passing in like manner to the nearest lineal ancestors and their descendants." If there are no relatives at all, the property "escheats" (passes) to the State of Texas.

2. *If the Intestate Leaves a Husband or Wife.* (a) If the intestate leaves a husband or wife then his estate (his separate

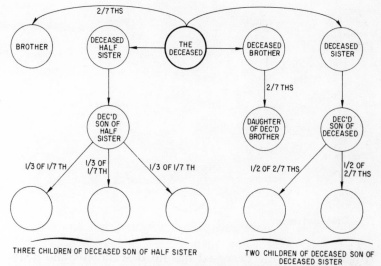

(Figure 2.5) If the deceased has no descendants and neither the father nor the mother survives, the whole of the estate will pass to the brothers and sisters of the deceased and their descendants.

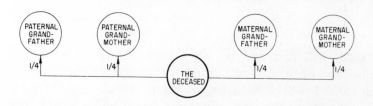

(Figure 2.6) If the deceased has none of the previously mentioned relatives, but is survived by grandparents, the estate will be divided into two equal portions, one of which shall go to the maternal grandparents and the other to the paternal grandparents.

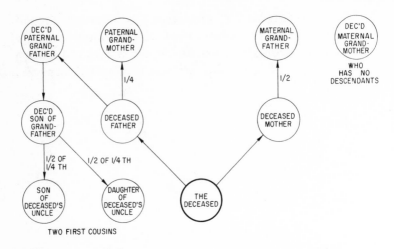

TWO FIRST COUSINS

(Figure 2.7) If the deceased has no descendants and is not survived by father or mother or their descendants but is survived by grandparents and their descendants on each side, then as before, the estate will be divided into two equal portions, one of which will go to the maternal grandparents and their descendants and the other to the paternal grandparents and their descendants.

estate) will pass and be inherited as follows (Figure 2.9): one-third of the personal property (movable property, money in bank, livestock, vehicles, corporate stocks, bonds, etc.) to his surviving wife and two-thirds to his children and their descendants, if he has a deceased child or children survived by descendants; and the homestead and one-third of his other real property (lands, minerals in the land, and houses) to his surviving wife as a life estate to be used and enjoyed by her during her lifetime with the remainder passing after her death to his children and their descendants along with the other two-thirds interest in the real property. (b) if the intestate has no child or children, or their descendants, the

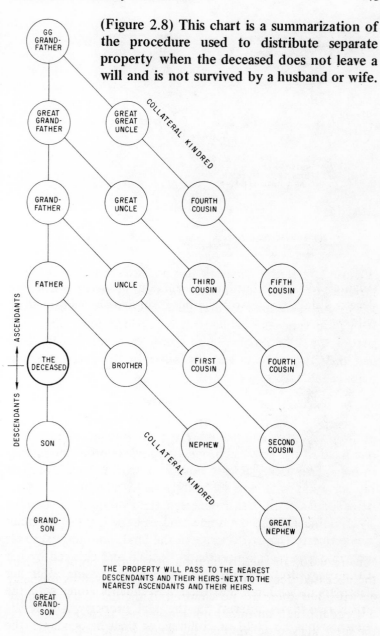

(Figure 2.8) This chart is a summarization of the procedure used to distribute separate property when the deceased does not leave a will and is not survived by a husband or wife.

THE PROPERTY WILL PASS TO THE NEAREST DESCENDANTS AND THEIR HEIRS-NEXT TO THE NEAREST ASCENDANTS AND THEIR HEIRS.

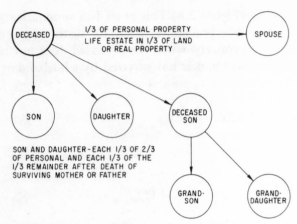

(Figure 2.9) Distribution of separate property when the deceased does not leave a will but is survived by a husband or wife.

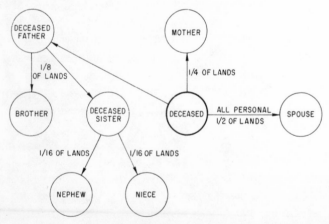

(Figure 2.10) In the distribution of separate property when the deceased does not leave a will and is survived by husband or wife, but there are no children of the deceased nor their descendants and no father nor mother nor their descendants, the surviving spouse will take the whole estate in fee.

surviving spouse (Figure 2.10) will inherit all of the personal property and one-half of the real property, without remainder to anyone else with right to sell it or to pass it by will, and the other one-half of the real property passes according to the laws of descent and distribution to the kindred of the deceased; provided, however that if the deceased has neither father nor mother nor any brother or sister, or their descendants, the surviving spouse will receive and inherit the whole estate of the deceased spouse.

Note: The foregoing illustrations deal only with separate property of the deceased—not community property.

Community Estate

The community estate is owned in equal shares by the husband and wife. When one of them dies, the survivor's one-half of the community estate is not affected, and the survivor will inherit the deceased's half of the community property if there are no children of the deceased or their descendants. If there are children of the decreased, or their descendants, they will inherit the deceased's half of the community estate, subject, however, to the survivor's right to use the homestead as a life estate. No rent is due the children for its use.

Passage of property by inheritance can better be understood if one keeps in mind that kinship derives from a common ancestor, or ancestors. For example, first cousins are relatives because they have the same grandparents. Brothers are related to each other because they have the same parents. A person is related to his uncle because his grandparents are the uncle's parents.

Inheritance *per capita* instead of *per stirpes* occurs when a person dies intestate leaving as his only heirs relatives of the same class relation to him (Fig. 2.12). It is rather unusual but it does sometimes happen. If the deceased leaves heirs that are related to him in different degrees of kinship, then the rule will not apply, and the inheritance will be *per stirpes*.

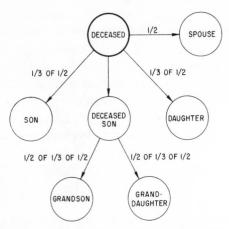

(**Figure 2.11**) **In the distribution of the community estate when the deceased left a surviving spouse and children and their descendants, the surviving spouse will take one-half of the community estate (that being the part already owned by the surviving spouse), and the children and their descendents will inherit the other half from the deceased, subject, however, to the right of the surviving spouse to a life estate in the homestead.**

Matters Affecting and Not Affecting the Right to Inherit

Persons Not in Being. If a child of an intestate is born to the surviving wife after his death, that child will inherit from the father the same as if it had been born before the father's death. Such a child would also be entitled to participate in the father's estate if the father should leave a valid will in which he provides benefits for his other children. In this case, the child born after his father's death would by law participate on an equal basis with the other children.

Heirs of Whole and Half Blood. When a person dies intestate and his property is inherited by his collateral kindred (which would be the case if he had no children, no wife, no father nor mother, nor other ascendants or de-

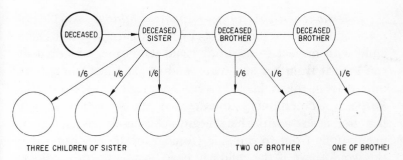

THREE CHILDREN OF SISTER   TWO OF BROTHER   ONE OF BROTHEI

(Figure 2.12) Inheritance per capita instead of per stirpes, which is rather unusual, means that if a man dies intestate, leaving no wife surviving him, and no children or their descendants, and his parents are deceased, and his sister and two brothers are deceased, but they are each survived by children, the children will be given equal shares because they are all the same class relation to the deceased.

scendants in the direct line) those of the half blood will inherit only half as much as those of the whole blood of the same class. For example, a half-brother or half-sister would inherit only half as much as a whole-brother or whole-sister. However, if all of those inheriting should be of the half blood, they would inherit whole parts.

Aliens. By provision of our constitution and statutes, aliens can inherit property in Texas.

Convicted Persons and Suicides. It does not matter that a person may have been convicted of a crime, he can inherit from his kindred and they can inherit from him, and the estates of those who die intestate by destroying their own lives will pass and be inherited the same as if they had met natural deaths. Under provisions of the Insurance Code, however, if a person who is a beneficiary under a life insurance policy intentionally causes the death of the insured, he forfeits his right to receive the benefits of the policy. The benefits would go to the next of kin of the insured.

Inheritance Rights of Illegitimate Children. An illegitimate child has the same rights of inheritance as a legitimate child with respect to its mother and its mother's kindred. It can inherit from her and them, and she and her kindred can inherit from the child. It is considered legitimate also for the purpose of determining homestead rights. A mother living in her homestead with her illegitimate child has the same exemptions from forced sale (foreclosure by creditors) that she would have if the child had been born in lawful wedlock. A child born of a common law marriage is in law considered legitimate for all purposes, inheritance rights, homestead exemptions, etc.

Advancement Brought into Hotchpotch. It so often happens that a father or mother will advance to one of the children (give to that one out of his or her estate) a portion of the family fortune or accumulation, and later when the parent dies intestate the child who received the gift or advancement comes forward for a portion of the intestate's remaining estate. If the child who received the gift or advancement brings back the amount he received so that it can be added back to the intestate's estate and can be distributed to the children along with the other assets, there can be no question about that child's right to participate in the distribution of the estate. It may be that he received a tract of land as an advancement and then sold it so that he cannot return that particular tract of land; however, it suffices if he returns, or "brings into hotchpotch," the value of the advancement. In bringing an advancement back into hotchpotch, it is not necessary that the money or other thing of value be physically returned. The value of the advancement can be added to the sum total of the intestate's estate, and when the division is made the value of the advancement can be subtracted from the amount awarded to the child who received the advancement.

Now, there is no difficulty when the one receiving the gift or advancement treats it as an "advancement." The law, however, provides that "every gratuitous *inter vivos* transfer is deemed to be an absolute gift and not an advancement unless proved to be an advancement." So here we have some difficulty when the child who received a gift or advancement contends that it was a gift and insists that he should share in the remaining estate on an equal basis with the other children. He has the law in his favor, and the burden is upon the other children to refute the legal presumption. If they fail to prove that it was in fact an advancement, intended by the parent to be an advancement to the child out of his future inheritance, then the child who received it can retain the gift and also participate with the other children in equal shares of the intestate's remaining estate.

The choice lies mainly with the one receiving the gift or advancement. Under any circumstance, he can keep the gift or advancement, whichever it may be, if he considers it more valuable than a further share in the intestate's estate. But if in fact it is proved to be an advancement, and not an out-right gift, the one who received it cannot keep it and also participate in the distribution of the remaining assets of the intestate's estate.

Passage of Title upon Simultaneous Death. Particularly in the case of deaths in fires consuming residences and in automobile accidents, storms, floods, etc., we have questions arising as to which person survived the other. This is important because the time of death of the persons involved will often determine the course an inheritance will take. An interesting example is where a man and his wife who own a considerable community estate are both killed in an automobile accident and are not survived by any child or children or their descendants. If it can be proved that the husband died first, then the whole of the community estate will pass to and be inherited by the wife's kindred. If it can be proved that the wife died first, then the whole of the community estate will pass to and be inherited by the husband's kindred.

The deaths may be separated only by minutes, but in law it is the same as months or years.

If, in such deaths resulting from a common accident, it develops that it cannot be determined which death preceded the other, the law provides that the estate will be inherited in equal shares by the kindred of the wife and the kindred of the husband; that is, equal shares will pass to each group. But in such simultaneous deaths it may be that the property rights are not exactly equal. The husband or the wife may have separate property and the other may not. In this instance the law provides that for the purpose of their estates it shall be considered that each one survived the other, and this means that neither will inherit from the other, leaving each one's estate to pass to his or her other heirs.

The law, however, leaves the husband and the wife to inherit from each other if it can be determined which preceded the other in death, even by seconds. Here is another impelling reason why people should make wills. An attorney drafting a will can anticipate such occasions and provide for them in the will.

Survival of Beneficiaries. If property is disposed of so that the right of a beneficiary to have an interest therein is conditional upon his surviving another person and the two meet death from a common cause under such circumstances that it cannot be determined which died first, it will be presumed that the beneficiary did not survive. This means that his heirs will not inherit the property.

But if property is given alternatively to one of two or more beneficiaries with the right of each being dependent upon his surviving the other or others, and they all meet death under circumstances so that it cannot be determined in which order they died, the property will be divided into as many equal portions as there are beneficiaries, and the heirs of each will inherit a portion.

Joint Owners. If stocks, bonds, money in bank, or other personal property is owned so that one of two persons will be entitled to it upon the death of the other and they both die under such circumstance that it cannot be determined which survived the other, the property will be divided into two equal parts and the heirs of each will inherit a part. If there are more than two persons owning the property, it will be divided into as many shares as there are owners, and the heirs of each owner will inherit a share.

Insured and Beneficiary. When the insured and the beneficiary under a life or accident policy meet death under such circumstances that it cannot be determined who died first, the proceeds of the policy will be distributed as if the insured had survived the beneficiary, meaning that the proceeds will pass to the estate of the insured and be inherited by his heirs or be distributed according to the terms of his will if he leaves a valid will.

If those dying under the circumstances mentioned above leave writings (contracts or wills) showing their intentions that their property not follow the courses provided by law, then the writings, if clearly understandable, will be effective instead of the applicable provision of the law.

Federal and State Taxes Upon Estates of Decedents

The United States government and the State of Texas impose a tax upon estates of decedents that are valued above the exemptions or credits allowed, and these taxes apply the same whether the decedent left a valid will or died intestate.

The federal government, in taxing estates of decedents, allows a "credit" of $47,000 against the tax itself. This is the equivalent of an "exemption" of $175,625. If the value of an estate is less than $175,625, no tax will be due.

Table 2-1
Rate Schedule for Computing Tentative Tax
of Citizens or Residents

If Taxable Amount is:	The Tax is:
0 to $10,000	18% of such amount
$10,000 to $20,000	$1,800 plus 20% on excess over $10,000
$20,000 to $40,000	$3,800 plus 22% on excess over $20,000
$40,000 to $60,000	$8,200 plus 24% on excess over $40,000
$60,000 to $80,000	$13,000 plus 26% on excess over $60,000
$80,000 to $100,000	$18,200 plus 28% on excess over $80,000
$100,000 to $150,000	$23,800 plus 30% on excess over $100,000
$150,000 to $250,000	$38,800 plus 32% on excess over $150,000
$250,000 to $500,000	$70,800 plus 34% on excess over $250,000
$500,000 to $750,000	$155,800 plus 37% on excess over $500,000
$750,000 to $1,000,000	$248,300 plus 39% on excess over $750,000
$1,000,000 to $1,250,000	$345,800 plus 41% on excess over $1,000,000
$1,250,000 to $1,500,000	$448,300 plus 43% on excess over $1,250,000
$1,500,000 to $2,000,000	$555,800 plus 45% on excess over $1,500,000
$2,000,000 to $2,500,000	$780,800 plus 49% on excess over $2,000,000
$2,500,000 to $3,000,000	$1,025,800 plus 53% on excess over $2,500,000
$3,000,000 to $3,500,000	$1,290,800 plus 57% on excess over $3,000,000
$3,500,000 to $4,000,000	$1,575,800 plus 61% on excess over $3,500,000
$4,000,000 to $4,500,000	$1,880,800 plus 65% on excess over $4,000,000
$4,500,000 to $5,000,000	$2,205,800 plus 69% on excess over $4,500,000
Over $5,000,000	$2,550,800 plus 70% on excess over $5,000,000

If the value of the estate is greater than $175,625 there will be a federal tax on it after the owner's death, and the amount of the tax can be estimated by computing the tax, without regard for any exemption, using the schedule in Table 2-1, and then subtracting $47,000 from the tax arrived at. This applies to all except those whose tax outlook has changed because of gifts made during or prior to the current tax year.

For taxable estates of $40,000 or more, the federal government allows certain credits for state death taxes, but the State of Texas assesses an additional tax on the estate that is equal to the amount of the credits allowed by the federal government. Therefore, the benefit of the credits allowed goes to the state and not to the tax paying estate.

The State of Texas bases its inheritance tax upon the amount received by each beneficiary or heir, and the exemptions it allows are based upon relationship of the beneficiaries to the deceased, and they are divided into classes:

Class A includes husband or wife and their direct descendants, any direct lineal descendant or ascendant of the decedent, the legally adopted child of decedent, any direct lineal descendant of adopted child of decedent, the husband of a daughter and the wife of a son.

For property passing to beneficiaries (or a beneficiary) in Class A during the period beginning September 1, 1978 and ending through August 31, 1982 the first $200,000 in value is exempted from the tax; for the period beginning September 1, 1982 and ending through August 31, 1985 the exemption is $250,000; and for the period beginning September 1, 1985 the exemption is $300,000. If there are more beneficiaries than one, the exemption is divided among them according to the amounts received.

After the above mentioned exemptions, property passing to Class A beneficiaries is taxed as follows:

On any value not exceeding $50,000 .... 1 %

On any value between $50,000 and $100,000 .... 2 %

On any value between $100,000 and $200,000 .... 3 %

On any value between $200,000 and $500,000 .... 4 %

On any value between $500,000 and $1,000,000 .... 5 %

On any value exceeding $1,000,000 .... 6 %

Class B includes the United States when the benefits passing to the government are to be used in the State of Texas. For Class B the first $25,000 will bear no inheritance tax.

Class C includes brothers and sisters of decedent and their direct lineal descendants. The first $10,000 of the estate will bear no inheritance taxes.

Table 2-2
Inheritance Tax Rates After $25,000

Over	But Not Exceeding	The Tax Rate is
$ 25,000	$ 50,000	1%
50,000	100,000	2%
100,000	200,000	3%
200,000	500,000	4%
500,000	1,000,000	5%
1,000,000	— — — —	6%

Table 2-3
Class C — Tax Rates

Over	But Not Exceeding	The Tax Rate is
$ 10,000	$ 25,000	3%
25,000	50,000	4%
50,000	100,000	5%
100,000	250,000	6%
250,000	500,000	7%
500,000	750,000	8%
750,000	1,000,000	9%
1,000,000	— — — —	10%

Table 2-4
Class D Tax Rates

Over	But Not Exceeding	The Rate is
$ 1,000	$ 10,000	4%
10,000	25,000	5%
25,000	50,000	6%
50,000	100,000	7%
100,000	500,000	10%
500,000	1,000,000	12%
1,000,000	— — — —	15%

Table 2-5
Class E Tax Rates

Over	But Not Exceeding	The Rate is
$ 500	$ 10,000	5%
10,000	25,000	6%
25,000	50,000	8%
50,000	100,000	10%
100,000	500,000	12%
500,000	1,000,000	15%
1,000,000	————	20%

Class D includes uncles and aunts and their direct lineal descendants. The first $1,000 passing to any of them will bear no inheritance taxes.

Class E includes the United States when the benefits are not to be used in this State and all other persons, institutions, organizations, corporations and associations not included in the Classes A, B, C, and D. The first $500 will bear no inheritance taxes when received by any in Class E.

However, the foregoing provisions will not apply, which means no tax will be collected on any bequest, devise or gift to the United States, or a religious, educational, or charitable organization, which is, in writing and prior to the payment of the tax, irrevocably committed for use exclusively within the State of Texas. The terms religious, educational, or charitable organization include a youth organization or program for physical fitness, character development, and citizenship training or similar program.

3. Property: Personal, Real and Corporate

Americans traditionally are landowners. One of the first concerns of English colonists was to acquire land on which they could build homes. George Washington was a land surveyor and the owner of extensive lands centering around his impressive estate at Mount Vernon. John Adams, the second president, was the son of a farmer. Thomas Jefferson, the third president, who owned Monticello, surrounded his mansion with a complete farming domain. James Madison was the son of a planter. Andrew Jackson received much of his compensation for legal fees in land, and after serving as the seventh president, returned to his land near Nashville, his beloved Hermitage. Robert E. Lee, a great military leader, loved his native Virginia and his home, Arlington.

Incidents of Ownership of Land

Unlike many foreign countries, the United States government, along with the other states including the State of Texas recognizes complete ownership of land. There are some limitations, but generally this means the owner of a tract of land owns the vegetation growing upon it, the water in its strata below the surface, and all minerals. Theoretically at least, this ownership goes to the center of the earth terminating at a mere point.

However, this ownership implies severability or the right to sell out of the land any or all of the minerals and other rights. So when one is acquiring land, he should find out what

58

has been done by prior owners. A part or all of the minerals may have been sold by a prior owner; or an oil, gas, and mineral lease may have been sold; or timber on the land has been sold and the purchaser is to remove it at a later date; or the fresh water rights have been sold. In all such instances, one purchasing the land recognizes those prior severed and outstanding interests and is subject to them.

Land titles originate from what is commonly termed the "sovereignty of the soil." Before Texas became a state, it was an independent nation, the Republic of Texas. Before it was a republic it was one of the states of Mexico and it was originally a possession of Spain.

Each of these sovereign powers, during its ownership of the land which is now Texas, was the "sovereignty of the soil" and could grant title to the land. Mexico, and Spain before it, in transferring the title to the land did not part with the minerals. It was those governments' theory that the minerals belonged to the government and no minerals should be privately owned. Mexico presently claims title to minerals in all lands within its borders.

When Texas became independent of Mexico, it adopted the English rule which considered minerals the property of the land owner. As a state, Texas has the same rule, and as a result, one who owns the land owns the minerals in it unless there has been a severance. Even the Spanish grants and the Mexican grants are considered by the State of Texas to have conveyed the minerals with the soil, even though those governments did not so intend it at the time the grants were made.

However, in 1897, the Texas Legislature passed a law that provided that thereafter sales should be without the minerals, and from that date, purchasers acquiring lands from the state took the lands with the mineral rights reserved by the state. In these sales there was a severance of all of the mineral rights from the soil.

But in 1919, the legislature enacted the so-called "Relinquishment Act," which appointed the owner of the soil as the state's agent for leasing minerals in the land. For his services, the agent (the owner of the surface of the land) is given a share in the returns from the lease.

Land Grants from the Sovereignty

The first conveyance out of the sovereignty of the soil is generally referred to as a "grant." By scanning records in the various counties, or those in the General Land Office in Austin, one will find that the Spanish government made many land grants before Mexico gained her independence from Spain and many were made by the Government of Mexico before Texas gained her independence from Mexico. Likewise, the Republic of Texas continued to make land grants, and Texas still follows the practice. It may seem that these governments were extravagant in granting, in some instances, such large tracts of land to people who settled upon the soil or to people who had rendered military or other service to the sovereign. The large grants can be accounted for by understanding that these several governments were anxious to have people settle upon the land and make it productive and thereby create wealth. Moreover, the governments desired to give people title to the land so it could be taxed and bring in revenue for support of the government.

The Original Survey or Measurement of the Land

It was the practice of these early governments to require the owner of the land grant to have the land surveyed at his own expense. Of course, in the early days few men were qualified to make accurate land surveys, and often a man who knew very little about surveying would be designated as the public, or official surveyor in a colony. It is probable that some of them did not possess surveying instruments. Moreover, there were no roads leading to the lands they were to survey, and transportation was slow and difficult. So it could be expected that some surveys would be inaccurate, some of them so much so that the poorly delineated lines could not be followed or not any or only some of the corners could be found. But people moved in and occupied the land and it was not the government's policy to move them out because of the inaccuracy of the land survey. Even after Texas became a state, the legislature passed acts intended to validate all of these Spanish, Mexican and Republic of Texas land grants.

Despite all of this, some of these old surveys have been challenged, but even with the inaccuracies they have been hard to invalidate. Even the State of Texas has filed proceedings against some of the old titleholders, mainly on the grounds that outlines of a survey include more land than the grant specified. It is only reasonable to expect that those first surveyors would be generous with the man applying for the land since he was paying them for their work. Because of the surveyors' generosity, most of these old surveys contained more, rather than less, land than the grant specified. In one instance where the state sued, the excess land mapped out by the surveyor amounted to eleven leagues. A league is 4,428 acres of land, and eleven leagues amount to a sizeable pasture —48,708 acres. Regardless of this excess, the courts supported those claiming the land under the grant. It is a rule in Texas that if the surveyor's footsteps can be traced and the corners he described and designated can be found, the survey cannot be defeated because of excess land within its outlines, even eleven leagues of excess land. It is often jocularly said that those frontier surveyors measured the land with a coonskin and threw in the tail for good measure.

Land Deeds

Voluntary conveyances of land, after the original grant, are made by deeds. A deed properly made is a written instrument reciting a consideration, containing words of grant, describing the land conveyed so that it can be located, and generally containing some warranty (or guarantee) of title. They fall into three general classes:

The *general warranty deed.* The grantor agrees to defend the title that is given to the grantee, his heirs, executors, administrators, successors, and assigns against all persons who may claim it against them. In it, he even binds his executors and administrators to do so. In this situation, if the title fails, the grantor can be sued for the loss suffered by the purchaser.

The *special warranty deed.* The grantor warrants the title only against those who may claim it by, through, or under him, the grantor. He does not guarantee that the title is good against any and all persons who may later claim it, but he does guarantee that he, himself, has not sold or encumbered the land.

The *quit claim deed.* The grantor does not guarantee or warrant anything. He does not even claim that he has the title, but in effect, he says such title as I have, I hereby convey. If the title fails, he is not responsible.

There is also another kind of deed sometimes used which is a different version of the quit claim deed. It is one in which the grantor, where the warranty clause would ordinarily be written, finishes it with, "but this conveyance is without warranty of title," or other words to that effect. Here again, the grantor frees himself of responsibility if the title fails.

Necessity for Title Examination or Title Insurance

When one is purchasing land, it is necessary that he assure himself that he is getting a good title. It is not sufficient that the man or the company selling him the land warrants the title. The one who sells the land may not be financially responsible or may not continue to be financially responsible so that a loss could be recovered against him. There are two general methods commonly used, and they are both effective in assuring the purchaser that he is receiving good title.

In the first method, the purchaser may require of the seller that he furnish a complete abstract of title. This is supplied by an abstracter, generally a corporation chartered for the purpose and under bond to guarantee the accuracy of its work. The abstract is a compilation of all of the deeds and other records in the county in which the land is located that affect, or have any bearing on, the title to the land involved. It will contain a copy of all of those documents and constitutes a complete history of the title to the land. With this abstract, the purchaser, before he pays the consideration or becomes obligated for it, places it with his attorney for examination. The attorney will review the title's whole history and give a written opinion to the purchaser. If the attorney shows or states in his opinion that the purchaser will be receiving a good title by the proposed deed from the seller, or that the title is, at the time the abstract is closed, good in the seller, then the purchaser can depend upon that opinion and close the trade.

In the second, the purchaser may require that the seller furnish a guaranteed title, or title insurance, by a title insurance or title guaranty company. This title policy, or title insurance policy, should be delivered to the purchaser's attorney so he can make sure that the "exceptions" that may be contained in it do not leave too much risk for the purchaser to bear. If the purchaser's attorney states that the title insurance is in order, and that the purchaser is properly protected, then the purchaser can feel confident that he is receiving a good title by the deed from the seller.

In each of these instances, it should be kept in mind that the warranty in the deed and the title insurance protect the purchaser against loss only to the extent of the land's purchase price. One might think that, if he purchases a tract of land for $1,000 and has a general warranty in his deed or has title insurance and the land later is worth $10,000 and the title fails, he would be entitled to recover under the warranty or the insurance policy the current land value ($10,000). That is not the rule. He would only be able to recover the purchase price.

Both of these methods are extensively used, and a purchaser should be governed by his attorney's advice as to which one he chooses.

Necessity for Recording the Deed

As soon as the transaction is closed, the purchaser should place his deed of record in the county clerk's office in the county where the land is located. If the transaction is handled by a title insurance company or title guaranty company, that company will record the deed. When the deed is recorded, it is notice that the land described in the deed belongs to the person named as the purchaser, and all persons having any dealings pertaining to that tract of land are bound by the notice given by the recording of the deed.

If the purchaser fails to record his deed, he is subject to risks from different directions:

1. The seller might forget that he has sold the land and sell it to someone else who does not know about the previous sale, and in this case, the second purchaser, if he is truly an innocent purchaser, will own the land.

2. The seller might forget that he has sold the land and borrow money and give a mortgage on the land to secure the loan, in which case, if the loan is not paid, the lender of the money might foreclose his mortgage and the first purchaser would lose his title to the land.

3. The seller might be sued for some other obligation and a judgment against him would create a lien against the land, and the purchaser may then lose the land.

There are other reasons why a deed should be recorded, but those listed are sufficient to show that a purchaser should lose no time in getting his deed of record.

Vendor's Lien

In the sale of land, more often than otherwise, part of the consideration is paid in cash and the balance of it is represented by promissory vendor's lien notes to be paid at later specified dates. The deed, by which title is conveyed, states the amount to be paid and describes briefly the notes that are signed by the purchaser, and it stipulates that a vendor's lien is retained to secure payment of the notes, the interest, and attorney fees, if placed with an attorney for collection. It often also mentions that the notes are further secured by a *deed of trust* executed by the purchaser to a named trustee.

The Deed of Trust

In the sale of real property, i.e. land, buildings, etc., the usual procedure is for the seller to give the purchaser a deed, which is generally a warranty deed (but not always so) reciting the consideration paid and agreed to be paid by the purchaser for the property. The purchaser receives the deed from the seller, and at the same time, pays the cash consideration, which is only part of the total consideration. The purchaser also signs vendor's lien notes to the seller to evidence the deferred payments to be made. At the same time, he signs a deed of trust to a trustee who is chosen by the seller, and by this deed of trust, the purchaser conveys the title to the land to the trustee. However, this transferring of the title is in trust to secure the payment of the notes, that are also described in the deed of trust, and conditioned so that if the notes are paid as they become due, the deed of trust will be of no further force and effect. This means that the title will then be the purchaser's by virtue of the deed from the seller, and not kept by the trustee. To clear his title of record, the purchaser must obtain from the seller a release of the vendor's lien and the deed of trust lien, and this instrument should be placed on record in the county clerk's office.

But if the purchaser fails to pay the notes, or any of them as they become due, the seller will call upon the trustee to sell the property at public auction in accordance with the authority granted to him in the deed of trust and apply the proceeds to the payment of the notes.

The particular virtue of the deed of trust is that the seller does not have to go to court to prove that default has been made in payment of the notes. The trustee has full authority, within the limits in the deed of trust, to post notices of sale and actually sell the property as a protection to the seller's interests. Of course, this must not be done wrongly or unjustly. The trustee is not authorized to make the sale unless the purchaser is actually in default, and it is very seldom that this mistake is made.

If there is a default, and the property is sold by the trustee, anyone may go to the sale and bid on the property. The successful bidder must pay cash for the property, and the trustee will deed the property to him. The trustee then pays the notes, if he receives enough money at the sale to do so, and, if there is any money left over, he pays it to the man who made the notes. If the amount received is insufficient to pay the full amount of the notes and the interest, he applies it as far as it will go, and then the seller may sue the maker for the balance due on the notes. The notes constitute a personal obligation of the maker, and he has no escape if what is received at the trustee's sale is inadequate.

Enforcing the Vendor's Lien Without the Deed of Trust

If the sale of the land is made for part cash and part vendor's lien notes, and no deed of trust is executed by the purchaser, as is mentioned above, then the enforcement of the vendor's lien necessitates court action. The holder of the notes cannot of his own volition take over the property or sell it at public auction, as the trustee in the deed of trust could do when a deed of trust is used. The one holding the defaulted notes must bring a suit in the district court, since it involves title to land, and he must prove to the court's satisfaction that he is the owner of the notes or note on which he sues, that default has been made, that he has demanded payment and that payment has not been made, and that the amount he sues for is still due and unpaid. If the court is satisfied with the proof offered, a judgment will be entered against the maker of the notes for the principal sum due, the interest, and the attorney's fee. This judgment itself will constitute a lien against the land in favor of the plaintiff (the one who brings the suit). In due time, an execution will be issued by the court clerk directing the county sheriff, in which the land is located, to levy upon the property and to sell it at public auction. Due notice of sale will be given and at the courthouse door on the appointed date, the sheriff will offer the land for sale and will sell it to the highest bidder for cash. The sheriff will make the purchaser at the sale a deed to the land, and he will apply the proceeds to payment of the note or notes and the interest after deducting the court costs and his fees.

If the proceeds of the sale are sufficient to defray the expenses, the note or notes, interest, and the attorney fees, then the purchaser will owe no more, but he has lost his land. If the sale's proceeds are insufficient to satisfy the judgment in its entirety, the deficiency will stand as a remaining amount due on the judgment or as a deficiency judgment against the maker of the notes, and he may be faced with a levy upon and sale of other property to satisfy it.

Ownership of Land in Indivision – Partition

Frequently, several people acquire title to a tract of land so that each owns a fractional interest in it. This often results from inheritance; for example, one owning land may die intestate leaving several lawful heirs and this results in the heirs owning the land in indivision.

Under certain circumstances, it may be desirable to continue to own the land in indivision, but generally, the owners will ultimately want their respective shares given to them separately so that each one will own a separate piece of acreage.

If there are only two people owning the land in indivision, the partition of it between them should be simple, but it is not always so. It has been suggested that the one desiring to divide the land should draw a plat and cut the land into two parts and let the other owner choose his half. If there are more than two owners the problem is not so easy, and the greater the number of owners, the more difficult the problem becomes. However, if the owners can all agree, the land can be cut into as many parcels as there are owners, with all parcels having equal value, as near as may be reasonably determined, and a drawing is held so that each will receive a share, and all parties can enter into a partition deed to carry the drawing into effect.

But if no agreement on the method of division can be reached, the person or the persons desiring to divide the property can bring a suit for partition in the district court. No one is obligated to leave his land in indivision if he desires to have it partitioned.

It sometimes is desirable to leave the minerals in indivision, particularly if a portion of the land is in production. It has happened that a family will partition inherited land, minerals and all, and later find that one or more of the partitioned tracts produce oil or gas and the others do not. However, again if the several owners are agreeable, they may partition the land, minerals and all, and then join together in making oil, gas and mineral leases, all of them signing the same lease and describing all of the land in the lease. This is particularly desirable in the case of small tracts, say 5, 10, 15, or 20 acres each. Thus they pool and unitize their land for the purpose of the lease so that if oil or gas is discovered on any part of the land, they all will receive a royalty according to the amount of acreage owned, regardless of on whose tract the well may be located. After the lease is terminated, whether the land was productive or not before the leases's termination, the land is no longer pooled.

Of course, under the pooling provisions contained in most oil, gas and mineral leases, the same thing can be accomplished. But if the owners of the several tracts make separate leases, it is the lessee who decides how the tracts are to be unitized. If the landowners join in one lease, however, they can also provide that if any part of the larger tract is put into a unit, the whole tract must be included. But even if they do not make such a provision and only part of the land is included in a producing unit, then all of the landowners will participate in the returns from that part that does go into the unit.

Minerals in the Land

Under our American ownership system, the minerals in the land belong to the landowner, unless the rights have been transferred or otherwise severed from the land. Minerals are considered part of the land or realty. This is different from the rules in many foreign countries where the minerals belong to the government, not to the individual who owns the land.

But minerals, which include oil and gas, can be sold out of the land or severed from it in whole or in part, even as a landowner may sell an undivided interest in his land itself. When one sells a tract of land without reserving the minerals, he sells the minerals with the land, even though no mention is made of minerals in the land deed.

The minerals in Texas land that are most valuable in the aggregate and most traded are oil, gas, and sulfur. Most of the sulfur found in this state is in the cap rock of salt domes. Oil and gas are found in porous formations in the earth, such as sand strata, porous limestone, cap rock of salt domes, etc.

Since the oil and gas industry has never been able to develop oil and gas finding techniques into an exact science, much of the land in Texas has potential value for oil and gas leasing, or oil, gas, and sulfur leasing, or oil, gas and mineral leasing, even though it may never produce.

The oil, gas, and mineral lease is the document most commonly used when a landowner sells to the one buying the lease a right to explore his land for minerals, develop them, and market them. Usually the lease reserves for the land-owner, or mineral owner, a portion of the minerals that may be found, produced, and marketed, and this retained or reserved interest is known as "royalty." It is usually 1/8th of the oil and gas, free of cost, into the pipeline and one dollar or more per long ton of sulfur mined and marketed. While the royalty on oil and gas is usually 1/8th, it may be more or less, according to the trade made between the landowner and the one buying the lease. Also the lease has a "primary term," say five years, during which the lease can be kept effective by paying annual rentals, and the lease will name a bank as the land or mineral owner's agent to receive the rentals. At the end of the primary terms, the one buying the lease will lose the lease unless he is then producing oil, gas, or other minerals from the land or carrying on operations upon the land for that purpose. If oil, gas, or other minerals are produced upon the land during the primary term, then no delay rentals are necessary to keep the lease effective as long as production continues. Production will keep the lease effective as long as it continues after the end of the primary term, even though production began after the end of the lease's primary term, but was a result of operations started on or before the end of the primary term and continued till production began.

There are many different forms of oil, gas, and mineral leases commonly used. Most major oil companies have their own forms which they prefer to use, and they differ from company to company in some respects, sometimes only in minor detail. But the leases generally follow a common pattern such as the form one can buy at stationery stores.

Royalty is Free of the Cost of Producing It

The royalty reserved under the lease's terms is produced into the tanks or into the pipeline to which the wells may be connected free of the production costs, but not tax free.

Pooling and Unitization

Most modern lease forms provide for the pooling or unitization of the land covered by the lease with other lands or leases in the immediate vicinity. This enables the operator of the leases to form units of more or less uniform size so that the oil in the pool, or common reservoir, can be produced without drilling excess wells. It also enables the operator to do a better job for the royalty owners. By pooling and unitizating, the operator can come nearest to delivering to each royalty owner shares in the royalty oil and gas produced on the basis of the amount of royalty interest he owns in the pooled unit. To illustrate: If A owns 80 acres of land which he has leased with pooling privileges, and the operator forms a 160-acre unit by putting A's 80 acres in with another tract of 80 acres, then A will own one-half of his original fraction of royalty, but he will have it under a tract twice the size of his original tract. If he has a 1/8th royalty under his 80 acres, then he will have a 1/16th royalty under the 160-acre unit. With such a unit, it does not make any difference to A whether the well is drilled on his 80 acres or on the other half of the unit. He participates in the royalty just the same.

Overriding Royalty

The royalty reserved in an oil, gas and mineral lease by a land or mineral owner is commonly called "base royalty," but there is another kind of royalty often created called "overriding royalty." If the lease holder sells the lease to another operator for the purpose of exploration and/or drilling, he most likely will reserve a fractional interest in the oil, gas, and other minerals (say 1/32nd) in the assignment wherein he specifies that such royalty be paid or delivered to him free of the production cost. This is overriding royalty. The operator holding a lease may sell a fractional part of the oil, gas, and other minerals to be produced under terms of the lease and specify that such fractional part shall be paid to or delivered to the purchaser free of the production cost. In this case, he has sold an overriding royalty which he has carved out of his working interest.

When Minerals are Severed From the Land

Sometimes all of the minerals are sold out of the land, or a landowner may sell the land and reserve all of the mineral rights. If this happens, the one who owns the minerals has the same rights with respect to the minerals as he would have if he owned the land with the minerals. He can sell part or all of the minerals, carve out and sell royalty interests in the minerals, or he can lease the land for oil, gas, and mineral development.

The one who owns the land without owning any interest in the minerals cannot prevent the mineral interest owner or the one who leased the rights from coming upon the land to develop the mineral estate. One acquiring a lease from the mineral interest owner has the same rights that he would have if the minerals had not been severed from the land. If he does not do the land any more damage in his operations than is reasonably necessary, he will not owe the land owner any damages for his operations. The one who owns the land without any interest in the minerals is compensated by the lower price that he had to pay for the land, and he is charged with full knowledge when he buys the land that mineral production operations may be carried on upon the land to his inconvenience and reasonable damage.

Damages to Fences, Crops and Timber Upon the Land

Most oil, gas, and mineral leases provide that the one buying the lease will be responsible for damages to fences, growing crops, and timber upon the land caused by his operations. But even if a lease does not include this provision, the one who carries on such operations and causes damage will be responsible to the owner. It has been held repeatedly by the courts that an oil operator holding a valid oil and gas lease, or oil, gas and mineral lease, has the right to use as much of the surface of the land and a roadway into the location as is necessary to his operation. Controversies more often arise when the landowner leases his land for oil, gas and other minerals, and, either before or afterward, leases the same land to another for agricultural purposes. The responsibility of the oil operator is little changed because of the agricultural lease. The tenant farmer is inclined to be far less tolerant toward the oil operator because he, the tenant farmer, will not benefit from the possible results from the operations in developing the minerals. If the operator of an oil, gas and mineral lease goes upon agricultural land when no crops are growing upon it, as in the winter time, then he does not damage any growing crops in his operations. This is a different situation than going in the middle of a field with growing crops, making a road and occupying two or three acres for the drill site. On the other hand, if the operator goes on the land when there are no crops growing, then spring comes and the tenant farmer gets ready to plant, especially if the agricultural lease is older than the oil lease, the tenant farmer has a valid complaint that the landowner and the operator must answer.

Railroad Commission Regulation of Oil and Gas

Under Texas laws, the Railroad Commission is charged with regulating the oil and gas business in the state in its several phases — production, transportation, refining and marketing. Before any well can be drilled in search of oil and gas, a permit must be obtained from the oil and gas division of the Railroad Commission, and that permit is for a specific location which cannot be changed without the commission's permission.

The permit is granted without charge to the applicant when the application is in order and shows the proposed location to be "regular," which is not requiring exception to the spacing or other rules of the commission. But every permit requires the applicant to contact the Water Development Board and receive a direction as to the amount of surface casing required to protect the fresh water sands from pollution. Once the permit is issued and the applicant begins his operations, then he must make following reports to the commission (a) a completion report to show how the well was completed, a dry hole or a producer, including a driller's log of the well to show the various strata or formations encountered in the drilling process; (b) if the well is a dry hole, a plugging record must be furnished to show how the well was plugged. The rules require that the well be filled with mud and that it have cement plugs at such depths as will prevent the flow of salt water into fresh water zones and prevent the escape of fluid from the well onto the surface of the ground. (c) if the well is a producer, then a potential test must be made and reported to show how much oil or gas the well is capable of producing and (d) a report must be made to show the oil or gas purchasers whom the operator has authorized to receive the production from the well; and before these purchasers can move such products from the lease, they must have written authorization from the Railroad Commission.

Each month after the well is put on production, the operator must make a report to the Railroad Commission showing the amount of production from the well during the last or preceding month, and the amount sold during the month, and the amount on hand in stock tanks at the end of the month. Heavy penalties are assessed on those making false reports.

A barrel of oil is defined by statute as 42 gallons, and a cubic foot of gas is defined as that amount of gas necessary to fill one cubic foot of space with a standard pressure of 14.65 pounds per square inch (which is atmospheric pressure at sea-level) at a standard temperature of 60 degrees Fahrenheit.

Eminent Domain

It is recognized by the laws of the State of Texas that it is necessary for the state or U. S. Government or their subdivisions to build public roads, streets, courthouses, libraries, post offices, military installations, public schools, water works, sewers and other structures for the public good. It is also recognized that railroads, telephone and telegraph lines, pipelines for gas or oil transportation or other products are necessary for all of the people, and therefore the right of "eminent domain" is an unusual power available to acquire real estate at a fair cost for building or construction of these necessities. Otherwise, general progress may be blocked to the injury of all. This is a case where individual rights must be subordinated to the public interest. But property taken in this manner or "condemned," must be fairly and adequately compensated for, a protection which is guaranteed to the property owner by Section 17, Article 1 of the *Texas Constitution,* under the "Bill of Rights."

If the government, or its subdivision, a corporation, or any other entity having the right of eminent domain, fails to make a settlement with the owner of needed real estate, a petition can be filed with the county judge in the county where the property is located, requesting the condemnation of the property and naming the owner. The petitioning party and the property owner can themselves name three commissioners whose duty is to appraise the property to be taken, if they are approved by the county judge. But if the parties cannot agree upon the commissioners or if the county judge does not approve of those chosen (which would be an exception to the general practice) then the judge will appoint the commissioners.

These commissioners then, after giving the interested parties notice of the time and place, hold a hearing where both parties have the right to be heard and present evidence as to the value of the property to be taken, the resulting damage to other property, if any, of the owner or the value increase of the property, if any, which reasonably could be expected to result from the intended use of the property. The commissioners must make a statement in writing to the county judge based upon the evidence given at the hearing.

The notices for such a hearing must be served upon the interested parties at least five full days before the hearing date, and the hearing must be at a convenient place near the property in question or at the county seat. The person serving the notices of hearing is generally the county sheriff, his deputy, or a constable, but any person qualified to testify may serve and return the notices.

The commissioners' report to the county judge shall give the damages they assessed to be paid by the party who is taking the property and the costs that have accrued in the proceedings and the party or parties on whom the costs shall fall, including a $3 fee per day for each commissioner for each day the commissioners have served.

If either party is dissatisfied with the decision, the party may, within ten days after the decision has been filed with the county judge, file his objections in writing, giving his grounds of objection. The adverse party shall be cited and the cause shall be tried and determined as in other civil cases in the county court.

If no objections to the decision are filed within ten days, the county judge will have the decision recorded in the minutes of the county court, and will make the decision the judgment of the court and issue necessary orders for its enforcement.

An appeal from the judgment of the county court may be taken as in other civil cases. If the appeal is by the state or federal government, or some subdivision of either, no appeal bond is to be posted by the appellant. If the appeal is by a private citizen or anyone else, not the state or federal government or their subdivisions, a bond is required. But if an appeal is taken, the county court's judgment is not suspended. Of course, if the appellate court makes a different decision from that of the county court, the appellate court's decision and judgment will become effective and set aside the county court's judgment.

On appeal, the losing party pays the costs. For example, if a railroad company wants to condemn a piece of land belonging to a person to be used as a railroad station site and obtains judgment in the county court for possession of the land and in the judgment the price of the land is fixed, should the property-owner be dissatisfied because the price is too low, he can appeal the case and on appeal he can obtain a judgment for a higher price than was fixed by county court. Then the railroad company will have to pay the costs. However, if on appeal the property-owner does not obtain judgment for a higher price, he must pay the costs.

In condemnation proceedings under the right of eminent domain, the one condemning the property does not obtain the fee title to the property condemned. He obtains the use of the property only to serve the purpose which he claims is the reason he needs the property. To illustrate, if a pipeline company brings an action under the right of eminent domain to build and operate a pipeline across A's land, and the company obtains judgment giving it the right to do so, the company does not acquire the fee title to the land; or the title to the minerals in the land, or the grazing rights. The only right acquired is to build and operate a pipeline over and across the land. A still owns the land, but his use of it is subject to the right of the pipeline company to build and operate a pipeline. The pipeline company has an "easement."

The Law of Limitation

Actions for Land and the So-Called "Squatter's Rights"

"Limitation" as the word is here used means: (a) the time during which a person owning or claiming land has a right to commence a lawsuit to recover land in possession of another; and (b) the time that the one in possession must hold it adverse to the owner or claimant in order to perfect his title to it. If limitation (time) runs against the owner for sufficient time that he loses his title to the one in possession, then the owner has lost his title "by limitation", the one in possession has perfected his title "by limitation." One who takes possession of land without the consent of the owner is commonly called a "squatter."

The statutes dealing with limitation describe the several different kinds, three, five, ten, and twenty-five years. The one we are most often confronted with is the ten year limitation, and the article is quoted in full.

Ten Years' Possession

"Any person who has the right of action for the recovery of land, tenements or hereditaments against another having peaceable and adverse possession thereof, cultivating, using or enjoying the same, shall institute his suit therefor within 10 years next after his cause of action shall have accrued, and not afterward. The peaceable and adverse possession contemplate, in this article, as against the person having the right of action, shall be construed to embrace not more than one hundred and sixty acres, including the improvement, or the number of acres actually enclosed, should the same exceed 160 acres; but when such possession is taken and held under some written memorandum of title, other than a deed, which fixes the boundaries of the possessor's claim and is duly registered, such peaceable possession shall be construed to be coextensive with the boundaries specified in such instrument." *Vernon's Annotated Civil Statutes.*

Depending upon which side of the litigation a person may be on, this can be a very harsh rule. For instance, if a person has legitimate title to a piece of land and then finds that some other person has been living on it or using it as his own for ten years, he then loses title to it. That is the way the law provides that the title can be passed. It is not necessary that the one in possession pay any taxes during the ten-year period, and the titleholder may himself be paying the taxes each year as they accrue. But even under these circumstances the titleholder can and will lose his title to the one living on his land if he does not bring suit within the ten year period to oust the one in possession, if that one in possession uses the provisions of this article in his efforts to hold the land. But the person in possession, in order to perfect his title under this ten year statute, must hold the land without the consent of the true owner. If he is in possession and using the land by the owner's permission, he is recognizing the owner's rights to the land, and this will defeat the possessor if he attempts to take the title. In order to perfect his title, the one in possession must at all times during the ten years treat the land as if it belonged to him and not at anytime during such period recognize or acknowledge that the land belongs to anyone else.

Moreover, this man in possession of a portion of a large tract may, if he is well advised, perfect his title to 160 acres, even though he may have only a small portion of the land actually enclosed, by occupying it for ten years. If he enclosed a tract larger than 160 acres and possesses it without the knowledge or consent of the record title holder for ten years, he perfects his title to the amount he has fenced.

Under this statute it is use and occupancy of the land for ten years, at all times without recognizing the owner's rights, that perfects the title for the one in possession. He may pay taxes or he may not do so. The paying of taxes is not required under this statute for the one in possession to perfect his title.

Three Years Possession

"Suits to recover real estate, as against a person in peaceable and adverse possession thereof under title or color of title, shall be instituted within three years next after the cause of action accrued, and not afterward." *Article 5507, Vernon's Annotated Civil Statutes.*

Title, as used in the foregoing article is defined by statute as a regular chain of transfers from, or under, the sovereignty of the soil. By a regular chain, it is meant with none of the links missing. Color of title is defined as a consecutive chain of such transfers down to such person in possession, without being regular, as if one or more of the memorials or muniments are not registered, or not duly registered, or have some other irregularity; or when the party in possession shall hold the same by a certificate of headright, land warrant, or land scrip, with a chain of transfers down to him in possession. To hold the land under three years' possession, one must have something in the nature of record title.

Five Years Possession

"Every suit to recover real estate as against a person having peaceable and adverse possession thereof, cultivating, using or enjoying the same, and paying taxes thereon, if any, and claiming under a deed or deeds duly registered, shall be instituted within five years next after cause of action shall have accrued, and not afterward. This article shall not apply to one in possession of land, who deraigns title through a forged deed, and no one claiming under a forged deed, or deed executed under a forged power of attorney shall be allowed the benefits of this article." *Article 5509, Vernon's Annotated Civil Statutes.*

To perfect title under this statute, the one in possession must be able to prove: (a) that he has been in peaceable and adverse possession of the land for full five years; (b) that he claims under a deed or deeds duly registered or recorded in the county in which the land is located; and that his deed is not forged; (c) that he had paid the taxes currently each year, which means before they became delinquent.

There are conditions that will defeat one in possession in perfecting title by limitation or delay the starting of the limitation period, and examples are presented when the one owning the property is under some disability at the time the adverse possession starts, such as:

1. The owner of the land may be a minor, in which case the period of limitation will not start to run until the owner is no longer a minor,

2. The owner may be insane, in which case the limitation period will not start to run until the owner regains his sanity,

3. The owner may be serving a sentence in prison, in which case the limitation period will not start to run until his release therefrom,

4. The owner may be serving in the military service during war, in which case the limitation period would not start to run until the military service or the war ends.

The Twenty-Five Year Statute of Limitation

One holding possession of real estate, using and enjoying it continuously for twenty-five years, under a deed or deeds or other instrument which have been recorded in the deed records of the county in which the real estate is located, will thereby perfect his title regardless of whether the owner may be under some disability as mentioned under conditions 1 through 4 above.

Once the limitation period has started running in favor of the one in possession, with respect to any of the periods mentioned above, the only thing that will stop it or interrupt it is a suit to remove the person in possession. If the person having the right to sue for removal of the one in possession delays bringing suit until the full period has run, whichever period it may be, then he has lost his right.

Moreover, the use and possession of the land does not have to be all by one person. One who takes possession adverse to the landowner may occupy it for a time and then deliver possession to another who continues to hold possession to the end of the period. The owner has then lost his title the same as if the same person had continued in possession, because under the law, the second one to hold can "tack" the time of his possession onto the time of one before him. There, however, must be privity of estate between them, which is agreement between them for the holding of the property.

Minerals in the Land Under Adverse Possession

If the minerals in the land are intact, which means that they have not been severed or sold out of the land, then when the title to the land has been perfected by limitation it will include the minerals. But if the minerals have been severed from the land before the limitation period starts, then the minerals would not be included in the title to the land. The "squatter" would not get the minerals, unless, of course, he used the land in a way that would serve as notice that he was also claiming the minerals. He could do this by drilling for the minerals and producing them and continuing the appropriation during the full limitation period. If he did that without interruption, he would thereby acquire the minerals also, even though they had been previously severed from the land. This is not likely to happen, for the reason that one drilling for and producing oil, gas, or other minerals must show good title to the purchaser of such minerals before he can sell them, unless, of course, the producer of the minerals is the same one who refines and sells them.

Once the limitation period starts to run, severing the minerals during the period will not save them. It is necessary that a suit be brought for the purpose of ousting the "squatter" before the end of the period. Coverture, (or marriage), does not prevent the running of limitation on land against a married woman.

Assignment For Creditors

Sometimes a man finds he is unable to pay his debts, and when this happens he may be forced into bankruptcy. However, if he still has enough assets so that when they are applied to his debts no creditor will receive less than one-third of his claim, he may be discharged from further liability to his creditors.

He accomplishes this by making an assignment for the benefit of his creditors. The assignment will include all of his property, except items exempt from forced sale. He will not be discharged from liability to any creditor who does not receive as much as one-third of the amount due and allowed in his favor as a valid claim against the debtor's estate.

The assignment made in bankruptcy proceedings must be in writing, acknowledged, and recorded in the same manner provided by law for real estate conveyances. It must contain an inventory of debtor's property and it must include the following:

1. A list of all of the debtor's creditors;
2. The place of residence of each creditor, if known;
3. The sum owed each creditor, and the nature of the debt or demand;
4. The consideration of such indebtedness in each case, and the place where such indebtedness arose;
5. A statement of any existing judgment or security for the payment of any such debt;
6. An inventory of all such debtor's estate at the date of such assignment, both real and personal, and any existing encumbrances, and all relative vouchers and securities and the value of the estate.

The person making the assignment must make a sworn statement to the truth of the assignment which he must sign.

When the assignment is made, the assignee (the one receiving the assets from the debtor) gives notice of his appointment within thirty days by publishing the notice in some newspapers printed in the county where the assignor resides, if there is such a newspaper in the county, and if not then in the nearest newspaper to the place of business of the person making the assignment. This publication is to be continued once each week for three consecutive weeks. In addition the assignee gives notices to each of the listed creditors by mail.

Acceptance by Creditors

The creditors of the one making the assignment who consent to the assignment must give notice to the assignee within four months after the assignee's notice is issued. A creditor who does not consent will not be entitled to any benefits under the assignment. A creditor who had no actual notice may consent to the assignment at any time before distribution of the assets, and he will thereby be entitled to his portion of the distribution. Any creditor who receives any portion of his claim from the assignee is presumed to agree to the assignment.

The assignee is required to give bond as fixed by the county or district judge binding him to a faithful discharge of his duties. Also, he must record the assignment in the county where he resides and in each county where any of the assigned property may be located. He is obligated to make distribution of the assigned property or to sell it and distribute the proceeds from the sale to the creditors according to the amounts of the claims filed and approved. If the assignee fails to act promptly as the law provides, he may be removed and may be replaced by another to act as assignee in his place.

Inasmuch as a creditor who does not agree to the assignment cannot receive any benefits under the assignment, and the one making the assignment must assign all of his property except that which is exempt from forced sale, it is wise for a creditor to accept it promptly; otherwise he will not be able to collect anything on his claim.

Landlord and Tenant

The Landlord's Lien

If the owner of farm land rents or leases it to a tenant with the owner furnishing only the land, and the agreed rent to be paid to the owner is not in excess of one-third of the grain and one-fourth of the cotton; or if the owner furnishes the land and everything else, except the labor, and the agreed rent to be paid to the owner is not in excess of one-half of the grain and one-half of the cotton, the law provides that the landowner can place a lien upon the crops to secure his share of the crops grown or his portion of the value of the crops grown. If the agreed rents exceed the shares mentioned, the lien is not created.

This lien will continue as long as the produced crops remain upon the rented or leased land and one month afterwards. If the crops are stored in a warehouse off the premises, the lien will continue as long as the crops remain in the warehouse. The tenant has no right to remove the crops from the land where they were grown without the landlord's consent. If he does remove the crops from the land and has the landlord's consent to do so, the lien is not invalidated. As a practical matter, the landlord generally gives his consent for the tenant to remove the produced products to a market.

However, if the tenant removes the products covered by the crop lien, without the landlord's consent, and the landlord feels that he might not receive his share of the products or the value of his share, the landlord has the right to apply to a justice of the peace for a distress warrant directing that the removed products be seized and disposed of according to law so that landlord and tenant each will receive his rightful share.

Rights of Tenant

The tenant has a corresponding protection under the law to protect himself against failure of the landlord to comply with his part of the agreement. If the landlord fails to furnish what he agrees to supply, he will be responsible for damages to the tenant. To secure the tenant's right to recover against the landlord, the law provides a lien upon the land and other things belonging to the landlord but in possession of the tenant which are not exempt from forced sale, including the landlord's share of the crops produced on the land.

Owners of Building Lien

If the owner of a residence or warehouse, or other building rents or leases it or a portion of it to a tenant, the law gives him a preference lien upon all the tenant's property, or sub-tenant of the tenant in a residence, warehouse, or other building for the payments of rents due and to become due. In order to secure the lien for rents that are more than six months due, it is necessary for the person leasing or renting any storehouse or other building used for commercial purposes, to file in the county clerk's office in the county in which such building is located, a sworn statement of the amount of rent due, with the name and address of the tenant and/or subtenant, a description of the rented premises, the date that the rental contract began and the date that it terminates.

When the tenant or subtenant owing rent money is about to leave the rented or leased building, or is about to remove his property, the landlord has the right to apply to a justice of the peace for a distress warrant. If the distress warrant is issued and served upon the tenant or subtenant, then he is forbidden to remove his property from the building pending payment of the rent. If he violates the orders contained in the distress warrant and removes his property from the premises without making full settlement of the rents due, he will be subject to penalties that may be imposed by the court.

The Statute of Frauds

It is the intention of the law that frauds are not to be perpetrated upon the people of this state. Therefore, lawsuits cannot be brought in any of the state's courts to enforce certain agreements unless the agreements or promises, or some memorandum thereof, are in writing and signed by the party to be charged or by some person authorized by him. These agreements include:

1. A suit to charge an executor or administrator upon any promise to answer any debt or damage due from his testator or intestate, out of his own estate;

2. A suit to charge any person upon a promise to answer for the debt, default or miscarriage of another;

3. A suit to charge any person upon any agreement made upon consideration of marriage;

4. A suit upon any contract for the sale of real estate, or upon any contract to lease real estate for a longer term than one year;

5. A suit upon any agreement which is not to be performed within the time of one year from the making;

6. A suit for the collection of a commission for the sale or purchase of oil and/or gas minerals leases, oil and/or royalties, minerals or mineral interests, or a suit for commission for the sale of land.

In the absence of these provisions in the law, people could be subjected to much harassment and expense in defending themselves against claims that are not well founded. Of course, there are instances where people take advantage of these provisions of the law to defeat claims that are morally just, but the benefits of this law far outweigh the disadvantages.

Conveyances to Defraud

"Every gift, conveyance, assignment or transfer of, or charge upon, any estate real or personal, every suit commenced, or decree, judgment or execution suffered or obtained and every bond or other writing given with intent to delay, hinder or defraud creditors, purchasers, or other persons of or from what they are, or may be, lawfully entitled to, shall, as to such creditors, purchasers or other persons, their representatives or assigns, be void. This article shall not affect the title of a purchaser, for valuable consideration, unless it appears that he had notice of the fraudulent intent of his immediate grantor, or of the fraud rendering void the title of such grantor." *Article 3996, Vernon's Annotated Civil Statues.*

Probably one of the most prevalent attempts to fraudulently convey is in the case where a property owner finds himself in financial difficulties with creditors and transfers the title of his property to a relative or close friend for no consideration of any value, or for a consideration far below the property value. The courts in well-presented cases have consistently held such conveyances void when used as attempts to evade creditors.

If a person conveys his property to another in an effort to hide it from creditors, the courts will not aid him in his effort to recover it, even though he has otherwise satisfied his creditors in the meantime so that he is not in debt when he brings suit to recover his property. One who receives title from a person trying to hide his property from his creditors can hold title against his grantor, even though he cannot hold against his grantor's creditors. If he sells the property and keeps the consideration, his grantor cannot have the court's aid to recover what he received for it. The purchaser can hold the property against the true debtor-owner, even though he knew it was conveyed by the debtor to hide it from his creditors.

There is a maxim in law often quoted by the courts and attorneys in such cases; "Whoever comes into a court of equity must come with clean hands."

Gifts

"No gift of any goods or chattels shall be valid unless by deed or will, duly acknowledged or proven up and recorded, or unless actual possession shall have come to, and remained with, the donee or someone claiming under him." *Article 3998, Vernon's Annotated Civil Statutes.*

Of course, a gift given to hide property from creditors would not be valid against creditors even if the requirements of this statute were actually met. But this statute is not concerned primarily with the protection of creditors. It is intended to define the necessary procedure to make a gift of movable property (as distinguished from real estate). Its effect can be better understood by an example.

John Doe may say to his friend Mr. Roe, "You like my white horse so much that I am going to give him to you." If no more is said or done, John Doe has done nothing more than signify his intention to give the horse to Mr. Roe. No actual gift has been made. If John Doe says to his friend, Mr. Roe, "You like my white horse so much that I have decided to make you really happy, and therefore I give him to you." With that John Doe has not yet made a gift until he delivers this horse to Mr. Roe, or makes out a bill of sale and gives it to Mr. Roe and lets him take possession of the horse. The gift, to be effectual, must be complete and this includes delivery of it into the physical possession of the recipient.

Loss of Title by Loan

If one lends another person any personal property (the law calls this class of property a chattel) and the use of the property or the possession of it continues for two years without any demand for its return by the lender, the lender has no remedy against the borrower's creditors or purchasers of the property. After that length of time without any demand for return of the property, the ownership is presumed to be in the borrower or one claiming under him in possession of the property. The lender, however, may still have a right of action against the borrower for conversion (taking property without paying any consideration for it) of the property. He would have a good cause of action if he brings suit within two years after he discovers that the borrower has converted the property, or permitted it to be converted. The lender, in order to protect himself against loss of the loaned property, could have required the borrower to return it before the end of two years, or he could have, at the time of lending, required the borrower to execute a chattel mortgage which the owner could have placed in record in the county where the property was situated, and this would have served as notice of the owner's rights to the property.

chattel mortgage

A Purchaser of Merchandise at Retail is Protected

One purchasing merchandise from retail dealers is under no obligation to investigate the retailer's authority to sell the merchandise because the law provides that any mortgage, deed of trust, or other form of lien attempted to be given in such an instance shall be void against one who purchases in parcels in the due course of retail business.

This statute is a protection for the public. On the other hand, if one is to buy out the retail merchant or dealer and take over his store or a substantial portion of it in bulk, then a different rule applies for the protection of that merchant or dealer's creditors. Anyone contemplating such a purchase must demand and receive from the seller a sworn statement showing a list of all of his creditors and the amount owed to each. At least ten days before closing the purchase and paying for the store or dealership and the stock of goods and fixtures, or a part thereof, he must notify each creditor personally or by registered mail of his contemplated purchase. This gives the creditors a chance to come forward, if they fear that the seller will not pay them, and assert their rights to that portion of the purchase price that will satisfy their claims against the merchant or dealer. This is commonly referred to as the "Bulk Sales Law."

Corporations, Partnerships and Limited Partnerships

Corporations

Corporations may be organized under the Texas laws to do business in this state for profit, or they may be organized as nonprofit corporations.

The nonprofit corporations often are organized for such undertakings as the dissemination of some religious belief, knowledge of art, promotion of patriotism, or other things not forbidden by law and which are not intended to result in a monetary profit.

Most corporations doing business in this state are for profit. If a corporation obtains its charter from the State of Texas, it is known as a domestic corporation, and if it obtains its charter from some other state it is known as a foreign corporation. A foreign corporation desiring to do business in the State of Texas must obtain a permit from the Secretary of State before starting business within this state. Otherwise, the corporation will be faced with penalties for failure to do so, and it will be at great disadvantage in court if it chooses to sue or is sued in this state.

Two of the principal advantages of doing business as a corporation are: (a) it shields the stockholder from personal liability for causes of action in court against the business, and; (b) it affords accumulation of a greater capital aggregate for the business through investments by many persons.

Three or more people may decide to organize a corporation to do business in Texas, and they make application to the Secretary of State for a charter. The application must track the statutes and meet all of the requirements and contain all information required by law. Of course, it is necessary to have an attorney to prepare the application since the average man would not know the steps to take. The procedure is not complicated for the one who knows how and is experienced in such matters. With a proper application and all of the requirements, the Secretary of State will issue a "charter" which will show, among other things, the corporation's name, the purpose or purposes for which it is organized, the amount of the authorized capital, and the names and addresses of the incorporators. The charter is the evidence of authority of the corporation to do business in Texas.

To begin business in the state, those interested in the corporation (the stockholders) hold an organizational meeting at which the following things are usually done: (a) a board of directors is elected; (b) by-laws of the corporation are adopted that prescribe the manner in which the corporation is to conduct its business, fill vacancies on the board, etc., and, (c) a corporate seal and form of stock certificate are adopted. The board of directors then carries on the corporation's business until their successors are elected. To accomplish this, the board of directors elects the corporation's officers, usually a president, a vice president, a secretary and a treasurer. Large corporations may have any number of other officers which the board may think are necessary to carry on the corporation's business. One person may hold two or more offices in the corporation, but the president of the corporation cannot be also the secretary. Board members may be, and generally are, officers of the corporation.

One who invests money in a corporation receives a stock certificate showing the number of shares he holds in the corporation, and usually is entitled to vote at stockholders' meetings, casting his votes according to the number of shares of stock he holds. He also receives income from the corporation according to the number of shares he holds, if the corporation makes profits and pays dividends.

Partnerships

When two or more persons join together in a business undertaking, without incorporating, sharing profits and losses of the business, and without filing a declaration in the county clerk's office in the county in which they do business, they are partners. As partners they are both, or all of them individually, liable for the debts and other obligations of the business, and one of the partners acting for the partnership will bind the other or all of them. Many people in business are partners without knowing that they actually occupy such status and that they are individually liable for the whole debt or obligation of the business. For this reason a wealthy man generally shuns a partnership. He realizes that if the business should become heavily indebted and required more than all of the business' assets to discharge, he might be sued individually for the deficit. This is quite different from the status of a stockholder in a corporation. When the corporation's assets have been consumed by creditors, proceedings cannot be brought against the individual stockholders. The stockholder can lose his investment, but with that loss his liability stops: not so with a partnership.

On the other hand, a partnership is a most convenient way for two or more persons to group themselves together to carry on a business. It is not legally necessary that any partnership agreement be put in writing. Two or more persons may agree to start operating a business together and begin work, and they have a partnership — this is known as a general partnership. It is not necessary that their interests in the business be equal. They may be equal, and if there is no agreement between them that one shall have a greater interest, then it is presumed their interests are equal. But the partners may agree between the two of them, or among the several of them, that one or more of the partners will have a larger interest, and this generally arises when one or more of the partners are equipped to render more service to the business. Frequently this is the case when an older doctor or older lawyer takes a young member into the firm.

While it is not legally necessary to the existence of a partnership that a written agreement be signed by the members, it is quite often desirable, and it very frequently is done. The written agreement, which almost always should be prepared by an attorney, lets the partners better understand their relationship, and they are less likely to have misunderstandings in the course of business. There are exceptions to the rule, but when the partnership agreement is drafted by a competent attorney and it is fully understood and signed by the partners, the business is off to a better start, and it is more likely to be successful and to last longer.

The Limited Partnership

The limited partnership, if it is properly organized and kept on this basis, does afford a limited liability to the "limited partner." In this case, the man of some wealth may be limited in his liability to the amount of money or other things of value he puts into the business. For example, A, who is wealthy, decides to join B and C in a business undertaking. B and C are young and vigorous and they propose to do the work and worry of the business, but they are lacking in capital. A is willing to invest the necessary money for the business to get started, but he feels that he must be protected against personal liability beyond the investment he puts into the business. In other words, he is willing to risk the investment, but he must be protected against suit for more.

So, the three go to their lawyer and have him draft the articles or declaration of the limited partnership, giving the amount each partner is investing in the business and declaring each partner's status. A is a "limited partner" and B and C are "general partners" (the number may be only one or more, and there can be more than one limited partner). With this document properly drawn and executed and filed in each county in which the limited partnership is to do business, A will occupy somewhat the same status as a stockholder in a corporation, but B and C are individually liable for the obligations of the partnership.

4. Damage Suits and Complaints

With just daily living, it is not unusual for a person to damage another person or his property. He may negligently bump into another's automobile and damage or destroy it or injure the person. He may dam up a creek on his own land and back water up onto the land of his neighbor upstream and cause damage to growing crops or pasture grasses, or he may spray his own lands to kill weeds and permit the spray to be blown across over his neighbor's land where it kills growing crops or fruit trees. A person may become angry and assault some other person and injure him without good cause, or he may in anger kill some person without good cause. These are a few of the ways he could commit some act that would result in a damage suit.

If the person injured or damaged demands retribution and it is not promptly made, the one committing the injury to the person or damage to his property will probably find himself in court answering a damage suit. Sometimes these suits result in judgments for large sums of money. But in every instance, the damage must be real and not just imagined. For example, when someone is spraying his lands to poison weeds or bushes, the neighbor has no cause for action unless he is actually damaged. It is not sufficient in court that he presents a claim that could result if the spray is blown over his land. It is the duty of the one spraying to exercise care so that he does not permit the spray to be blown over the neighbor's land, and if he uses the spray and the neighbor is not damaged, the neighbor has no cause for action.

There was a case where a land salesman sold a tract of valley land to an unsuspecting purchaser on the premise the land was in an irrigation district and that irrigation water was available. When the purchaser made preparations to plant crops on the land he discovered that no irrigation water was available to the land as the seller had assured him. The purchaser went to his lawyer to hire him to bring suit against the seller for actionable fraud. The lawyer asked, "How do you know that the water will not be available at the time you need to irrigate? You have not planted any crops yet, and thus far you have not been damaged. If you go ahead and plant the crops, and then the water is not available, you will then have a cause for damage, since the crops will die and you will thereby suffer a loss."

A person may be damaged by falsely spoken or written words against his character. This is especially true in the case of persons in public life. If someone states publicly, or publishes in a newspaper, etc., or broadcasts over radio or television falsely that a priest, minister, or rabbi is of bad and immoral character, or that a public official, the county judge, mayor, or a legislator is dishonest and unworthy of public trust, he exposes himself to the possibility that he will be sued for damages by the offended person. If he is unable to sustain the truth of his statements, the damages assessed against him may be very great. A judgment may be rendered against him for actual or compensatory damages and in addition, punitive or exemplary damage to punish him for a great wrong.

But it is not only public officials and priests, ministers, and rabbis who are entitled to collect damages, but any other persons can have the aid of the courts in claiming damages for wrongs against them. It is interesting though, that a remark made and published about one person may give rise to a damage suit, whereas, if it is made about another it can have no damaging effect. An example is where a statement published about a businessman indicating he is insolvent and cannot pay his bills may be greatly damaging to him and give rise to a damage suit, but if the same remark is made about a member of the clergy it may not be damaging at all; in fact it may be beneficial to him if his parishioners become aware of the situation.

Limitation of Personal Actions

As in suits for regaining possession of land, there are also limitations of time in which one may bring suits in personal actions. If the one having the right to sue permits the limitation period to pass without bringing his suit, he loses his right to sue.

Actions to be Commenced in One Year

1. Actions for malicious prosecution or for injuries done to the character or reputation of another by libel or slander.
2. Actions for damages for seduction, or breach of promise of marriage.

In these instances, death of the injured person or death of the one doing the wrong will not extinguish the right to bring the suit if it is brought within the time period. Suit can be brought in behalf of the injured person in the name of his estate, if the injured one has died, and against the estate of the one committing the wrong, if that one has died.

Actions to be Commenced in Two Years

1. Actions of trespass for injury done to the estate or property of another.
2. Actions for detaining the personal property of another, and for converting the property to one's own use.

3. Actions for taking and carrying away the goods and chattels of another.

4. Actions for debt where the indebtedness is not evidenced by a contract in writing.

5. Actions upon stated or open accounts, such as the accounts of persons who buy on credit from stores.

6. Actions for injury done to the person of another.

7. Actions for injury done to the person of another which causes death, and in this instance the two-year period will run from the date of death — not from the date the injury occurred.

8. Actions against a city government or the commissioners' court, and others that may be involved, for the closing of a street or roadway, other than a state highway. If the city or county closes a street or roadway and relinquishes possession of the land which the street or roadway occupied, then anyone not in possession of the land but claiming it or an interest in it, or claiming that the street or roadway should be reopened, must bring his suit within the two-year period or lose his right to sue on the cause. The one in possession of the land abandoned for street or roadway purposes will gain full title to the land by possessing it for two years, if during the two-year period he is undisturbed by any suit to recover it.

Actions to be Commenced in Four Years

1. Actions for debt where the indebtedness is evidenced by or founded upon any contract in writing — for example, promissory notes.

2. Actions for the penalty or for damages on the penal clause of a bond to convey real estate.

3. Actions by one partner against his co-partner for a settlement of the partnership accounts, or upon mutual and current accounts concerning the trade or merchandise between merchant and merchant. The cause of action will be

considered as having occurred upon the termination of the dealings the partners conducted together.

4. Suits for recovery on the bond of any executor, administrator or guardian, and the four-year period commences upon the death, resignation, removal, or discharge of the executor, administrator, or guardian.

5. Actions on foreign judgments, where judgment has been rendered in some other state, or in the District of Columbia, or in some foreign country, will be barred in four years, if such action is also barred in the place where the judgment was rendered.

6. Actions requiring the specific performance of a contract for the conveyance of land.

7. Actions involving the contest of any will, and the four-year period runs from the date that the will is admitted to probate. If the action is based upon a claim of forgery or fraud in the making of the will, the action may be brought within four years after the discovery of the forgery or fraud.

8. All other actions, other than for recovery of land, where the law has not provided a specific limitation period, shall be barred in four years.

Limitation After Death

In case of the death of a person against whom or in whose favor there may be a cause of action, the law of limitation is suspended until 12 months after his death, unless an executor or administrator qualifies prior to that time. In that event, the running of limitation is delayed only until such qualification.

If the full limitation period has run against the right to sue, no acknowledgment of the justness of the claim made subsequent to the time it became due can be admitted as evidence at the trial, unless the acknowledgment is in writing and is signed by the person to be charged.

In making contracts, persons, firms, or corporations cannot legally agree or stipulate to shorten the time for suing to less than two years.

No limitation is effective against the state, a county, a city or a school district, meaning any of these organizations can bring suit against one in possession of its land in disregard of the limitation periods already discussed. However long a "squatter" may stay in possession of land belonging to one of these organizations, he cannot perfect his title to it.

Abatement of Nuisances

Incorporated cities generally have power and authority under their charters to abate nuisances, which is the stopping or preventing of a nuisance. This is particularly true where the health of citizens of the city is endangered, some sanitation ordinance is being violated so that disease is likely to spread, or where some constantly annoying noise is maintained to disturb the rest of people and endanger health. An example is a family in a closely settled community which keeps livestock such as cows, hogs, or chickens penned in the back yard in violation of a city ordinance, thus attracting flies or rats to the neighborhood; or the animals make loud and disturbing noises at night disturbing sleep. Another situation is where a nearby neighbor keeps dogs penned close to another person's house and fails to keep the pen sanitary, and it creates a health hazard; or the dogs howl and bark at night and disturb the neighborhood residents' sleep.

The city will generally aid a complainant in instances of this kind and bring action against the offending party and abate the nuisance. It is fairly easy to obtain relief if the complainant can show that the acts in question constitute a violation of a city ordinance. It is more difficult if the one creating the nuisance is carrying on a business not forbidden by ordinance. In such an instance the city may not be willing to give its aid, and the complainant may have to bring suit and try to prove the validity of his complaint.

By law, some acts are declared to be common nuisances, and the state acting by the county attorney, district attorney, or the attorney general will abate the nuisance. An example is where a guise is used of operating a boarding house, country club, garage, rent car stand, or other place the public commonly uses for board or lodging, or congregates for business or pleasure, but where intoxicating liquors are kept and sold or given away, particularly to minors, or such places are used for gambling or for prostitution. Any person knowingly maintaining such a place is guilty of maintaining a declared nuisance.

When a place is kept for gambling, or is a disorderly or bawdy house, any interested citizen may bring suit to abate the nuisance. If proper proof is given, an injunction to prevent the continued use of the place for such purposes can be obtained. While a private citizen can bring and prosecute such a suit, it is better to seek the aid of law enforcement officers first.

There are other nuisances that are borderline, such as the blowing of automobile horns disturbingly near one's home, bad odors from manufacturing plants, the spilling of garbage on the street in front of one's home. These nuisances are often too difficult to abate, maybe because the acts are not consistently repeated, or the offender cannot be definitely identified. Anyone intending personally to abate a nuisance would do well to explain his complaint to an attorney and receive an opinion from him as to whether he has a provable case, before he incurs other expense. But this does not mean that one should hesitate to abate a continuing, unnecessary annoyance which could be proved to be a real nuisance.

Workmen's Compensation Insurance

Prior to the enactment of the Workmen's Compensation Laws, about 50 years ago, it was brought to the legislature's attention that many workmen were being injured, and sometimes killed, in the course of their work. It was pointed out often there was no kind of compensation available for the injured, or for the relatives of the ones who lost their lives. If a workman was injured on the job, or if he lost his life accidentally, then under the common law rule, he, or those representing him after his death, had to prove that his employer was negligent and that the negligence brought about the injury or death. This proof was the only basis for recovering damages against the employer. If the proof could not be given, recovery was not made, even though the workman may never be able to work again because of his injury, or his family would be forced into poverty because of his death. In trying such cases, the employer could defeat recovery by showing that the injury or death was caused by acts of a fellow workman, or that the injured workman was negligent and caused or contributed to the injury or death. Or the employer could show that the workman knew of the danger involved and that the workman assumed the risk of the employment.

Moreover, it often happened that if the injured workman or the representatives of the workman who lost his life did succeed in proving negligence on the employer's part, there still could be no compensation recovered because the employer was financially unable to respond.

These conditions resulted in great hardship for workmen, and it posed a threat to employers. An employer was constantly in danger of being brought to financial ruin by a lawsuit from an employee. This sometimes made able men reluctant to become employers, men who were fully capable of furnishing extensive employment to people of this state. This reluctance tended to slow down commerce and reduce full employment and lessen opportunities for workmen.

It became apparent that legislation was necessary to establish some kind of plan to protect the workman and his family, regardless of the fact that the workman recognized and assumed the risk of the employment, or that he was injured through no negligence of the employer, or that he, himself, was negligent and that his negligence contributed to his injury, or that his injury resulted from acts of a fellow workman. On the other hand, it was recognized that men willing and able to run businesses and furnish employment must be protected against damage suits that could penalize them out of business.

The Workmen's Compensation Law was adopted to fill these needs. It requires every employer with three or more workmen to carry workmen's compensation insurance, except persons, firms, or corporations operating any steam, electric, street, or interurban railway as a common carrier. These exceptions are governed by other laws. The law does not apply to employers having fewer than three employees. However, once an employer subscribes to the insurance and is recognized as complying with the law, he continues to be protected, even though he may later have fewer than three employees. If an employer does not subscribe to the insurance and comply with the other requirements of the law, then he operates at his own risk. If an employee is injured while working, the employer cannot defend himself in court on the grounds that: (a) the employee assumed the risk of the work involved; (b) the injury or death of the employee was caused by acts of a fellow workman; (c) the injury or death was caused in whole or in part by negligence of the employee, himself.

This is a real whip to make employers comply with the law. If an employer complies with the law, then he is not subject to damage suits by his employees for their injuries or deaths suffered while on the job. The employees must file their claims with the Industrial Accident Board in Austin which administers the law. This board will hear the employee's case and make an award. If the employee is not satisfied with the award, he can appeal his case to the district court, and from there, to the Court of Civil Appeals.

An employer who is to be protected under the law is required to give notice to his employees by posting notices in the plant or other place where the employees work that he subscribes to the insurance. If he fails to give the notice, he is not protected. The employee will be subject to the law's provisions, unless at the time of his employment he gives his employer notice in writing that he expects to exercise his rights under the common law with respect to injuries or death that he may suffer in the course of his employment. If he gives such a notice, and he is permitted to work after the notice is given, then the employer would not be protected against a damage suit by that employee for injuries he may receive, but the common law defenses would be available to him.

Benefits Provided to Workmen Under the Law

First, if an employee is injured in the course of his employment, he is entitled to medical attention, including a doctor's service, dressings for his injury, and if required, hospitalization and nursing. The law recognizes chiropractic service to be the same as a doctor's or physician's service. This service, being the ordinary or usual service rendered by physicians, chiropractors, hospitals, and nurses, may continue, free to the employee, as long as is necessary to cure the injury. It includes, when necessary, artificial limbs, their fitting and training in their use, and reasonable rehabilitation of the employee.

If the injury does not cause disability or incapacity for work for as much as one week, no compensation will be paid to the employee for loss of time, but if the disability continues for more than one week, the compensation will start on the eighth day of disability. If the disability continues for four weeks or longer, then the compensation will cover the entire time of disability, including the first week.

Rate of Compensation

If death results from the injury, the deceased's legal beneficiaries will be paid a weekly payment equal to 60 percent of his average weekly wages, but not more than $49, nor less than $12 per week for a period of 360 weeks. If death occurs after a total or partial incapacitation for which compensation has been paid, the incapacitation period will be deducted from the total period of compensation allowed for death.

If the deceased leaves no legal beneficiaries to receive the benefits payable under the law, then the association will pay the expenses of his last sickness resulting from the injury, and in addition a funeral expense of $500. If the deceased leaves legal beneficiaries, and he is buried at the beneficiaries' expense, or at the expense of his employer or any other person, then the association will pay the person bearing the funeral expenses an amount not to exceed $500.

If the injury results in total incapacity to work, then while the incapacity continues, the association will pay the injured employee 60 percent of his average weekly wages, but not more than $49, nor less than $12 per week, limited in any case to 401 weeks.

If the injury results in partial incapacity, the association will pay 60 percent of the difference between his average weekly wages before the injury, and his average weekly wage earning capacity when partially disabled, but in no case more than $49 per week, and the period covered by the compensation will never exceed 300 weeks. However, in no case can the period of compensation for total and partial incapacity exceed 401 weeks from the date of injury.

Injuries Constituting Total and Permanent Incapacity

The following injuries are considered as bringing on total and permanent disability (but there are others also): (a) total and permanent loss of the sight of both eyes; (b) the loss of both feet at or above the ankles; (c) the loss of both hands at or above the wrists; (d) a similar loss of one foot and one hand; (e) an injury to the spine resulting in permanent and complete paralysis of both arms or both legs or of one arm and one leg; (f) an injury to the skull resulting in incurable insanity or imbecility.

Other Particular Provisions of the Law

The law is very extensive, giving particular injuries and the weeks of compensation that will be paid for them. For example, the loss of a thumb means 60 percent of the average weekly wages during sixty weeks, and for the loss of the index finger, 60 percent of the average weekly wages during forty-five weeks etc., limited in each case to a maximum of $49 and a minimum of $12 per week. These are too long and involved for inclusion here.

Attorney's Fees

The attorney's fees that injured persons are charged for representation before the Industrial Accident Board are regulated by the board. They are limited to 25 percent of the total recovery in favor of the injured employee, plus expenses that are incurred by the attorney in the preparation and presentation of the claim. If an appeal is taken to the district court from the award made by the Industrial Accident Board, then it is lawful for the attorney to contract with the injured workman for as much as 25 percent of the total recovery. The court, however, will allow the attorney a fee which it considers fair and reasonable based upon the services rendered in bringing the case before the court, but limited in all cases to 30 percent of the total recovery. If an attorney takes an appeal from the award of the board and does not make an additional gain for his client over the board's award, he is not entitled to any fee except that allowed by the board in the first instance. Moreover, while a claim is pending before the Industrial Accident Board, and before any award is made by the board, if the association (the insurer) files a written statement with the board admitting full liability and tendering the maximum amount of compensation allowed by law, then no attorney's fees will be allowed in the case.

What To Do When Sued

When suit is brought against anyone for any cause, a "citation" will be served upon the person being sued, which is the official notice from the court, signed by the court clerk or his deputy. The citation shows when the suit was filed, and by whom, and the nature of the cause of action, and indicates the time in which the person sued should answer in court.

This notice should not be ignored, for if it is, a default judgment will be entered in the case against the person sued. The law assumes that if the allegations in the plaintiff's petition are not denied, they are true and a judgment will be rendered on the plaintiff's petition without a trial. The defendant, the one who is sued, should take the citation to his attorney, talk the case over with him, and arrange employment and the amount of the attorney fee to be paid. It does not suffice that the cause stated appears to be unfounded or unjust. If it is indeed an unfounded case, it will be easy to defend if it is handled by a capable lawyer.

However simplified we seek to make court procedure, it is too technical for the layman, and if he does undertake to defend himself without the assistance of a lawyer, he may overlook the most fundamental defense at his command and lose the case on a technicality. The petition itself may be defective so that an advantage could be gained by initially lodging an

defective petition

exception against it, or a plea in abatement, and this defect ordinarily would not be detected by one not skilled in court procedure. The judge might be sympathetic, but he is the judge, and he cannot serve as the advocate for either party in court. The judge and the jury are bound by the law and the facts proved by admissible evidence in the case, and the defendant must be prepared with his evidence. The strict rules of evidence, which are not in easy reach of any layman, and which often are the lawyer's hardest work in a case, may defeat the unskilled. These rules work both ways, and no one dares go into court unprepared to use them in keeping out testimony, exhibits, etc., which do not belong in the case. If any of this material does get in over objections, then proper exceptions should be preserved so that the wrong can be considered on appeal, if an appeal is taken.

Moreover, answering the plaintiff's petition is a technical matter which requires a lawyer. As mentioned, it is sometimes necessary to file and urge preliminary pleas before answering to the merits of the case. Sometimes a case can be won by an exception, or plea in abatement, and presenting the laws applicable to the allegations in the plaintiff's petition. The average man could hardly be expected to be acquainted with such procedures, much less how to meet the various legal strategies that may be used against him during the trial.

One should rarely, if ever, decide to represent himself in a lawsuit that amounts to more than a small sum, say $50 or $100, and even in these small cases he is likely to have fewer regrets if he employs a competent legal counselor. It has been said that "One who represents himself in court has a fool for a client." There is some virtue in knowing when to be scared.

Arbitration

Arbitration in its simplest form is a method of settling disputes without going to court. Example: A and B have made an agreement to cultivate a certain tract of land with the understanding that they will contribute equally in labor and expenses and share the returns in the same way, but during the busy season one of them gets sick and is unable to do as much as the other; thus a dispute arises. When the harvest is in and the returns are to be divided, there is a difference of opinion between them as to how much each should receive out of the net returns. When each one concludes that the other is unreasonable, they call in C, who is a disinterested party and known by both of them to be a fair man. They agree that if C will decide between them they will each be bound by his decision. C accepts the responsibility, hears both sides and makes his award to each, which they accept. They have settled their dispute by arbitrations.

This is a very quick, inexpensive and effective way of arriving at a settlement. By this method, the dispute was settled in a day or two or an hour or two, when had the parties gone to court, they may not have had the settlement in weeks, months, or a year or two. The key to the quick settlement here was the agreement by the parties that they would be bound by the arbitrator's decision.

But arbitration does not always carry with it the disputants' agreement that they will be bound by the arbitrator's decision. One might agree to an arbitration of the dispute reserving the right to appeal.

In order to promote the effectiveness of arbitration, the ground rules are given in the statutes, and they can be summarized as follows:

Agreement

When a dispute between persons or parties is to be settled by arbitration, it is necessary that the interested parties sign an agreement to arbitrate. In this agreement each one should state whether he reserves or waives the right of appeal. The "plaintiff," or the one who is asserting a claim, will name one arbitrator, and the "defendant," the one who is resisting the claim, will name one arbitrator in the written agreement. Those named as arbitrators must have the qualifications of a juror and must not be related to the parties in the dispute, or interested in the results of the decision to be made, and they must be 21 years old or over. The agreement should also establish the method of choosing an "umpire" who is the third arbitrator. This third arbiter may be chosen by the first two arbitrators or he may be appointed by the court or the court clerk, according to the wishes of the disputants.

If the amount in dispute is $200 or less, exclusive of interest, the agreement shall be filed with some justice of peace in the county where the disputants reside. If the matter in dispute exceeds $200, exclusive of interest, but does not exceed $500, the agreement is filed with the county clerk, since the county court has exclusive original jurisdiction in matters involving amounts from $200 to $500. If the amount involved is over $500 but does not exceed $1,000, the agreement may be filed either with the county clerk or the district clerk, because the county court and the district court have concurrent original jurisdiction in matters involving such amounts. But if the amount involved exceeds $1,000, the agreement must be filed with the district clerk, since the district court has exclusive original jurisdiction when such an amount is involved.

Designation of the Day of Trial
(Assuming the agreement was filed in justice court)

Upon filing the agreement, the justice of the peace or the county or district clerk, as the case may be, will designate a day for the trial, not less than two days after the filing date. Each party will inform the clerk, or the justice of the peace, of the names of the witnesses he wishes to have notified to be present at the trial, and the clerk or the justice of the peace will issue notices to those witnesses to be present to give testimony at the trial.

Oath of Arbitrators

When the arbitrators are assembled for the trial, the justice of the peace, or the clerk, will administer to each of them the following oath: "You do solemnly swear that you will fairly and impartially decide the matter in dispute between the parties, according to the evidence adduced and the law and equity applicable to the facts proved. So help you God."

The Trial

The arbitrators will then administer the necessary oath to the witnesses, and the trial will proceed as in court, the plaintiff holding the affirmative, and entitled to open and close the argument. (NOTE: Since it is not required that the arbitrators have qualifications other than that of a juror, it cannot be expected that the proceedings before a board of arbitration would involve such strict rules of evidence as would be found in other courts, particularly the district courts).

The Award of Judgment

After the arbitrators have conducted the hearing, they make a written decision which is filed with the justice of the peace, or the clerk, as the case may be, and this becomes the judgment in the case. It has the same force and effect that it would have if the case had been tried in court.

An appeal may be made in any case involving, exclusive of interest, more than $20, unless the right of appeal was waived in the agreement to arbitrate.

Once a party to a dispute signs an agreement to arbitrate, he is bound by that method of settling the dispute. If he refuses to proceed with the arbitration, his refusal may be pleaded in bar of any action for the same cause in court.

Arbitration between Employer and Employee

The procedure in arbitration between employer and employee is similar to that already given, except that the proceeding is more exacting, and it is under and returnable to the district court, and there are five arbitrators, instead of three, and the submittal is in writing. Arbitration of labor disputes should be handled by competent attorneys. Such disputes often wind up before the National Labor Relations Board or in a federal court.

Civil Trial Procedure

The author is aware there is much grumbling about the waste of time in the courtroom and recognizes lawyers feel that the greatest loss of their time is in the courthouse. All good judges would save time of everyone concerned in the courtroom — litigants, lawyers, witnesses and jurors — if it could be done without losing the court's ultimate goal — justice. But when two Texas citizens, or any others who have a right to, come into court for a redress of wrongs or for a defense of rights, the main duties call for the best that democracy can give, and the necessary time required to attain it becomes relatively unimportant.

The judge is bound by the duties of his high office to conduct a fair and impartial trial, and the lawyers are bound by their profession and by law to represent their clients to the best of their abilities. Indeed, the judge and the lawyers are subject to heavy penalties provided by law and to severe discipline by their professional organization for failure to discharge their duties. The jury is under oath to give a fair and impartial verdict according to the evidence and the law presented to them. The witnesses are sworn to tell the truth and the law provides severe penalties if they fail to do so.

With few exceptions, trials are well-conducted, everyone who is a part of the court personnel does his duty, and justice is achieved. Moreover, this American system of jurisprudence, based upon the English common law, more particularly defined and delineated by our United States and Texas Constitutions, the laws passed by our legislative bodies, and the decisions of our higher courts, is probably the best means of settling disputes that there is in the world. Everyone should spend some time in the courtroom observing this democratic process in operation.

Origin

Trial procedures developed from methods used in settling family disputes, because the family was the earliest organized unit of society. It still remains the basic one. Before there were any courts, families, by necessity, had rules, not written rules, but rules, nevertheless, that were understood. The father was first in command, the mother second, and then the children in order of age.

In any family, disputes arise among children, and a wise parent will take time to listen to the children about both sides of the question. Each child involved should be permitted to tell his side of the story without interruption from the opposition, letting each child name his witnessess to bear out his testimony. The parent's wisdom and the information from the children help make the decisions that set things right.

This is a trial and trial procedure in its simplest form, and it is the natural beginning of respect for law and order. As children grow up, they learn to appreciate the need for justice and lend their efforts toward its effectiveness.

But since disputes arise outside of the family where parental authority does not extend, it became necessary to establish some authority with jurisdiction over families and individuals and their relationships with each other. And so, over a considerable time, we have arrived at the present system designed for orderly solutions to disputes. More than any other people in the world, the English speaking people have gone to great lengths to provide means for settling disputes around the council table. We believe that when men grow in wisdom and moral being, they are willing to use the council table for settling disputes, instead of trial by physical combat. Therefore, let us study a lawsuit from its beginning to its end in a district court where strict rules apply.

A controversy has arisen between two citizens of this state, and it has grown out of complicated and involved business so that each man honestly believes that he is right, or at any rate, each one has decided to go through a lawsuit rather than yield to the other. One man has made his demands upon the other and has served notice that unless his demands are met a suit will be filed to enforce them. His demands are flatly refused.

So, the first man explains the whole matter to a lawyer. The lawyer decides from the story that it is a dispute that can be settled only by litigation, and he becomes the man's representative. He may talk to the opposing party, or write him one or two letters, but he soon draws up a petition to the district court (for it involves in this case an amount over $1000 which puts it within the jurisdiction of that court). He then calls his client in and reads the petition to him and they agree that the cause of action is correctly stated. The man who is starting the suit is called the "plaintiff," and the man against whom the suit is brought is called the "defendant," which is how they are referred to in the petition which the lawyer is preparing to file. The plaintiff gives his lawyer the amount required by the district court clerk as a cost deposit, and the lawyer files the petition in the district court. Besides

service of citation

defining the purpose of the suit, this petition requests that the defendant be cited to appear and answer the suit, and that the plaintiff be granted the relief to which he is entitled. With this petition, the lawyer gives a copy of it to the clerk so it can be delivered to the defendant when he is served the citation which the clerk will issue.

The district court clerk will immediately issue a citation and the citation is the official notice from the court to the defendant that he is being sued, what the suit is about, and it states the date on which the defendant must answer.

The clerk passes the citation, with a copy of the plaintiff's petition attached, to the county sheriff, or his deputy, or to a constable, and the citation instructs the officer to serve it upon the defendant and make a return to the court showing where and when he served it. The officer serves the citation with the attached petition upon the defendant. Thus, the defendant knows that he has been sued, the amount, or other relief asked by the plaintiff, and the date on or before which he must file his answer.

Now the defendant sees a lawyer and tells him his side of the case and hires him to represent him in the case. The defendant's lawyer prepares and files his answer in the case within the limited time. In that answer, the defendant's lawyer denies everything, not admitting anything stated in the plaintiff's petition, thereby showing that he expects to protect every legal right his client has, and he either sends this to the plaintiff's lawyer, or leaves him a copy with the district court clerk.

So each side is then aware of the nature of the pending fight. Both sides talk to prospective witnesses, each trying to find those whose testimony can help its own purpose or defeat the opposition.

Before the trial date, the attorneys will make sure that witnesses are summoned to attend the trial, unless they are satisfied that the witnesses will attend without a summons.

Also, before the trial date, one side or the other decides that the trial should be before a jury. That side then deposits $5 with the district clerk and requests a jury for the trial.

On the trial date, the court calls for order and the clerk reads the case's number and style, and the judge asks the attorneys if they are ready for trial. If one or the other is not ready, the judge will hear his excuse and grant a delay, or he will overrule the motion for delay or postponement. But in this particular situation, both sides announce they are ready.

The clerk then orders the jury panel to stand and hold up their right hands and be sworn in, and he administers the following oath: "You, and each of you, do solemnly swear that you will true answers give to all questions propounded to you concerning your qualifications as a juror, so help you God."

The clerk will then hand the plaintiff's attorney and the defendant's attorney identical lists containing 24 names. The attorney for the plaintiff will tell the jury panel the nature of the lawsuit and then question the panel as a group about their qualifications. If he finds any he believes to be disqualified to serve on the jury, he will address the judge and "challenge the juror for cause." The judge will rule on the challenge and sustain or overrule it. If he sustains it the person's name is erased from the list. If he overrules it the name is left on the list, which means that the judge does not believe that the person is disqualified. After this general questioning, the plaintiff's attorney generally will question the members of the panel individually, to learn more about their individual attitudes toward the kind of case that is to be tried and other pertinent facts.

Next, the defendant's attorney will make his statement about the nature of the case to be tried, and he will question the panel in much the same manner as the plaintiff's attorney did, but of course, seeking to eliminate those who may be disqualified or who may have some prejudice that would be against the interests of the defendant. If the challenges made for cause by the attorneys and sustained by the judge reduce the number on the panel to less than twenty-four, the judge will call for additional prospective jurors to bring the number on the lists back to twenty-four, and the new ones called are questioned by the attorneys.

With the challenges for cause disposed of and the number on the lists brought back to twenty-four, each side is allowed six "peremptory challenges" or "scratches," which are made by simply drawing a line through the names of the objectionable ones without the necessity of stating a reason. Thus a full panel of twelve jurors are left on the list after each side makes six scratches, even if each side scratches different names.

After the attorneys have made their scratches and have handed the clerk their changed lists, the clerk reads out the first twelve unscratched names, and these file into the jury box as their names are called. After they are in place, the judge, or the clerk under the judge's direction, will command the jurors to stand, raise their right hands, and be sworn in with the following oath: "You, and each of you, do solemnly swear that in all cases between parties which shall be to you submitted, you will a true verdict render, according to the law as it may be given you in charge by the court and to the evidence submitted to you under the rulings of the court; so help you God."

If the witnesses have not been sworn in previously, the clerk will order all witnesses in the case to stand and raise their right hands and be sworn in with the following oath: "You and each of you do solemnly swear that the evidence which you are about to give in this case will be the truth, the whole truth, and nothing but the truth, so help you God."

It may be desirable to the attorney on either side, or both of them, to have witnesses "put under the rule." Either attorney may address the court "Your Honor, we invoke the *Do this*

Put under the rule.

rule." Whereupon the judge will tell the witnesses that the rule has been invoked and that they should remain outside the courtroom until their names are called to testify and that they should not discuss the case among themselves or with anyone else. The witnesses then leave the courtroom, but remain in the halls where they can hear their names as they are called to the witness chair. The judge will order the attorneys to proceed.

1. The attorney for the plaintiff will read his petition.

2. The defendant's attorney will read his petition.

3. The plaintiff's attorney will briefly state to the jury the nature of the plaintiff's case or claim and the supporting facts he expects to prove.

A court reporter is ready to take down, word for word, what is said and other things that transpire during the trial proceedings:

4. The plaintiff's attorney will then introduce his evidence by calling to the witness chair one witness at a time and asking him questions designed to draw testimony that will establish plaintiff's claim.

5. The defendant's attorney will cross-examine, if he chooses, each witness as he concludes his direct testimony.

As the questioning by the plaintiff's attorney proceeds, and exhibits are offered in evidence. The defendant's attorney will object to any question which he believes calls for inadmissible testimony, evidence and exhibits which he thinks are not proper for the plaintiff to offer (in fact, to any testimony and exhibits that he hopes to keep out). He gives his reasons for the objection such as "It is hearsay," or "The question is leading," (meaning that the attorney suggests the answer he expects by the way he asks his question), or "It is irrelevant and immaterial to any issue in this case," or other reasons why he thinks the testimony should not be admitted.

As he makes his objections, counsel stands and addresses the judge thusly: "Your Honor, we object to the question because it is irrelevant and immaterial."

The judge will immediately rule on the objection by "sustaining" the objection, which means that the witness should not answer the question, or by "overruling" the objection, which means that the witness should answer the question.

If the judge sustains the objection, the plaintiff's attorney (if he really believes the question is important and that it should be admitted) will make an "exception" to the court's ruling, which is generally done by stating so that both the judge and the court stenographer can hear it, "Please note our exception."

Sometimes the attorneys' views differ so greatly on what should be admitted and what should not be admitted in evidence that arguments develop over points of law. Often, in a closely contested proceeding, the judge will have the jury leave the courtroom while the Judge hears argument from the attorneys and then he rules on the dispute. This part of the proceeding is also recorded by the stenographer, for it will compose part of the case's record. The attorneys, for both sides, must assure that the record is well-made so that if he is ruled against wrongly by the Judge, the error may be righted on appeal, if an appeal is taken.

The plaintiff's attorney must continue with the introduction of evidence until he has "made out his case," for if he does not prove a *bona fide* cause of action, he will, upon proper motion of the defendant's attorney, lose his case. The judge will instruct the jury to find for the defendant, which is known as an "instructed verdict." But an attorney with a well-prepared case will not stop short. He will develop his case fully and to the point where, in the absence of contrary proof by the defendant, he will win his case. If he has made out a *bona fide* case, and the defendant can offer nothing to disprove it, then an "instructed verdict" will result for the plaintiff.

Finally, the plaintiff's attorney exhausts his supply of evidence, and he concludes that he should "rest" his case.

When the plaintiff's attorney rests, the defendant's attorney will probably make a motion for an instructed verdict for the defendant, claiming that the plaintiff has not presented a *bona fide* case. The judge will rule on the motion by granting it or overruling it. If he grants the motion, the case comes to an abrupt end in the defendant's favor, which does not happen often. If he overrules the motion, the burden of proceeding shifts to the defendant. This means that the judge believes the plaintiff has stated and proven a *bona fide* case and if the defendant does not properly refute it, the plaintiff should have a judgment against the defendant.

This is somewhat like ball players shifting from "field" to "bat." The defendant must be heard if he desires to be heard, and he almost always does.

6. The defendant's attorney will then state briefly the nature of his defense and the facts relied on to support it.

7. The defendant's attorney will then introduce his evidence in an effort to disprove or tear down the case that has just been made out against his client. As he puts his witnesses on the stand and questions them in an effort to elicit testimony favorable to the defendant, the opposing attorney objects to questions which he thinks call for inadmissible testimony; and he has a right to cross examine each witness at the conclusion of the direct testimony.

The defendant's attorney proceeds with witness after witness, and with exhibits, to show his side of the lawsuit favorably until he has covered as best he can the whole scope of defense, because both the defendant and the plaintiff will be confined, after the defendant rests, to rebutting the testimony or evidence.

8. After all of the defendant's evidence has been presented, the plaintiff may introduce further testimony to rebut that given by the defendant, but he cannot offer any new testimony as original evidence, except in particular instances when the judge believes it is necessary to arrive at justice.

9. After all the rebuttal evidence offered by the plaintiff is in, the defendant may offer testimony to rebut that last offered by the plaintiff.

10. After all of the evidence on both sides is in, the judge will prepare his charge to the jury with the assistance of the attorneys on both sides. If it is agreeable to both sides it can be a "general charge," in which case the judge instructs the jury on the law applicable to the case. Each side is given a copy of the charge before it is given to the jury, and time is allowed for the attorneys to prepare written objections to the charge, which they file with the court reporter, as the charge itself is filed, as part of the case's record.

But if either side demands it, the charge to the jury will be in the form of "special issues" which are questions prepared by the judge for the jury to answer, and these are intended to cover the basic phases of the case, so that answers to them will constitute a "verdict." The answers to the questions will determine the outcome of the lawsuit. They will show who won and the extent of his victory. This is a very technical part of a lawsuit, and each side has a right to prepare and submit to the judge special issues and instructions to the jury. The judge decides which of these special issues are to be submitted to the jury and the instructions that are to be given.

The attorneys will make timely objections if the judge does not submit the issues and instructions requested, or if the judge changes them materially, and these objections or "exceptions" become a part of the record. These exceptions are recorded by the court reporter as they are made, and sometimes they become important on appeal.

11. Finally, when the issues are composed and the judge is satisfied with them, and the exceptions by the attorneys have been recorded, the judge will read the charge to the jury, including the special issues, and if the case is submitted on special issues, he will also read the definitions he considered

necessary and give explanatory instructions, but he will not comment on the evidence or the credibility of the witnesses.

Following the charge to the jury by the judge, the attorneys are permitted to address the jury, first the plaintiff's attorney and then the defendant's attorney, followed by a rebuttal by the plaintiff's attorney. The judge will allow them the time he believes the nature of the case demands.

12. After the attorneys' arguments are concluded, the jury retires to consider its verdict. If they agree, they return into open court with their verdict in writing, and the foreman of the jury hands the written verdict to the clerk. The judge calls the court to order and inquires whether they have reached a verdict. If they answer that they have, the judge directs the clerk to read it.

13. The clerk reads the jury's verdict. The losing party generally requests a poll of the jury and this request is always granted. To poll the jury, the verdict is read to them collectively, whether it be on a general charge or on special issues, then they are asked individually if that is their verdict. If any juror answers negatively, the jury is sent back for further deliberation. Either side has the right to require a poll of the jury.

14. Once the jury has agreed and has returned its verdict, the judge renders the judgment in the case based upon that verdict.

As a practical matter, the winning party's attorney prepares and submits to the judge a draft of the judgment he thinks should be rendered in the case, also giving a copy to the opposing counsel for his consideration. The opposing counsel may offer suggestions for some change, or he may even write and submit to the judge and the opposing counsel the kind of judgment he thinks should be entered in the case. Ultimately, the judge approves and enters one of these drafts or makes changes and then approves and enters it as the judgment, or he may write it entirely by himself and enter it as the judgment in the case.

The foregoing is an outline of procedure in a trial before a jury. In civil cases like this example, the trial also can be held before the judge without a jury. In fact, if no jury is requested in advance, the trial is before the judge only.

The procedure is the same, except for the absence of the jury, but it is also somewhat more informal before the judge.

New Trial

Often the losing party will make a motion for a new trial, and in this motion he states, through his attorney, the errors which he thinks have been made in the case which entitle him to a new trial. When this motion is made, the judge generally will grant a hearing on it, at which the attorneys on each side will present to the judge their views of the law and its application to the procedure in the case. The winner tries to avoid a new trial and the loser tries to obtain one. The judge will grant or overrule the motion. If the motion is granted, then a new trial is ordered, unless the loser on the motion appeals from the judge's ruling. In some instances, the case will go up to a higher court on the judge's ruling on the motion and the question is ruled on by the Court of Civil Appeals. If the judge overrules the motion for a new trial, the mover (the losing party), if he believes he is right and the amount involved is worth the effort and expense, gives notice of appeal.

Appeal

When notice of appeal is made within the prescribed time, then the one taking the appeal, in order to get to the higher court, must post an appeal bond in an amount determined by the judge, or the clerk, to cover adequately the costs (in the court below and the estimated costs in the court above) for the reason that additional costs will be incurred on appeal. The bond may be in cash and posted with the clerk, or it may be by an approved bonding company or by two or more persons who have sufficient assets. After an adequate bond is posted with the clerk, the appellant may then order a transcript of the record in the case and take or send it to the Court of Civil Appeals. The appeal is almost wholly a function of the attorneys in the case, since no new testimony can be presented to the appellate court, and no witnesses can testify before that court. The case goes before the appellate court on the record made in the court below and the briefs that are presented by the attorneys in the case and their oral argument at the hearing.

The Court of Civil Appeals may affirm the initial judgment or reverse it. If that court affirms the initial judgment without change, then it is up to the appellant to take the case on to the Supreme Court of Texas, if it is a controversy that qualifies for consideration by that highest court; otherwise he has lost the case, and the initial judgment will be enforced.

The Court of Civil Appeals may reverse the initial judgment and remand the case for a new trial (which means that the motion for a new trial in the court below should have been granted in the first place) or it may reverse the judgment and render judgment in the case for the losing party if no other evidence is necessary to a proper conclusion of the litigation, or it may partially affirm the judgment below and partially reverse it.

The attorney for the aggrieved party must decide for his client what is to be done next after any such judgment, as he made the decision for appeal following the judgment in the court below. In the appellate courts, it is a matter of law and its application to the evidence presented in the court below, and this must be handled by the attorneys in the case.

5. The Texas Penal Code

The Texas Legislature of 1973 adopted a new Penal Code which became effective on January 1, 1974. Prior to this action much ground work and drafting had been done by a committee appointed by the Board of Directors of the State Bar Association of Texas, a committee appointed by the Texas District and County Attorneys Association and a committee appointed by the Texas Criminal Defense Lawyers Association. The final draft of the proposed new Penal Code was adopted by the 63rd Legislature at its regular session in 1973, and it was approved by Governor Dolph Briscoe on June 14, 1973. The new code seems to be a great improvement over the old Penal Code, but as it is presently written it did not repeal or supercede all provisions of the old code. Some provisions of the old code remain unaffected.

Objectives of the Code

The objectives of the new code are stated as follows:

"The general purposes of this code are to establish a system of prohibitions, penalties, and correctional measures to deal with conduct that unjustifiably and inexcusably causes or threatens harm to those individual or public interests for which state protection is appropriate. To this end the provisions of this code are intended, and shall be construed, to achieve the following objectives:

"1. to insure the public safety through:

"A. the deterrent influence of the penalties hereinafter provided;

"B. the rehabilitation of those convicted of violations of this code; and

"C. such punishment as may be necessary to prevent likely recurrence of criminal behavior;

"2. by definition and grading of offenses to give fair warning of what is prohibited and the consequences of violation;

"3. to prescribe penalties that are proportionate to the seriousness of offenses and that permit recognition of differences in rehabilitation possibilities among individual offenders;

"4. to safeguard conduct that is without guilt from condemnation as criminal;

"5. to guide and limit the exercise of official discretion in law enforcement to prevent arbitrary or oppressive treatment of persons accused or convicted of offenses;

"6. to define the scope of state interest in law enforcement against specific offenses and to systematize the exercise of state criminal jurisdiction."

Classification of Offenses and Punishments Prescribed for the Several Classes

Offenses fall into two general groups:

1. felonies which can be punished by sentences to the Department of Corrections (the penitentiary) or by death, and

2. misdemeanors punishable by jail sentences or fines.

Classification of Felonies and Punishments for them

Felonies are classified according to the relative seriousness of the offense into four categories.

1. capital felonies, punishable by death or a life sentence in the Department of Corrections;

2. felonies of the first degree, punishable by a life sentence or any number of years, not less than five nor more than ninety-nine in the Department of Corrections;

3. felonies of the second degree, punishable by a sentence of not less than two nor more than twenty years in the Department of Corrections, and in addition thereto a fine not to ex-

ceed $10,000 may be assessed, but the fine may not be assessed alone;

4. felonies of the third degree, punishable by a sentence of not less than two nor more than ten years in the Department of Corrections, and in addition thereto a fine not to exceed $5,000 may be assessed, but not the fine alone.

Classification of Misdemeanors and Prescribed Punishments for them

Misdemeanors are classified according to the relative seriousness of the offense into three categories:

Class A—punishable by a jail sentence not to exceed one year or a fine not to exceed $2,000, or both;

Class B—punishable by a jail sentence not to exceed 180 days or a fine not to exceed $1,000, or both;

Class C—punishable by a fine not to exceed $200. Conviction of a Class C misdemeanor does not impose any legal disability or disadvantage. It does not take away the right to vote or to hold public office.

Repeat or Habitual Felony Offenders

The repeat offender can bring upon himself increased punishment after the first conviction, as stated in the Penal Code.

"If it be shown on the trial of a third-degree felony that the defendant has been once before convicted of any felony, on conviction he shall be punished for a second-degree felony.

"If it be shown on the trial of a second-degree felony that the defendant has been once before convicted of any felony, on conviction he shall be punished for a first-degree felony.

"If it be shown on the trial of a first-degree felony that the defendant has been once before convicted of any felony, on conviction he shall be punished by confinement in the Texas Department of corrections for life, or for any term not more than 99 years nor less than 15 years.

"If it be shown on the trial of any felony offense that the defendant has previously been finally convicted of two felony offenses, and the second previous felony conviction is for an offense that occurred subsequent to the first previous conviction having become final, on conviction he shall be punished by confinement in the Texas Department of Corrections for life."

Burden of Proof

Every person is presumed to be innocent until he has been proven guilty beyond any reasonable doubt, and the burden of proving a person guilty rests upon the State of Texas. One may be charged with an offense and may be brought into the courtroom for his trial, but this does not raise any presumption of his guilt. Lawfully he remains innocent until he has been proven guilty, and the degree of proof must be such that it removes all reasonable doubt from the minds of those who are to pass sentence upon him (the judge or the jury).

Repeat and Habitual Misdemeanor Offenders

"If it be shown on the trial of a Class A misdemeanor that the defendant has before been convicted of a Class A misdemeanor or any degree of felony, on conviction he shall be punished by confinement in jail for any term of not more than one year nor less than 90 days.

"If it be shown on the trial of a Class B misdemeanor that the defendant has been before convicted of a Class A or Class B misdemeanor or any degree of felony, on conviction he shall be punished by confinement in jail for any term of not more than 180 days nor less than 30 days."

There is no enhancement of punishment for one convicted of a Class C misdemeanor, even though he may have been convicted before of any offense or any number of offenses, misdemeanors or felonies.

Reduction of the Degree of Offense

By the Penal Code, courts have been given novel discretion in some instances. A court may set aside a judgment or verdict of guilty of a felony of the third degree and enter a judgment of guilt and punishment for Class A misdemeanor, if the court believes that justice would be better served because the defendant is a first offender or that he is the kind of person that can be rehabilitated.

Also, if a person has been found guilty of an offense, then during the sentencing hearing (the hearing in which his punishment is to be determined) he may make admission of other offenses he has committed but for which he has not been convicted and ask the court to take them into consideration in fixing his punishment for the offense of which he is convicted. If the court does so, then thereafter the defendant cannot be prosecuted for the offense or offenses which he confesses to the court. This enables the person who is in multiple troubles to "clean the slate" at this one trial. These are new provisions in Texas law.

Criminal Intent (without actually committing the intended offense)

> "A person commits an offense if, with specific intent to commit an offense, he does an act amounting to more than mere preparation that tends but fails to effect the commission of the offense intended."

For example, a man who holds a grudge against a police officer makes up his mind to murder him and takes his gun and draws a bead on the officer and fires his gun, but his aim is poor and the other person is not hit by the bullet. He actually intended and attempted to commit the offense, but his efforts failed. If his efforts had succeeded, he could have been prosecuted for a capital felony, but because his efforts failed he could be prosecuted and convicted for an offense one category lower than the intended offense, in this case a first-degree felony.

The same rule holds for attempts to commit offenses of lower degree. The actor or offender can be prosecuted for an offense one category lower than the offense he intended to commit.

Criminal Conspiracy

> "A person commits criminal conspiracy if, with intent that a felony be committed:
>
> 1. he agrees with one or more persons that they or one or more of them engage in conduct that would constitute the offense; and
>
> 2. he or one or more of them performs an overt act in pursuance of the agreement."

One person alone cannot commit criminal conspiracy. There must be two or more involved, an agreement must be made, and there must be an overt act in pursuance of the agreement. The coconspirators can be prosecuted for the offense one category lower than the offense which they agreed to commit.

Punishment of Corporations or Associations

A corporation or association is a "legal entity," but it is not susceptible of being put in prison. If it is convicted of an offense its punishment has to be by fine. If it is convicted of an offense for which a fine is provided, its punishment is the fine provided for the offense of which it is convicted. If under the law the offense is a felony of whatever category or degree, the court may fix a fine not to exceed $10,000. If the offense is a Class A or Class B misdemeanor, the fine is any amount fixed by the court not to exceed $2,000. If it is a Class C misdemeanor the fine will not exceed $200. However, if the court finds that the offense committed by the corporation or association resulted in financial gain to the offender, in lieu of the fines otherwise provided, the court may assess a fine of any amount not to exceed twice the amount of the gain.

Offenses Against the Person

With the foregoing general provisions and definitions in mind we turn now to the several groups of offenses that are made punishable by law, and the first and most serious are offenses against the person. Here is where the capital offenses will be found.

Capital Murder

If a person knowingly and intentionally causes the death of another and the other
1. is a peace officer or fireman who is lawfully acting in the discharge of his duty and who the person knows is a peace officer or fireman; or
2. the person intentionally commits a murder in the course of committing or attempting to commit kidnapping, burgulary, robbery, aggravated rape, or arson; or
3. the person commits the murder for remuneration or the promise of remuneration or employs another to commit the murder for remuneration or the promise of remuneration; or
4. the person commits the murder while escaping or attempting to escape from a penal institution; or
5. the person, while incarcerated in a penal institution, murders another who is employed in the operation of the penal institution; that person in any case commits a capital felony punishable by the death sentence or for a life sentence in the Department of Corrections.

From the present day viewpoint it does not appear likely that we shall see a death sentence actually executed in Texas in the near future. Judges of our criminal courts ceased to set dates for carrying out death sentences even before the Supreme Court of the United States in the case of Furman vs. Georgia held that the death penalty is unconstitutional as providing for cruel and unusual punishment in violation of the eighth amendment.

Murder (less than capital)

> "A person commits an offense if he:
> 1. intentionally or knowingly causes the death of another;
> 2. intends to cause serious bodily injury and commits an act clearly dangerous to human life that causes the death of another; or
> 3. commits or attempts to commit a felony, other than voluntary or involuntary manslaughter, and in the course of and in furtherance of the commission or attempt, or in immediate flight from the commission or attempt, he commits or attempts to commit an act clearly dangerous to human life that causes the death of another."

An offense committed under any of the three types mentioned is a felony of the first degree, punishable by a sentence of life in the Department of Corrections or for any number of years not less than five nor more than 99.

Voluntary Manslaughter

> "A person commits an offense if he caused the death of another under circumstances that would constitute murder except that he caused the death under the immediate influence of sudden passion arising from an adequate cause"

"Sudden passion" is defined as passion directly caused by and arising out of provocation by the individual killed or another acting with the person killed which produces passion at the time of the offense and is not solely the result of former provocation. "Adequate cause" is cause that would ordinarily produce a degree of anger, rage, resentment, or terror in a person of ordinary temper, sufficient to render the mind incapable of cool reflection. Voluntary manslaughter as above defined is a felony of the second degree, punishable by sentence to the Department of Corrections for not less than two years nor more than twenty with or without a fine not to exceed $10,000, but not by the fine alone.

Involuntary Manslaughter

If a person recklessly causes the death of another, or if while he is intoxicated he, either by accident or mistake, operates a motor vehicle so that he causes the death of another, he is guilty of committing a felony of the third degree and he is punishable by sentence to the Department of Corrections for any number of years not less than two nor more than ten, and a fine not to exceed $5,000, but not by the fine alone.

Evidence

In the trial of cases of murder or voluntary manslaughter both the state and the defendant are permitted to offer testimony to show any and all facts about the circumstances surrounding the killing and the prior relationship of the person accused and the deceased. It was by similar provisions in laws of evidence in other states that the famous Clarence Darrow, as defense attorney, could, in his own words, "so inflame the jury that they would want to dig up the deceased and kill him again." On the other hand an able prosecuting attorney may be able to convince the jury that the defendant is a very bad actor.

Criminally Negligent Homicide

A person commits an offense if he causes the death of another by criminal negligence, and the punishment for it is a jail sentence of not more than one year with or without a fine not to exceed $2,000—a Class A misdemeanor. The definition of criminal negligence is quite technical, but the substance of it is that it must be substantial and unjustifiable. Offenses of this kind often arise from negligent driving of motor vehicles.

Kidnapping and False Imprisonment

A person commits an offense if he intentionally or knowingly abducts another person; and this is a felony of the third degree. It is an affirmative defense to prosecution under this provision of the law that
1. the abduction was not coupled with intent to use or to threaten to use deadly force:
2. the actor (the one doing the abducting) was a relative of the person abducted; and
3. the actor's sole intent was to assume lawful control of the victim.

But generally when kidnapping is committed it is with the intent to
1. hold the person kidnapped for ransom or reward;
2. use him as a shield or hostage;
3. facilitate the commission of a felony or the flight after the attempt or commission of a felony;
4. inflict bodily injury on him, or her, or violate or abuse the victim sexually;
5. terrorize the victim or a third person; or
6. interfere with the performance of any governmental or political function.

This is known as aggravated kidnapping and it is a felony of the first degree unless the actor releases the victim voluntarily and in a safe place, in which event it is felony of the second degree.

False Imprisonment

People of this state have the right and privilege of free movement and when a person intentionally and knowingly restrains another, he commits the offense of false imprisonment which is a Class B misdemeanor unless he recklessly exposes the victim to substantial risk of serious bodily injury, in which event it is a felony of the third degree.

It is an affirmative defense against prosecution, however, if the person restrained was a child less than 14 years of age, and the actor was a relative of the child, and the actor's sole intent was to assume lawful control of the child.

Sexual Offenses

Rape

A person commits an offense if he has sexual intercourse with a female not his wife without the female's consent, and this is a felony of the second degree. If a person commits the act above mentioned or the rape is of a child and the actor

1. causes serious bodily injury or attempts to cause death to the victim or another in the course of the same criminal episode; or

2. compels submission to the rape by threat of death, serious bodily injury, or kidnapping to be immediately inflicted on anyone, the offense is a felony of the first degree.

Sexual Abuse

The law describes various sex abuses including deviate or abnormal sex activity and sets the penalties for their commission and most of such acts are felonies, and when they are committed against a child the punishment is one category higher than for such offenses involving adults. There is no punishment for such acts carried on between a man and his wife.

Indecency with a child

A person commits an offense if, with a child younger than 17 years and not his spouse, whether the child is of the same or opposite sex, he

1. engages in sexual contact with the child; or

2. makes indecent exposures to the child, knowing that the child is present, with intent to arouse or gratify the sexual desire of any person. However, it is a defense against prosecution for this conduct that the child was at the time of the alleged offense fourteen years or older and had, prior to the time of the alleged offense, engaged promiscuously in
1. sexual intercourse;
2. deviate sexual intercourse;
3. sexual contact; or
4. indecent exposure.
The offense is classed as a felony of the third degree.

Assaultive Offenses

Assault

A person commits an offense if he
1. intentionally, knowingly, or recklessly causes bodily injury to another, which is a Class A misdemeanor;
2. intentionally or knowingly threatens another with imminent bodily injury; or
3. intentionally or knowingly causes physical contact with another when he knows or should reasonably believe that the other will regard the contact as offensive or provocative. Offenses under 2 and 3 are Class C misdemeanors.

Aggravated Assault

If in committing assault, as mentioned above, the actor
1. causes serious bodily injury to another;
2. causes bodily injury to a peace officer in the lawful discharge of official duty when he knows or has been informed that the person assaulted is a peace officer; or
3. uses a deadly weapon;
he commits a felony of the third degree.

Deadly Assault on a Peace Officer

If a person who assaults a peace officer uses a firearm or other prohibited weapon and intentionally or knowingly causes serious bodily injury to the officer in the lawful discharge of official duty when he knows or has been informed that the person assaulted is a peace officer, he commits a felony of the first degree. He is presumed to have known that the person assaulted was a peace officer if the officer was wearing a distinctive uniform indicating that he was an officer.

Injury to a child

A person commits a felony of the second degree if intentionally, knowingly, recklessly, or with criminal negligence he causes serious bodily injury, serious physical or mental deficiency or impairment, or deformity, to a child who is 14 years of age or younger.

Reckless Conduct

A person commits a Class B misdemeanor if he recklessly engages in conduct that places another in imminent danger of serious bodily injury, for example pointing a gun at another whether or not the actor believes the gun to be loaded. If the victim consented to such reckless conduct it is an affirmative defense against prosecution.

Terroristic Threat

A person commits an offense if he threatens to commit any offense involving violence to any person or property with intent to
1. cause a reaction of any type to his threat by an official or volunteer agency organized to deal with emergencies;

2. place any person in fear of imminent serious bodily injury; or

3. prevent or interrupt the occupation or use of a building, room, place of assembly, place to which the public has access, place of employment or occupation, aircraft, automobile, or other form of conveyance, or other public place.

The offense is a Class B misdemeanor, except for (3) which is a Class A misdemeanor.

Offenses Against the Family

Bigamy

1. If a person is legally married and he

   A. purports to marry or does marry a person other than his spouse in this state, or any other state or foreign country, under circumstances that would, but for the actor's prior marriage, constitute a marriage; or

   B. lives with a person other than his spouse in this state under the appearance of being married; or

If a person is legally married and knows that a married person other than his spouse is married and he

   A. purports to marry or does marry that person in this state, or any other state or foreign country, under circumstances that would, but for the person's prior marriage, constitute a marriage; or

   B. lives with that person in this state under the appearance of being married,

he commits a felony of the third degree.

It is a defense to prosecution under the first provision above that the actor reasonably believed that his marriage was void or had been dissolved by death, divorce or annulment.

A lawful wife or husband of the actor may testify both for and against the actor concerning proof of the original marriage, and this includes a common law spouse.

Incest

A person commits a felony of the third degree if he engages in sexual intercourse or deviate sexual intercourse with a person he knows to be, without regard to legitimacy
1. an ancestor or descendant by blood or adoption;
2. his stepchild or stepparent, while the marriage creating the relationship exists;
3. his parent's brother or sister of the whole or half blood;
4. his brother or sister of the whole or half blood or by adoption;
5. the children of his brother or sister of the whole or half blood or by adoption.

Interference with Child Custody

A person commits an offense if he takes or retains a child younger than 18 years out of this state when he
1. knows that his taking or retention violates a temporary or permanent judgment or order of a court disposing of the child's custody, or
2. has not been awarded custody of the child by a court of competent jurisdiction and knows that a suit for divorce, or civil suit or application for habeas corpus to dispose of the child's custody, has been filed.

It is a defense to (2) above that the actor returned the child to this state within seven days from the date of commission of the offense. An offense under these provisions is a felony of the third degree. This new provision is intended to fill a gap or hiatus in the law that has long been a frustration to parents, attorneys, judges and law enforcement officers. Now, when the relationship between parents reaches the state where a court must decide between them, the one not awarded custody of the child will do well to leave the physical custody of the child where the court places it. It is taking the child out of the state and purportedly out of the jurisdiction of the court that makes the offense so serious.

While it is an offense to interfere knowingly and intentionally with the custody of a child under 18 years of age by enticing it from the custody of the parent or guardian or the person standing in the stead of the parent or guardian, this offense is classed only as a Class B misdemeanor, if the child is not carried out of the state.

Criminal Nonsupport

A person commits a Class A misdemeanor if he intentionally or knowingly fails to provide support that he can provide and that he is legally obligated to provide for his children younger than 18 years, or to his spouse who is in needy circumstances. This applies to the wife as well if the husband is in needy circumstances. The class of offense is increased to a felony of the third degree if the actor has been convicted one or more times for the offense or commits the offense while residing in another state. The deserted spouse and children are provided with the services of a public prosecutor and of law enforcement personnel to enforce the husband's (or wife's) duty to support the family.

Having now dealt with offenses against the person and offenses against the family, our attention now turns to offenses against property, which can, like the afore mentioned offenses, carry heavy penalties.

Offenses Against Property

The following is a verbatim quotation of an article that takes the place of many articles in the old code:

"Art. 28.03, Criminal Mischief.
    "A. A person commits an offense if, without the effective consent of the owner:

"1. he intentionally or knowingly damages or destroys the tangible property of the owner; or

"2. he intentionally or knowingly tampers with the tangible property of the owner and causes pecuniary loss or substantial inconvenience to the owner or a third person.

"B. An offense under this section is:

"1. a Class C misdemeanor if (a) the amount of pecuniary loss is less than $5 or (b) except as provided in Subdivision (4) (B) of this subsection, it causes substantial inconvenience to other

"2. a Class B misdemeanor if the amount of pecuniary loss is $5 or more but less than $20;

"3. a Class A misdemeanor if the amount of pecuniary loss is $20 or more but less than $200;

"4. a felony of the third degree if (a) the amount of pecuniary loss is $200 or more but less than $10,000, (b) regardless of the amount of pecuniary loss, if the actor causes impairment or interruption of public communications, public transportation, public water, gas, or power supply, or other public service, (c) regardless of the amount of pecuniary loss, the property is one or more head of cattle, horses, sheep, swine, or goats, (d) regardless of the amount of pecuniary loss, the property was a fence used for the production of cattle, horses, sheep, swine, or goats, or (e) regardless of the amount of pecuniary loss, the damage or destruction was inflicted by branding one or more head of cattle, horses, sheep, swine, or goats.

"5. a felony of the second degree if the amount of pecuniary loss is $10,000 or more."

If the one committing the offense is a part owner of the property damaged or destroyed and he does not have consent of the owners, he is subject to the penalties above set forth.

Robbery

A person commits a felony of the second degree if, in the course of committing theft and with intent to obtain or maintain control of the property, he

1. intentionally, knowingly, or recklessly causes bodily injury to another; or

2. intentionally or knowingly threatens or places another in fear of imminent bodily injury or death.

Robbery generally involves taking property from the person or possession of another, and it is often associated with violence. If the robber causes serious bodily injury to another, or uses or exhibits a deadly weapon the offense is a felony of the first degree.

Burglary

If, without the consent of the owner, a person goes into or remains concealed in a habitation or building not then open to the public and attempts to commit a felony or theft, he commits burglary which is a felony of the second degree. It is not necessary that the one committing the crime enter the habitation or building with whole body. He may reach in with an arm or hand or poke through a window or other opening a fishing pole or other object to retrieve the objects he is trying to steal, and he commits the offense. Moreover if the premises entered are a habitation, or if any party to the offense is armed with explosives or a deadly weapon, or if any party to the offense injures or attempts to injure anyone in effecting entry or while in the building or in immediate flight from the building, the offense is a felony of the first degree. It has long been recognized by the courts that a burglar is a potential killer.

Burglary of a Coin Operated Machine

This kind of burglary is a Class A misdemeanor.

Burglary of Vehicles

One who breaks into a vehicle with intent to commit a felony or theft commits a felony of the third degree. The breaking in may be into any part of the vehicle, the trunk or the main body of it, and vehicle in this sense means automobiles, trucks, enclosed tractors, road graders, a vessel, steamboat or railroad car.

Theft

The offense of theft has several elements: intent to deprive the owner of property, obtaining possession of it or exercising control of it (other than real estate), unlawfully. Thus a person who receives or conceals stolen property is guilty of theft the same as the one who steals it originally.

The offense is

1. a Class C misdemeanor if the value of the property stolen is less than $5;
2. a Class B misdemeanor if
    A. the value of the property stolen is $5 or more but less than $20; or
    B. the value of the property stolen is less than $5 and the defendant has previously been convicted of any grade of theft;
3. a Class A misdemeanor if the value of the property stolen is $20 or more but less than $200;
4. a felony of the third degree if
    A. the value of the property stolen is $200 or more but less than $10,000, or the property is one or more head of cattle, horses, sheep, swine or goats or any part thereof under the value $10,000;
    B. regardless of value the property is stolen from the person of another or from a human corpse or grave; or
    C. the value of the property stolen is less than $200 and the defendant has been previously convicted two or more times of any grade of theft;
5. a felony of the second degree if the value of the pro[stolen is $10,000 or more.

Theft of Trade Secrets

Often businesses, such as the Coca Cola Company, have secret formulas, or like oil companies, have geophysical maps, which mean very much to those companies in their businesses. They are known as trade secrets, and if someone without the consent of the owner makes a copy of the formula or of the map, he commits a felony of the third degree.

Theft of Service

A person commits theft of service if, with intent to avoid payment for service that he knows is provided only for compensation
1. he intentionally or knowingly secures performance of the service by deception, or false token; or
2. having control over disposition of services of another to which he is not entitled, he intentionally or knowingly diverts the other's services to his own use or benefit or to the benefit or another not entitled to them. An example is the often complained of practice by a county or city commissioner who uses the equipment and personnel of the county or city to build improvements on his private farm.

Intent to avoid payment is presumed if the actor absconds without paying for the service in circumstances where payment is ordinarily made immediately upon rendering of the service, as in hotels, motels, restaurants, and comparable establishments.

The offense is
1. a Class C misdemeanor if the value of the service stolen is less than $5;
2. a Class B misdemeanor if the value of the service stolen is $5 or more but less than $20;
3. a Class A misdemeanor if the value of the service stolen is $20 or more but less than $200;

4. a felony of the third degree if the value of the service stolen is $200 or more but less than $10,000;

5. a felony of the second degree if the value of the service stolen is $10,000 or more.

Bad Checks

post dated checks

If a person issues and passes a check when he does not have money on deposit with the bank or other drawee on whom the check is drawn or does not have sufficient funds in the bank or with the drawee to pay the check and all other outstanding checks he has issued and passed, he is presumed to intend to commit theft, except in the case of a postdated check. One who accepts a postdated check is on notice that there are at that time insufficient funds on deposit to redeem the check. However, if one does so issue and pass a bad check, he can prevent prosecution, if within ten days after due notice to him of the bank's refusal to pay the check, he redeems or pays the check. The former law provided a penalty only if by issuing and passing a bad check the one issuing and passing it defrauded the payee, or caused him to part with property or services. So if a person owed an account and gave a bad check in payment of it, he did not actually induce the payee to part with property or services, and no offense was committed. Not so under the new code. The issuing and passing of a bad check is an offense. It is a Class C misdemeanor. But the one who seeks to prosecute must give notice to the offender that his check has been refused by the bank. The notice may be by registered or certified mail with return receipt requested, or by telegram with report of delivery requested, and addressed to the issuer at his address shown on

1. the check or order;
2. the records of the bank or other drawee; or
3. the records of the person to whom the check was issued or passed.

If notice is properly given, it is presumed that the notice was received within five days after it was sent.

Unauthorized Use of a Vehicle

A person commits a felony of the third degree if he intentionally or knowingly operates another's boat, airplane, or motor propelled vehicle without the consent of the owner.

Aggregation of Amounts involved in Theft

Formerly it was possible for a thief to commit a series of misdemeanor offenses in one single foray while the aggregate of the value of the separate amounts or properties taken would amount to enough so that if they were added together they would equal that of a felony offense, and he could be prosecuted only for each offense separately. Now the offenses can be aggregated or added together often resulting in prosecution for a felony offense. An example is where one sells a thousand tickets to a nonexistent show or event at a dollar each. He can be prosecuted for a felony.

Fraud

In fraud as in theft when amounts are obtained pursuant to one scheme or continuing course of conduct, whether from the same or several sources, the conduct may be considered as one offense and the amounts added together in determining the grade of offense. In actual practice, however, prosecution under this provision probably will be rare rather than frequent.

Fraud involves deception and it takes on many forms of cheating and theft. By necessity the statutes dealing with fraud are technical and full of definitions too long and numerous to be presented in full in a book of this kind, but a fair discussion is here given dealing with the more serious acts constituting the offense.

Forgery

"Forge" means:

1. to alter, make complete, execute, or authenticate any writing so that it purports

  A. to be the act of another who did not authorize that act;

  B. to have been executed at a time or place or in a number sequence other than was in fact the case; or

  C. to be a copy of an original when no such original existed;

2. to issue, transfer, register the transfer of, pass, publish, or otherwise utter a writing that is forged within the meaning of paragraph 1. above; or

3. to possess a writing that is forged with intent to use it to defraud.

"Writing" includes printing or any other method of recording information; it also includes money, coins, tokens, stamps, seals, credit cards, badges, and trademarks; and symbols of value, right, privilege, or identification.

Most forgeries, such as mentioned above are Class A misdemeanors; but if the writing is or purports to be a will, codicil, deed, deed of trust, mortgage, security instrument, security agreement, credit card, check or similar sight order for payment of money, contract, release, or other commercial instrument, it is a felony of the third degree.

It is a felony of second degree if the writing is or purports to be part of an issue of money, securities, postage or revenue stamps, or other instruments issued by state or national government or by a subdivision of either, or part of an issue of stock, bonds, or other instruments representing interests in or claims against another person.

Criminal Simulation

If, with intent to defraud, a person makes or alters an object, in whole or in part, so that it appears to have value because of age, antiquity, rarity, source, or authorship that it does not have; or he sells or passes an object so made or altered; or he possesses an object so made or altered, with intent to sell it or pass it; or he autheticates or certifies an object so made or altered as genuine or as different from what it is. This offense is a Class A misdemeanor.

Credit Card Abuse

We are people accustomed to credit, and credit cards have come into such extensive use that public policy demands that their use be protected almost to the extent that our legal tender "money" is protected. The misuse of credit cards in the various forms it takes on is a felony of the third degree.

False Statement to Obtain Property or Credit

A person commits a Class A misdemeanor if he intentionally or knowingly makes a materially false or misleading written statement to obtain property or credit for himself or another. Credit in this case includes a loan of money, furnishing property or services on credit, extending the due date of an obligation, comaking, endorsing, or guaranteeing a note or other instrument for obtaining credit, a line or letter of credit, and a credit card.

Fraud in Insolvency

When a person or company becomes insolvent or credit is so poor that creditors are about to take over and have a trustee for benefit of creditors appointed, and he or it cannot protect the business by raising the necessary cash, then no act must be done which would deceive or defraud the creditors, such as falsifying the record, concealing property of the business, encumbering it, or refusing to disclose facts to the trustee or receiver. A violation of this kind is a Class A misdemeanor.

Receiving Deposit, Premium or Investment in Failing Financial Institution

If a bank, building and loan association or other financial institution is in such failing condition that it cannot meet its obligations and an officer or employee receives a deposit which he knows that the business cannot make payment of on demand, or knows that the business is about to suspend operations or go into receivership, then to receive such deposit or to accept an investment in the business, knowing that the investment will result in a loss to the investor, is a Class A misdemeanor.

Deceptive Business Practices

While the law provides penalties for numerous offenses against businesses it also seeks to protect the consumer against offenses by businesses. A business or business firm, if it carries on a "deceptive sales contest," one in which it seeks to increase sales by offering prizes, or other instruments designed to enhance sales, commits a Class A misdemeanor. A sales contest honestly carried on is not forbidden, it is deception that is punished. For example, a business may advertise that it will give away 1,000 prizes when in fact it gives only 500, or that the prizes will be of certain value when the value is less, or the business may rig the drawing of prizes so that only certain people closely related to the business will draw a prize. Examples of other deceptive practices for which the same penalty is provided are: selling a mislabeled or adulterated product; using a scale or weight measure that shows a greater weight than the product sold actually has; advertising a product for sale as new or original when it is second hand, altered, rebuilt, reconditioned or reclaimed; advertising a product for sale with intent not to sell it as advertised, etc.

Commercial Bribery

The law binds a person in a position of trust to be faithful to his trust, and all of the following classes of persons are in positions of trust:

1. an agent or employee:
2. a trustee, guardian, custodian, administrator, executor, conservator, receiver, or similar fiduciary;
3. a lawyer, physician, accountant, appraiser, or other professional adviser;
4. an officer, director, partner, manager, or other participant in the direction of the affairs of a corporation or association.

A person in any such position of trust commits a felony of the third degree if he intentionally or knowingly solicits, accepts or agrees to accept any benefit as consideration for violating a duty to a beneficiary or for otherwise causing harm to a beneficiary by act or omission. These are breaches of duty that involve a bribe, not the simple and small neglect of duty.

Rigging Publicly Exhibited Contest

A person commits a Class A misdemeanor if, with intent to affect the outcome (including the score) of a publicly exhibited contest, he offers, confers, or agrees to confer any benefit on, or threatens harm to

1. a participant in the contest to induce him not to use his best efforts; or
2. an official or other person associated with the contest; or
3. he tampers with a person, animal or thing in a manner contrary to the rules of the contest; and the person who agrees to accept, or does accept, any benefit to affect the outcome of the contest or score also commits the offense.

If the offense is in connection with betting or wagering on the contest it is a felony of the third degree.

Misapplication of Fiduciary Property or Property of Financial Institution

A person commits an offense if he intentionally, knowingly or recklessly misapplies property (or money) he holds as a fiduciary (in trust) or property of a financial institution in a manner that involves substantial risk of loss to the owner of the property or to a person for whose benefit the property is held. An offense of this nature is

1. a Class A misdemeanor if the value of the property misapplied is less than $200;
2. a felony of the third degree if the value of the property is $200 or more but less than $10,000:
3. a felony of the second degree if the value of the property is $10,000 or more.

Securing Execution of Property by Deception

A person commits a felony of third degree if, with intent to defraud or harm any person, he, by deception, causes another to sign or execute any document affecting property or service or the pecuniary interest of any person. The offense is of the degree or category mentioned, without regard to the amount or property or money involved.

Fraudulent Destruction, Removal, or Concealment of Writing

A person commits a Class A misdemeanor if, with intent to defraud or harm another he destroys, removes, conceals, alters, substitutes, or otherwise impairs the verity, legibility, or availability of a writing, other than a governmental record, and writing in this case includes

1. printing or any other method of recording information;

2. money coins, tokens, stamps, seals, credit cards, badges, trademarks;

3. symbols of value, right, privilege, or identification; and

4. lables, price tags, or markings on goods.

It is a felony of the third degree if the writing

1. is a will or codicil of another, whether or not the maker is alive or dead and whether or not it has been admitted to probate; or

2. is a deed, mortgage, deed of trust, security instrument, security agreement, or other writing for which the law provides public recording or filing, whether or not the writing has been acknowledged.

Endless Chain Scheme

"Endless chain" means any scheme for the disposal or distribution of property whereby a participant pays a valuable consideration for the chance to receive compensation for introducing one or more additional persons into participation in the scheme or for the chance to receive compensation when a person introduced by the participant introduces a new participant. "Compensation" does not mean or include payment based on sales made to persons who are not participants in the scheme and who are not purchasing in order to participate in the scheme.

A person commits a Class B misdemeanor if he contrives, prepares, sets up, proposes, operates, promotes, or participates in an endless chain.

Offenses Against Public Administration

Bribery

A person commits a felony of the third degree if he confers or offers to confer any benefit on a public servant (an official of the government or some branch of it), party official or voter

1. with intent to influence the public servant or party official in a specific exercise of his official powers or a specific performance of his official duties; or

2. with intent to influence the voter not to vote or to vote in a particular manner.

A voter commits an offense of the same category if he knowingly accepts or agrees to accept any benefit on the representation or understanding that he will not vote or will vote in a particular manner. A public servant or party official commits an offense if he knowingly solicits, accepts, or agrees to accept any benefit on the representation or understanding that he will be influenced in a specific exercise of his official powers or a specific performance of his official duties, and his offense is a felony of the second degree.

No offense is committed if one talks with a public servant and, without giving or offering any benefit, tries to influence him to support or oppose some measure; and the public servant commits no offense if he agrees, without receiving a benefit or promise of benefit, to support or oppose the measure or proposal discussed, if the proposal itself is proper if supported or adopted. More light will be shed on such activity under "lobbying."

Coercion of Public Servant or Voter

A person commits a Class A misdemeanor if by coercion he

1. influences or attempts to influence a public servant in a specific exercise of his official powers or a specific performance of his official duty; or

2. influences or attempts to influence a voter not to vote or to vote in a particular manner.

Improper Influence

A person commits a Class A misdemeanor if he privately addresses a respresentation, entreaty, argument, or other communication to any public servant who exercises or will exercise official discretion in an "adjudicatory proceeding" to influence the outcome of the proceeding on the basis of consideration other than those authorized by law. "Adjudicatory proceeding," as the term is here used, means any proceeding before a court or any other agency of the government in which the legal rights, powers, duties or privileges of specified parties are determined. It is highly improper, and now an offense mentioned above, if during the trial of a case a lawyer who is party to the suit approaches the judge or any member of the jury privately and tries to influence his decision in the case. A lawyer should shun the appearance of such conduct by avoiding any private meeting with the judge, except that specifically called for by the judge, and if the judge calls for a private meeting with one of the attorneys in the case, he owes it to the opposing attorney to let him know the reason for the private conference. If he fails to do so he probably leaves lingering in the mind of the opposing attorney some doubt as to the judge's fairness and impartiality.

Tampering with Witness

One who gives or offers to a witness in an official proceeding anything of value to influence him to testify falsely, to withhold information, to elude a summons, or to absent himself from a legal proceeding to which he has been legally summoned, commits a felony of the third degree.

A witness or prospective witness in an official proceeding who knowingly solicits, accepts, or agrees to accept any benefit on the representation or understanding that he will be influenced thereby to commit one of the wrongs above mentioned, commits the same offense, a felony of the third degree.

Retaliation

A person commits a felony of the third degree if he intentionally or knowingly harms or threatens to harm another by an unlawful act in retaliation for or on account of the service of another as a public servant, or witness or informant.

Compensation for
Past Official Behavior

A person commits a Class A misdemeanor if he intentionally or knowingly offers, confers, or agrees to confer any benefit on a public servant for the public servant's having exercised his official powers or performed his official duties in favor of the actor or another.

The public servant commits an offense of the same degree if he intentionally or knowingly solicits, accepts, or agrees to accept any benefit for having exercised his official powers or performed his official duties in favor of another. This is new to Texas law. Such "gifts" may imply a promise of similar compensation for future favor.

Gift to Public Servant by Person
Subject to His Jurisdiction

A public servant having regulatory or investigative authority or who exercises discretion in awarding public contracts commits a Class A misdemeanor if he solicits, accepts, or agrees to accept any gift from one who will be affected by his decisions or investigations; and the person who will be affected commits an offense of the same degree if he offers, confers, or agrees to confer any benefit on a public servant that he knows the public servant is prohibited by law for accepting.

However, it is no offense if the thing given is a fee required by law, or if the gift is trivial like a pencil or token of little or no value or a meal offered the public servant as a courtesy in ordinary fellowship or comradrie, or a lawful contribution made under the election laws for the political campaign of an elective public servant.

Nepotism

No officer of the State of Texas nor any officer of any district, county, city, precinct, school district, or other municipal state subdivision, nor any officer or member of any state, district, county, city, school district or other municipal board, or judge of any court, created by or under authority of any general or special law of Texas, nor any member of the legislature, shall appoint or vote for, or confirm the appointment to any office, position, clerkship, employment or duty, of any person related within the second degree by affinity or within the third degree by consanguinity to the person appointing or voting, or to any other member of any such board, legislature, or court of which the person appointing or voting may be a member when the salary, fees, or appointee's compensation is to be paid, directly or indirectly, out of or from public funds or fees of office of any kind or character. It is provided that nothing herein contained, nor in any other nepotism law contained in any charter or ordinance of any municipal corporation of this state, shall prevent the appointment, voting for, or confirmation of any person who has been continuously employed in any such office, position, clerkship, employment or duty for a period of two years prior to the election or appointment of the officer or member appointing, voting for, or confirming the appointment, or to the election or appointment of an officer or member related to such employee in the prohibited degree.

This is a statute that gives much concern, and it is the basis of many opinions by the attorney general of the state. Some trouble arises because the law does not define degrees of kinship. It simply says, "related within the second degree by affinity or within the third degree by consanguinity," and it leaves officials, boards and judges in doubt as to just what "degree" of kinship a first cousin, second cousin, or third cousin may be to the official.

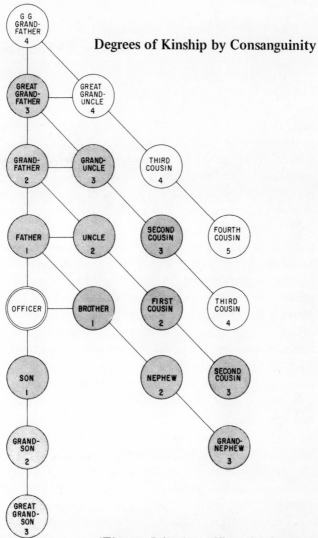

Degrees of Kinship by Consanguinity

(Figure 5-1) An officer having authority to appoint persons to office could not appoint anyone related to him within the third degree by consanguinity. Female relatives may be substituted in the circles, as aunt for uncle, mother for father, etc. Shaded circles show those within the prohibited degrees of kinship. Numbers indicate the degrees of kinship.

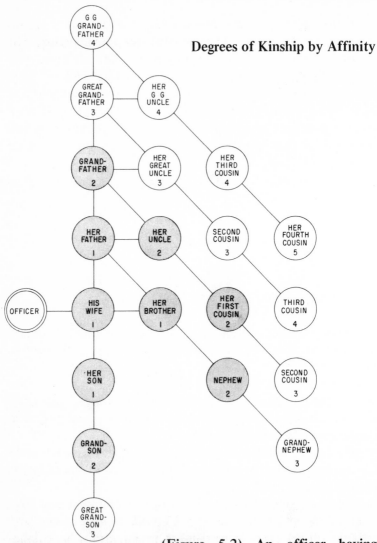

Degrees of Kinship by Affinity

(Figure 5-2) An officer having authority to appoint persons to office could not appoint anyone related to him within the second degree by affinity. Shaded circles show those within the prohibited degrees of kinship. Numbers indicate the degrees of kinship. Female relatives may be substituted in the circles, as aunt for uncle, etc.

Consanguinity means blood relation and affinity means relation by marriage. The penalty for violation of the nepotism laws is a fine of not less than $100 nor more than $1,000. It is interesting how strict our state laws are with respect to nepotism, when the United States Congress is just now giving its first serious attention to the matter. Heretofore, it has been common practice for congressmen to hire members of their own families and put them on the federal payroll.

Figures 5-1 and 5-2 will be helpful in determining degrees of kinship.

Abuse of Office

Official Misconduct

A public servant commits an offense if, with intent to obtain a benefit for himself or to harm another, he intentionally or knowingly
1. commits an act relating to his office of employment that constitutes an unauthorized exercise of his official power;
2. commits an act under color of his office or employment that exceeds his official power;
3. refrains from performing a duty that is imposed on him by law or that is clearly inherent in the nature of his office or employment;
4. violates a law relating to his office or employment.
Each of the above offenses is a Class A misdemeanor.

If the officer takes or misapplies anything of value belonging to the government that may have come into his custody or possession by virtue of his employment, or secretes it with intent to take or misapply it, or pays or delivers it to any person knowing that such person is not entitled to receive it, he commits a felony of the third degree.

Official Oppression

A public servant acting under color of his office commits a Class A misdemeanor if he
1. intentionally subjects another to mistreatment or to arrest, detention, search, seizure, dispossession, assessment, or lien that he knows is unlawful; or
2. intentionally denies or impedes another in the exercise or enjoyment of any right, privilege, power or immunity, knowing that his conduct is unlawful.

Misuse of Official Information

A public servant commits a Class A misdemeanor if, in reliance on information to which he has access in his official capacity and which has not been made public, he
1. acquires or aids another to acquire a pecuniary interest in any property, transaction or enterprise that may be affected by the information or
2. speculates or aids another to speculate on the basis of the information.

Perjury and Other Falsification

Perjury

A person commits a Class A misdemeanor if, with intent to deceive, and with knowledge of the statement's meaning
1. he makes a false statement under oath or swears to the truth of a false statement previously made; and
2. the statement is required or authorized by law to be made under oath.

Aggravated Perjury

The offense above mentioned becomes aggravated perjury if it is made in connection with an official proceeding and is material. A statement is material, regardless of the admissibility of the statement under the rules of evidence, if it could have affected the course or outcome of the official proceeding.

If one making a false statement of the class of aggravated perjury retracts his false statement before completion of the testimony at the official proceeding, and before it becomes manifest that the falsity of the statement would be exposed, he commits no offense.

False Report to Peace Officer

A person commits a Class B misdemeanor if he reports to a peace officer an offense or incident within the officer's concern, knowing that the offense or incident did not occur, if he makes such a report while knowing that he has no information relating to the offense or incident.

Tampering with or Fabricating Physical Evidence

A person commits a Class A misdemeanor if, while knowing that an investigation or official proceeding is pending or in progress, he
1. alters, destroys, or conceals any record, document, or thing with intent to impair its verity, legibility, or availability as evidence in the investigation or official proceeding; or
2. makes, presents, or uses any record, document, or thing with knowledge of its falsity and with intent to affect the course or outcome of the investigation or official proceeding.

There is no offense under this provision if the record, document, or thing concealed is privileged or is the work product of the parties to the investigation. It was under similar federal law that the hassle over the Watergate tapes became so intense.

Tampering with Government Record

It is a Class A misdemeanor if a person knowingly makes a false entry in, or false alteration of, a governmental record; or makes, presents, or uses any record, document, or thing with knowledge of its falsity and with intent that it be taken as a genuine governmental record; or intentionally destroy, conceals, removes, or otherwise impairs the verity, legibility, or availability of a governmental record.

Impersonating a Public Servant

It is a Class A misdemeanor for a person to impersonate a public servant with intent to induce another to submit to his pretended official authority or to rely on his pretended official acts.

Obstructing Governmental Operation

Failure to Identify as Witness

A person commits a Class C misdemeanor if he intentionally refuses to report or gives a false report of his name and residence address to a peace officer who has lawfully stopped him and requested the information.

Resisting Arrest or Search

If one intentionally prevents or obstructs a person he knows is a peace officer from effecting an arrest or search of the actor or another by using force against the peace officer, he commits a Class A misdemeanor. It is a felony of the third degree if the actor uses a deadly weapon to resist the arrest or search.

Evading Arrest

A person commits a Class B misdemeanor if he intentionally flees from a person he knows is a peace officer attempting to arrest him. If the attempted arrest is unlawful the actor who flees does not commit an offense.

Hindering Apprehension or Prosecution

A person commits an offense if, with intent to hinder the arrest, prosecution, conviction, or punishment of another for an offense, he

1. harbors or conceals the other;
2. provides or aids in providing the other with any means of avoiding arrest or effecting escape; or
3. warns the other of impending discovery or apprehension.
This offense is a Class A misdemeanor. It is a defense against prosecution under (3) if the person giving the warning was in fact trying to bring the one warned into compliance with the law.

Compounding

Phillips + Cannon

One who makes a complaint against another commits an offense if, after criminal proceedings have been started, he solicits, accepts, or agrees to accept any benefit in consideration of abstaining from, discontinuing, or delaying the prosecution of another for an offense. An offense of this kind is a Class A misdemeanor.

Escape

A person arrested for, charged with, or convicted of an offense commits an offense if he escapes from custody. This offense is a Class A misdemeanor. However, an offense under this provision of the law is a felony of the third degree if the actor

1. is under arrest for, charged with, or convicted of a felony;
2. is confined in a penal institution.
The offense becomes a felony of the second degree if the actor used or threatened to use a deadly weapon to effect his escape,

An official or employee of an institution that is responsible for maintaining persons in custody commits an offense if he intentionally, knowingly, or recklessly permits or aids the escape of a person in custody, and the offense is a Class A misdemeanor or a felony of the third degree, depending on the kind of prisoner aided, whether he is charged with or convicted of a misdemeanor or felony and whether he used a deadly weapon to escape.

Implements for Escape

It is a felony of the third degree to furnish an inmate in a penal institution a deadly weapon or anything else that may be useful for escape.

Bail Jumping and Failure to Appear

One who is released from custody with or without bond on condition that he subsequently appear commits an offense if he intentionally or knowingly fails to appear in accordance with the terms of his release. If the offense for which the person's appearance is required is punishable by fine only, then the offense is a Class C misdemeanor. If the offense for which the person's appearance is required is a felony then the person, by failing to appear, commits a felony of the third degree.

Barratry

It is a Class A misdemeanor if a person, with intent to gain a benefit for himself or harm another
1. institutes any suit or claim in which he knows he has no interest;
2. institutes any suit or claim that he knows is false;
3. solicits employment for himself or another to prosecute or defend a suit or collect a claim; or
4. procures another to solicit for him employment to prosecute or defend a suit or to collect a claim.

Hindering Proceedings by Disorderly Conduct

A person commits a Class A misdemeanor if he intentionally hinders an official proceeding by noise or violent or tumultuous behavior or disturbance, or if he hinders such a proceeding and continues to do so after explicit official request to desist.

Voter Registration and Election Laws

Prior to 1966, a Texas voter was required to hold a poll tax receipt showing that he had paid his poll tax, or had to hold an exemption receipt showing that he was exempt from the tax. The poll tax law is no longer effective in Texas due to a ruling of the United States Supreme Court, but voters must register in order to vote.

Election officers are charged with the duty to discharge their obligations faithfully in conducting elections. Penalties are provided for their misconduct, ranging from cash fines of up to $1,000 to jail sentences of no more than one year, to one-to-two year penitentiary sentences.

A person who knows he is disqualified to vote in an election and who votes anyway is subject to a penitentiary sentence of not less than two nor more than five years.

One who procures, aids, or advises another to vote at an election, knowing the person is not qualified to vote, or procures, aids, or advises a person to vote more than once at the same election can be fined not less than $100 nor more than $800, and he may be confined in jail not exceeding one month.

Anyone swearing falsely about his own qualifications to vote, or who swears falsely concerning the qualifications of a person wishing to vote and who is challenged as unqualified, is subject to confinement in the penitentiary for not less than two nor more than five years.

A person who willfully and falsely procures or persuades another to swear falsely about his voting qualifications shall be confined in the penitentiary for not more than three years, or be fined not exceeding $3,000.

A person voting illegally at a primary election or who procures another to vote illegally at the election is subject to a fine not exceeding $500, or he may be imprisoned in jail for not more than sixty days.

Voting in primary elections by two different political parties on the same day is punishable by a fine not to exceed $500.

Anyone who commits an illegal act while voting, such as showing his ballot to disclose his vote or giving the election judge a ballot other than the one the judge gave him at the polling place, can be fined not exceeding $500.

After the polls are closed on election day, the election officers have further duties. They must make returns, and deliver the ballot boxes with the ballots in them, etc. Failure to discharge those duties in accordance with law carries penalties of up to $1,000 and jail sentences up to six months. Anyone who forces or otherwise takes away an election return from any person entrusted with it or who willfully does any other act that obstructs the delivery of the return as directed by law, can be fined not exceeding $2,000.

If any act of rioting is committed at a public election place, or within one mile of the polling place, and is intended to disturb or influence the election, every person engaged in the riot can be fined not exceeding $1,000.

If any unlawful assembly meets at the election place or within a mile of it, that prevents the holding of the election, all persons engaged in the unlawful assembly can be fined not exceeding $500.

If any person disturbs an election by inciting or encouraging a tumult or riot, or causes any disturbance in the vicinity of any poll or voting place, he can be fined not less than $100 nor more than $500, and may also be imprisoned in jail not exceeding one month. The same penalty applies to anyone who uses force or intimidation to obstruct or influence a voter in the free exercise of the elective franchise.

If anyone other than a peace officer carries a gun, pistol, bowie knife or other dangerous weapon, concealed or unconcealed, on an election day, during the hours the polls are open within one-half mile of any poll or voting place, he can be fined not less than $100 nor more than $500, and may also be imprisoned in jail for not longer than one month.

Any person electioneering or loitering within 100 feet of the entrance of the election place or who hires a vehicle to convey voters to the polling place, or willfully removes ballots from the polling place, except as permitted by law, can be fined not exceeding $500.

If any magistrate or peace officer knowingly causes an elector (voter) to be arrested while attending, going to, or returning from an election, except in case of treason, felony, or breach of the peace, he can be fined not exceeding $300.

Candidates campaigning for an office are under heavy penalties if they fail to comply with the criminal laws governing their acts, and each person announcing his candidacy for office should make a careful study of the Articles 262 through 269 of the Texas Penal Code.

Children – Compulsory School Attendance, Employment of Children, Contributing to Delinquency of a Child

After the Texas legislature decided that it was fair to tax a person who has no children, so that another's children can be educated, it had then to consider the question whether that person had the right to keep his children out of school. The legislature decided that a person should be forced to send his children to school, if he was failing to do so. Thus, the compulsory school attendance law was enacted and this law carries punishment for the man who neglects to send his children to school.

Children are in a separate class from the adult with respect to employment. Any dangerous place or places where children may be exposed to immoral influences are "off limits" to them, and employers are held responsible when they expose children to such places through employment. It is not the law's intent that children should be forbidden to work; the intent is that when they work, they should be in places safe from physical danger and from moral danger.

Severe punishment is provided for adults who contribute to the delinquency of children. The following pages will show that the protection of children has had high priority with the legislatures of this state.

Compulsory School Attendance

It is the law in this state that parents shall send their children to school who are 7 years of age and not more than 17 years of age and who are not high school graduates, for the entire school term in the district in which they reside or in the district where they may be transferred. Failure of a parent to do so is punishable by a $5 fine for the first offense, $10 for the second offense and $25 for each offense thereafter, and each day constitutes a separate offense.

Of course, parents may send their children to a private or parochial school, instead of to the public schools. It is only required that children be sent to a suitable school, so their education may not be neglected.

Exceptions are:

1. Illness, or a state of health for which a reputable physician gives a certificate showing that school attendance is inadvisable and stating the period of time that such condition exists or may exist.

2. Any child who is blind, deaf, dumb, or feeble-minded, for the instruction of whom the school district has made no adequate provision.

3. Any child who lives more than 2½ miles from the school and no free transportation is provided.

4. Any child who is more than 16 years of age who has satisfactorily completed the ninth grade and whose services are needed for support of the parents or other person standing in parental relation to the child.

Habitual Truant

If any parent or person in the parental relation to any child within the compulsory school attendance ages presents proof that he or she is unable to compel the child to attend school, the person can be exempted from the penalties provided. The child may be proceeded against as an habitual truant and committed to the State Juvenile Training School or any other suitable school agreed upon between the parent or guardian and the Juvenile Court judge.

School Buses

School buses and other vehicles used as buses are required to be plainly marked on the front and on the rear in letters not less than six inches high with the words, *School Bus*. When a vehicle transporting children stops, any other motor vehicle approaching it from any direction must be brought to a complete stop before proceeding in any direction. If the school bus vehicle is receiving or discharging passengers, then any other motor vehicle should not start up or attempt to pass in any direction until the school bus vehicle has finished receiving and/or discharging passengers.

One who violates this provision is guilty of a misdemeanor and if convicted can be fined not less than $10 nor more than $500, or be confined in the county jail for not more than ninety days, or both fine and imprisonment. However, if death results to any person as a result of such a violation the offender shall be punished as is now provided by law otherwise for the death of such person.

Employment of Children Under Fifteen

Children of any age may be employed to work in private homes as nurses, babysitters, maids, yard servants or other similar work, which is presumed not too strenuous, or hazardous, and does not expose them to immoral influences. However, any child under 15 years of age may not be employed lawfully to labor in or about any factory, mill, workshop, laundry, or in a messenger service in cities of more than 15,000 population. The penalty for violation of this provision is a fine of not less than $25 nor more than $200, or imprisonment in jail for not more than sixty days, for the one employing the child.

Employment of Children Under Seventeen

Children under 17 years of age may not be employed lawfully to labor in any mine, quarry, or any place where explosives are used. They may not be sent for any purpose to any disorderly house, bawdy house, assignation house, or place conducted for immoral purposes if the employer is aware of the character and reputation of the places or if such information could be found by the employer upon reasonable inquiry. The fine for this violation is not less than $50 nor more than $500, or imprisonment in jail not to exceed 60 days.

Anyone who employs or controls any child under 15 years ofage and requires or permits the child to work more than 48 hours in any one week, or between 10 P.M. and 5 A.M. can be fined not less than $50 nor more than $500, or be imprisoned in jail not to exceed sixty days.

Contributing to the Delinquency of a Child Under 17 Years of Age

Anyone who commits acts toward a child under 17 years of age designed to debase or injure the child's morals, health, or welfare is guilty of contributing to the child's delinquency.

The offender is subject to a fine of not more than $500 or imprisonment in jail not to exceed one year.

Other offenses against children which are defined in the Penal Code and the punishment fixed include:

1. Enticing a child under 14 years of age to enter a vehicle, house, room, office or other place for the purpose of proposing sexual intercourse or fondling the child's sexual parts, or other related immoral acts, is punishable with a fine of up to $1,000 or a jail sentence of up to two years, or both the fine and imprisonment, or a penitentiary sentence for not more than ten years.

2. Knowingly and intentionally exposing one's private parts to a child under 16 years of age is punishable by a fine of not more than $2,000 or a jail sentence of not more than two years, or both the fine and jail sentence, or confinement in the penitentiary for not more than fifteen years.

These are not all of the offenses against children defined in the Texas Penal Code. However, all immoral and indecent acts toward children are forbidden by law and penalties are provided. It is the policy of the law in this state to give the utmost protection for children.

Offenses Against Reputation

Libel

Reputation is the character commonly attributed to a person or the esteem the public holds for a person. It is important, therefore, that one's reputation is not damaged unjustly because that person may be ruined in his community. Such statements include: that the person was guilty of some penal offense; that he has been guilty of some disgraceful act or omission which makes him unfit to move within respectable society; that he has some moral vice, or some physical or mental defect or disease that makes him unfit for respectable society and causes him to be generally avoided;

that he is of notorious or infamous character; or that he, in public office or as a candidate for a public office, is dishonest and unworthy or that he is guilty of some malfeasance while in office and is unworthy of the position.

To make, write, publish or circulate such statements is forbidden by law and is termed *libel.* Not only do these statements constitute grounds for a damage suit against the person committing the libel, they also constitute a criminal offense that is punishable by a fine of not less than $100 nor more than $2,000, or by imprisonment not exceeding two years.

Those who make, write, publish or circulate the statements, knowing them to be libelous, are guilty and subject to punishment. In some cases the truth of the statement or statements may be offered as a defense in damage suits or criminal prosecutions. This is particularly true when the supposed libel is against public officials and relates to their official conduct or where it is stated that the person is guilty of some penal offense with the time, place and nature of the offense being stated in the publication, or where the person is of notoriously bad or infamous character.

Slander

One who orally or otherwise falsely and maliciously, or falsely and wantonly, states that any married or unmarried female in this state is unchaste is guilty of slander and may be fined not less than $100 nor more than $1,000, and also may be imprisoned up to one year. Here again, the person slandered has cause to sue for damages against the slanderer.

The state in order to convict, and the plaintiff to recover damages, must prove that the spoken words were false. The person charged with the slander may prove the truth of the words or statements as a defense.

Publishing Another as a Coward

The offense of publishing that someone is a coward is punishable by a fine not to exceed $200.

Sending Anonymous Letters

To send to any person any anonymous letter or written instrument reflecting upon the integrity, chastity, virtue, good character or reputation of the person, or of any other person, or threatening the life of the person is an offense punishable by a fine of not less than $250 nor more than $1,000 and confinement in jail for not less than one nor more than twelve months. An *anonymous letter* is one where the sender does not sign his name, or does not sign his true and full name so he can obscure or place his identity in doubt; or where a fictitious name is signed or where any description of the sender is used in lieu of his name, such as "a friend," etc.

Offenses Against Public Order and Decency

Disorderly Conduct

A person commits an offense if he intentionally or knowingly

1. Uses abusive, indecent, profane or vulgar language in a public place, and the language by its very utterance tends to incite an immediate breach of the peace;

2. makes an offensive gesture or display in a public place, and the gesture or display tends to incite an immediate breach of the peace;

3. creates, by chemical means, a noxious and unreasonable odor in a public place;

4. abuses or threatens a person in a public place in an obviously offensive manner;

5. makes unreasonable noise in a public place or in or near a private residence that he has no right to occupy;

6. fights with another in a public place;

7. enters on the property of another and for a lewd or unlawful purpose looks into a dwelling on the property through any window or other opening in the dwelling;

8. discharges a firearm in a public place;

9. displays a firearm or other deadly weapon in a public place in a manner calculated to alarm;

10. exposes his anus or genitals in a public place and is reckless about whether another may be present who will be offended or alarmed by his act.

These are all Class C misdemeanors, except (9) and (10) which are Class A misdemeanors.

Riot

"Riot" means the assemblage of seven or more persons resulting in conduct which

1. creates an immediate danger of damage to property or injury to persons;

2. substantially obstructs law enforcement or other governmental functions or services; or

3. by force, threat of force, or physical action deprives any person of a legal right or disturbs any person in the enjoyment of a legal right.

A person engaged in the riot commits a Class B misdemeanor, but if the riot results in a higher offense like murder then his offense is the same as that higher degree of offense like felony of the first degree.

Obstructing Highway or Other Passageway

A person commits a Class B misdemeanor if, without authority, he intentionally, knowingly or recklessly

1. obstructs a highway, street, sidewalk, railway, waterway, elevator, aisle, hallway, entrance, or exit to which the public or a substantial group of the public has access, or any other place used for passage of persons, vehicles, or conveyances, regardless of the means of creating the obstruction and whether the obstruction arises from his acts alone or from his acts and the acts of others; or

2. disobeys a reasonable request or order to move issued by a person the actor knows to be or is informed is a peace officer,

a fireman, or a person with authority to control the use of the premises.

This provision, among other things, is intended to cover the take over of buildings and passage ways by protestors, as so frequently occurred in recent times.

It is no offense if those assembled or obstructing move promptly when the order to move is given, or if they are assembled to hear a speech by an authorized speaker on economic, religious, or political questions in a peaceable manner.

Disrupting Meeting or Procession

A person commits a Class B misdemeanor if, with intent to prevent or disrupt a lawful meeting, procession, or gathering, he obstructs or interferes with the meeting, gathering or procession by physical action or verbal utterance.

False Alarm or Report

A person commits a Class A misdemeanor if he knowingly initiates, communicates, circulates, or broadcasts a report of a present, past, or future bombing, fire, offense, or other emergency that he knows is false or baseless and that would ordinarily

1. cause action by an official or volunteer agency organized to deal with emergencies;
2. place a person in fear of imminent serious bodily injury; or
3. prevent or interrupt the occupation of a building, room, place of assembly, place to which the public has access, or aircraft, automobile, or other mode of conveyance.

Harassment

A person commits a Class B misdemeanor if he intentionally

1. communicates by telephone or in writing in vulgar, profane, obscene, or indecent language or in a coarse and

offensive manner and by this action intentionally, knowingly, or recklessly annoys or alarms the recipient;

2. threatens by telephone or in writing to take unlawful action against any person and by this action knowingly, intentionally or recklessly annoys or alarms the recipient or intends to annoy or alarm the recipient; or

3. places one or more telephone calls anonymously, at an unreasonable hour, in an offensive and repetitious manner, or without a legitimate purpose of communication and by this action intentionally, knowingly, or recklessly annoys or alarms the recipient or intends to annoy or alarm the recipient.

In this connection a person places a telephone call as soon as he dials a complete telephone number, whether or not a conversation ensues.

Public Intoxication

A person commits a Class C misdemeanor if he appears in a public place under the influence of alcohol, or any other substance, to the degree that he may endanger himself or another. It is not an offense if the alcohol or other substance was administered for theraputic purposes by a licensed physician.

Desecration of Venerated Object

A person commits a Class A misdemeanor if he intentionally or knowingly desecrates

1. a public monument;
2. a public worship or burial; or
3. a state or national flag.

"Desecrate" means deface, damage or otherwise physically mistreat in any way that the actor knows will seriously offend one or more persons likely to observe or discover his action.

Abuse of Corpse

A person commits a Class A misdemeanor if, not authorized by law, he

1. disinters, disturbs, removes, dissects, in whole or in part, carries away, or treats in a seriously offensive manner a human corpse;
2. conceals a human corpse knowing it to be illegally disinterred;
3. sells or buys a human corpse or in any way traffics in a human corpse; or
4. transmits or conveys, or procures to be transmitted or conveyed, a human corpse outside the state.

Cruelty to Animals

A person commits a Class A misdemeanor if he intentionally or knowingly
1. tortures or seriously overworks an animal;
2. fails unreasonably to provide necessary food, care, or shelter for an animal in his custody;
3. abandons unreasonably an animal in his custody;
4. transports or confines an animal in a cruel manner;
5. kills, injures, or administers poison to an animal belonging to another without legal authority or the owner's consent; or
6. causes one animal to fight with another.
It is an exception, however, if the person was or is engaged in bona fide experimentation for scientific research.

Shooting on Public Road

A person commits a Class C misdemeanor if he intentionally or knowingly shoots or discharges any gun, pistol, or firearm on, along or across a public road.

Promotion of Prostitution

A person commits a Class A misdemeanor if, acting other than as a prostitute receiving compensation for personally rendered prostitution services, he knowingly receives money or other property pursuant to an agreement to participate in the proceeds of prostitution.

Compelling Prostitution

A person commits a felony of the second degree if he knowingly
1. causes another by force, threat, or fraud to commit prostitution; or
2. causes by any means a person younger than 17 years to commit prostitution.

Abortion

An abortion in Texas by a physician, after medical consultation and advice, for the purpose of saving the life of the mother is not an offense. This applies to unwed mothers as well as to those lawfully married. An abortion for any other purpose is condemned by our laws and heavy penalties are provided for anyone causing an abortion, except for the one purpose above mentioned. However, in 1970 the famous case of Roe vs. Wade reached the Supreme Court of the United States, and the court held that such laws making an abortion an offense were unconstitutionally vague as not putting a physician on notice as to exactly what he might be held criminally liable for; and in 1973 an application for rehearing the same court (Supreme Court of the U.S.) held the whole array of abortion statutes unconstitutional, except that part protecting against prosecution for abortion to save the life of the mother. It is still an offense, punishable as murder, if one, not a physician, or a physician through malpractice, in an attempt to bring about an abortion, causes the death of a pregnant woman. Abortion has so many attendant dangers that anyone except a physician should not attempt it. A physician undertaking the operation should make sure that he is not operating under a cloud of malpractice.

Vagrancy

Persons charged with vagrancy are subject to a fine of not more than $200. The following classes of persons may be considered vagrants:

1. Persons known as tramps, who wander or stroll about in idleness and who are able to work, but have no property or means of support.

2. Persons who lead an idle, immoral or profligate life with no property to support them, but who are able to work and do not.

3. All persons able to work, but have no property to support them and have no visible or known means of a fair, honest and reputable livelihood.

4. All able-bodied persons who habitually loaf, loiter and idle in any city, town, village, railroad station, or in any other public place in this state for the better part of their time and who do not have regular employment or any visible means of support.

5. All persons trading or bartering in stolen property.

6. Every common gambler or person who, for the most part, maintains himself by gambling.

7. All companies of gypsies who, either in whole or in part, maintain themselves by telling fortunes.

8. Every able-bodied person who begs for a livelihood.

9. Every common prostitute.

10. All persons who are able to work and do not, but hire out their minor children or allow the children to be hired and live upon the children's wages without having any other means of support.

11. All persons over 16 and under 21 years of age, not in attendance at some educational institution and who are able to work and do not, having no property to support them or some known visible means of a fair, honest and reputable livelihood and whose parents or persons taking the parent's place are unable to support them.

12. All persons who advertise and maintain themselves in whole or in part as clairvoyants or foretellers of future events, or purport to have supernatural knowledge with respect to present or future conditions, transactions, happenings or events.

13. All males who habitually associate with prostitutes or continually loiter in or around houses of prostitution, or who receive financial aid or assistance from prostitutes without having visible means of support.

14. All persons who invite, entice or solicit any male to visit a bawdy house or disorderly house or other place used for unlawful sexual intercourse, knowing the purpose of going to such house, or who meet any female at a bawdy house or disorderly house for unlawful sexual intercourse.

15. All persons engaged in prostitution, lewdness or assignation.

16. All prostitutes who solicit, induce, entice or procure any male to visit a bawdy house or disorderly house or other place with her for unlawful sexual intercourse.

17. All persons who reside in, enter, or remain in any house, place, building or other structure, or who enter or remain in any vehicle, trailer, or other conveyance for prostitution, lewdness or assignation.

18. All persons who aid, abet or participate in any of these prohibited acts.

Additionally, persons who match cock fights or any fights between animals is subject to a fine of not less than $10 nor more than $100.

Obscenity

In the beginning it seems appropriate to give some definitions contained in the new code:

1. "Obscene" means having as a whole a dominant theme that
   A. appeals to a prurient interest in sex, nudity, or excretion
   B. is patently offensive because it affronts contemporary community standards relating to the description of representation of sex, nudity, or excretion; and
   C. is utterly without redeeming social value.

2. "Prurient interest" means a shameful or morbid interest in nudity, sex, or excretion that goes substantially beyond

customary limits of candor in description or representation of such matters.

Obscene Display or Distribution

A person commits a Class C misdemeanor if he intentionally or knowingly displays or distributes an obscene photograph, drawing, or similar visual representation or other obscene material and is reckless about whether a person is present who will be offended or alarmed by the display or distribution.

Commercial Obscenity

A person commits an offense if, knowing the contents of the material
1. he sells, commercially distributes, commercially exhibits, or possesses for sale, commercial distribution, or commercial exhibition any obscene material; or
2. he presents or directs an obscene play, dance, or performance or participates in that portion of the play, dance, or performance that makes it obscene; or
3. he hires, employs, or otherwise uses a person under the age of 17 years to achieve any of the purposes set out in (1) and (2) above.
An offense under (1) and (2) is a Class B misdemeanor, and under (3) it is a Class A misdemeanor.

Sale, Distribution, or Display of Harmful Material to a Minor

"Harmful material" in this instance means "obscene material." A person commits a Class A misdemeanor if, knowing the material is harmful
1. and knowing the person is a minor, he sells, distributes, exhibits, or possesses for sale, distribution, or exhibition to a minor harmful material;

2. he displays harmful material and is reckless about whether a minor is present who will be offended or alarmed by the display.

However, he commits a felony of the third degree if one hires, employs or uses a minor to do or accomplish or to assist in doing or accomplishing any of the acts mentioned in (1) and (2) above.

Offenses Against Public Health, Safety, and Morals

Weapons

Many weapons are defined in the penal code and designated as unlawful and they include the following: "club," which includes blackjack, nightstick, mace and tomahawk, but is not limited to those named. It may include also a heavy wooden stick or iron bar or a combination of them; "explosive weapon," "firearm", "firearm silencer", "handgun", "illegal knife", which includes a knife with a blade over five and one-half inches long, a throwblade knife, dagger, bowie knife, sword or spear; "knuckles"; "machine gun"; "short-barrel firearm", which means a rifle with a barrel length less than sixteen inches or a shotgun with a barrel length less than eighteen inches long.

Of course, one can own these things and display them as curios or antiques but carrying them around in public places is unlawful.

Unlawfully Carrying Weapons

A person commits a Class A misdemeanor if he intentionally, knowingly or recklessly carries on or about his person a handgun, illegal knife, or club. If he carries, on or about his person and into any place lawfully licensed for the sale or service of alcoholic beverages, any such weapon above named, he commits a felony of the third degree.

It is an exception, however, and not an offense if the person carrying any such weapon is a peace officer in the actual discharges of his duties as a peace officer, or he is a member of the armed forces or national guard or a guard employed by a penal institution. Neither is it an offense if the person is on his own premises or premises under his control, nor if he is traveling or engaging in lawful hunting or fishing or other lawful sporting activity. "Traveling" as used here means going on a journey—not just going downtown or to the corner grocery.

Places Where Weapons Prohibited

A person commits a Class A misdemeanor if, with a firearm, he intentionally, knowingly, or recklessly goes
1. on the premises of a school or educational institution, whether public or private without the permission or authorization of the institution; or
2. on the premises of a polling place on the day of election. Of course, it is an exception if he is a peace officer in the actual discharge of his duties.

Unlawful Possession of Firearm by Felon

A person who has been convicted of a felony involving an act of violence or threatened violence to a person or property commits a felony of the third degree if he possesses a firearm away from the premises were he lives. This provision even forbids him to hunt game with a gun away from the premise where he lives. It seems a bit harsh, and there probably will be some amendment of this feature of the law.

Prohibited Weapons

A person commits an offense if he intentionally or knowingly possesses, manufactures, transports, repairs, or sells
1. an explosive weapon;

2. a machine gun;
3. a short barrel firearm;
4. a firearm silencer;
5. a switchblade knife; or
6. knuckles.

An offense involving any of the first four above mentioned is a felony of the second degree; involving either of the last two is a felony of the third degree.

Unlawful Transfer of Firearm

A person commits a Class A misdemeanor if he
1. sells, rents, leases, loans, or gives a handgun to any person knowing that the person to whom the handgun is to be delivered intends to use it unlawfully or in the commission of an unlawful act;
2. intentionally sells, rents, leases, or gives or offers to sell, rent, lease, or give to any child younger than 18 years any firearm; or
3. intentionally, knowingly, or recklessly sells a firearm or ammunition for a firearm to any person who is intoxicated.

It is an exception in (2) above if the child is accompanied by his parent or guardian or the person who has custody of him or has written permission from the one in parental position.

Interstate Purchase

A resident of this state may, if not otherwise precluded by law, purchase firearms, ammunition, reloading components, or firearms accessories in contiguous states. Except for this provision federal law would prevent Texans from purchasing firearms in neighboring states.

Gambling

A person commits a Class C misdemeanor if he
1. makes a bet on the partial or final result of a game or contest or on the performance of a participant in a game or contest;

2. makes a bet on the result of any political nomination, appointment, or election or on the degree of success of any nominee, appointee or candidate; or
3. plays and bets for money or other thing of value at any game played with cards, dice, or balls.

It is a defense to prosecution under this provision that
1. the actor engaged in gambling in a private place;
2. no person received any economic benefit other than personal winnings; and
3. except for the advantage of skill or luck, the risks of losing and the chances of winning were the same for all participants.

Thus if gambling is done in a private home as a social affair no offense is committed, unless there is something rigged or unfair giving an advantage to one or more that is not available to others. It is public gambling that is proscribed.

Gambling Promotion

A person commits a felony of the third degree if he intentionally or knowingly does one of the following acts:
1. operates or participates in the earnings of a gambling place;
2. receives, records or forwards a bet or offer to bet; or
3. for gain, becomes a custodian of anything of value bet or offered to be bet.

Keeping a Gambling Place

A person commits a felony of the third degree if he knowingly uses or permits another to use as a gambling place any real estate, building, room, tent, vehicle, boat, or other property whatsoever owned by him or under his control, or rents or lets any such property with a view of expectation that it be so used.

Communicating Gambling Information

A person commits a felony of the third degree if he, with intent to further gambling, knowingly communicates information as to bets, betting odds, or changes in betting odds or he knowingly provides, installs, or maintains equipment for the transmission or receipt of such information.

Possession of Gambling Device or Equipment

A person commits a felony of the third degree if he knowingly owns, manufactures, tranfers, or possesses any gambling device that he knows is designed for gambling purposes or any equipment that he knows is designed as a subassembly or essential part of a gambling device; and the offense is the same if the device or part thereof is an altered device or part.

If the actor does as above mentioned with respect to gambling paraphernalia with intent to further gambling, he commits a Class A misdemeanor.

Testimonial Immunity

A party to a gambling offense may be required to furnish evidence or testify about the offense, but in this case he is exempt from prosecution for the offense. This is a design of the law to obtain evidence that may otherwise be impossible to obtain, and it is based upon the premise or theory that it is better to catch some of the offenders especially the leaders, even if one or more of the other offenders have to go free of punishment.

Miscellaneous Offenses

Conspiracy

A conspiracy is an agreement between two or more persons to commit a felony. This is a felony offense and is complete when a positive agreement is made to commit a felony even though the agreement is not carried out.

However, there must be a positive agreement with a threat to commit a felony. Contemplation of it is not sufficient to constitute the offense. The punishment for conspiracy when the agreement is to commit murder is imprisonment in the penitentiary for not less than two nor more than ten years. The penalty for any other conspiracy to commit a felony is not less than two nor more than five years in the penitentiary. If the parties to the agreement commit the felony they agreed upon, they are punishable for that offense also.

Conspiracy in Restraint of Trade

The following are examples of conspiracies in restraint of trade that are entered into by two or more persons, firms or corporations: (a) when they are engaged in buying or selling any articles of merchandise, produce, or any commodity and they enter into an agreement or understanding to refuse to buy from or to sell to any other person, firm, corporation, or association of persons, any article of merchandise, produce, or commodity; (b) when they agree to boycott, threaten, or refuse to buy from or sell to any person, firm, corporation, or association of persons for buying from or selling to any other person, firm, corporation, or association of persons; or (c) when they agree to boycott, or enter into any agreement or understanding to refuse to transport or deliver, receive, accept, erect, assemble, operate, use or work with any goods, wares, merchandise, articles or products of any other person, firm, corporation, or association of persons.

This does not apply, however, to employees who agree among themselves to terminate their employment, or to refuse to transport, deliver, receive, accept, erect, assemble, operate, use or work with the goods, wares, merchandise, articles, or products of their immediate employer, unless they are trying to coerce their employer into committing some kind of boycott against some other person, firm, corporation or association of persons.

The punishment for conspiracy in restraint of trade is confinement in the penitentiary not less than two nor more than ten years.

Farmers, Ranchmen, and Trades Unions

Laws dealing with conspiracy in restraint of trade do not apply to farmers, ranchmen, or laborers in trade unions or to trade unions themselves. A group of farmers may get together and agree not to sell their cotton until next July, or for any period of time, or until the price reaches a certain level. This is no violation, notwithstanding it is an agreement in restraint of trade. They may also agree not to sell to a certain buyer, and this is no violation. Likewise laborers and trades unions may agree not to work for a certain person or corporation, or they may by agreement and by working together persuade, or attempt to persuade, any workman or laborer, or a group of them, to quit the job or jobs held by them and they are not guilty of conspiracy. They may also agree not to work for any person, firm, or corporation, or to go on strike against their employer, and not be in violation of the law against conspiracies, because the law, specifically exempts them.

Entering the Enclosed Lands of Another to Hunt, Fish or Camp

It is unlawful to go upon another person's enclosed lands without the consent of that owner or his representative, for hunting animals or birds with a gun, or bow and arrow, or any other weapon capable of taking such animals or birds, or for fishing in any lake, stream, pond, or other body of water, or for camping. One guilty of this offense for the first time is subject to a fine of not less than $10 nor more than $50. For a second violation, one is subject to a fine of not less than $200 nor more than $500, and a third offense carries a jail sentence of not more than thirty days, or a fine of not less than $500 nor more than $1,000.

Permit for
Transporting Livestock

Any person driving a vehicle containing livestock or domestic fowl is required by law to have in his possession a permit showing his right to transport livestock or fowl if he goes on the highway or on, or across lands not his own. The permit can be in the form of a bill of sale describing the cargo and showing that the animals or fowl were purchased from the person who made the bill of sale, or it can be a statement from the owner of the animals or fowl showing that he has authorized the person driving the vehicle to transport them to a destination. If the driver does not have a permit, he is subject to a fine of not less than $25 nor more than $200 for each animal or fowl in the vehicle, unless when stopped or questioned by an authorized officer, he can show the name of the owner of the animals or fowl, the point of origin, and the destination and his right to transport them.

If the driver has a false or forged permit or if he makes a false statement in writing about his permit, he is subject to a fine of not less than $200 nor more than $500, or imprisonment in jail for not less than sixty days, nor more than six months, or both a fine and imprisonment in jail.

Want of Bill of Sale

When one is charged with theft of horses, mules, or cattle, and does not have a written transfer or bill of sale, this constitutes *prima facie* evidence against the accused that the possession was illegal.

Butchers and Slaughterers of Animals

Before anyone engages in the business of butchering animals and selling the meat, he is required to register his name and place where he will carry on such a business with the county clerk of that county. Failure to register is punishable by a fine of not less than $5 nor more than $25. This provision of the law does not apply to slaughter houses slaughtering as many as 300 cattle per day.

Illegal Marking and Branding

Anyone who marks or brands a horse, mule, ass, or cattle, or who marks any sheep, goat or hog, not his own, without the owner's consent and with intent to defraud, is subject to the same punishment as if he had stolen the animal. The same rule applies if he alters or defaces the mark or brand on another person's animal without his consent and with intent to defraud.

Texas Animal Health Commission

The Texas Animal Health Commission, was formerly known as the Live Stock Sanitary Commission. It consists of six members and they have the following qualifications: (a) practitioner of veterinary medicine; (b) dairyman; (c) practical cattle raiser; (d) practical hog raiser; (e) sheep or goat raiser; and (f) poultry raiser.

The commission is responsible for keeping informed about the livestock diseases in the state and supervising the officers whose responsibility it is to enforce the laws dealing with animal health and disease. The commission can hold hearings and issue rules governing the movement of livestock within the state, and into and out of the state to prevent the spread of animal diseases. Acting through its agents and representatives, the commission can condemn animals that have, or that were exposed to, deadly communicable disease. Their rules, decrees, and orders have the force and effect of law, and the Penal Code provides penalties for their violations.

The laws, rules and regulations adopted by the commission with respect to diseased livestock and for the prevention of livestock diseases are far too numerous and involved to be included in this book. Too, the rules are changed by necessity periodically and are generally local in scope. For this reason, it is suggested that anyone in any phase of the livestock industry in this state will be wise to meet with the nearest representative of the Texas Animal Health Commission and obtain all of the published material available that deals with his particular phase of the industry.

6. Regulatory Agencies

As a matter of practical operation, the State of Texas has set up a number of different regulatory agencies within the government to supervise and administer necessary policies and controls on a number of activities within the state. Included in these are the Commission of Labor Statistics that deals specifically with labor laws and policies, and the Department of Public Safety whose duty it is to patrol the highways, enforce traffic laws and protect the traveling public. Also, there is the Parks and Wild Life Commission whose duty it is to supervise the state parks and game reserves where wild life abounds as well as to enforce the laws governing hunting, trapping and fishing within the state. This commission, through its various subagencies, also seeks to preserve the wild life habitats and to facilitate the propagation of these game and fish species.

These agencies are but a few of those that the state government has provided to secure equal opportunities for all those living within its borders to enjoy the natural resources, rights, privileges, and protection afforded by this state.

Regulatory Agencies for Labor, Traffic and Wild Life
Labor

Commissioner of Labor Statistics

When this office of Commissioner of Labor Statistics was originally created, the legislature made it the commissioner's duty to collect and organize data concerning suitable sites for

194

industries in this state; and to correspond with prospective industries to induce them to establish industrial plants within the state. Now the duties of this office are more concerned with labor conditions relating to safety, elimination of hazards, means of escape from danger, educational and sanitary conditions surrounding laborers and their families, the means provided for the protection of life and health in factories, social surroundings of the workers, and labor of women and children and the hours of labor required of them.

The commission is required to make reports annually on these things, and looking into labor conditions, the commissioner and his agents may go into any industrial plant or factory to view the working conditions and talk to laborers, foremen, and the employer. If he or his agents find conditions unacceptable, it is their duty to give the employer written notice pointing out the objectionable conditions or practices. A manager or owner of such a place who does not correct the specified objectionable conditions may be proceeded against under the penal statutes and subjected to fines or imprisonment of not less than $25 nor more than $200, or not more than sixty days in jail, or both.

Eight Hour Work Day

Eight hours, with few exceptions, constitutes a legal day's work, and it applies to laborers working on construction for the state as well as for private industry.

Discrimination and Blacklisting

Any corporation, or receiver, or any agent, or officer of a corporation who discriminates against anyone seeking employment because of his having participated in a strike is subject to a jail sentence for not less than one month nor more than one year.

One is guilty of "blacklisting" if he places the name of any former employee on any list or in any book, or publishes it in a newspaper, periodical, or letter intending to prevent him from securing employment with any other employer, or prospective employer. This is punishable by not less than $50 nor more than $200 fine, or imprisonment in jail for not less than thirty nor more than ninety days.

It is not an offense, however, for the former employer to give, upon the request of the discharged employee or prospective employer, a true statement giving the reasons for the discharge, and the statement cannot be used against the former employer as a cause for an action for libel, either civil or criminal.

Servants or Employees Not to be Coerced

No person, firm, or corporation, nor the representatives of any employer may lawfully coerce or require any servant or employee to deal with or purchase any article of food or clothing, or merchandise of any kind whatever from any person, corporation, association, or company or at any place or store. No employee may be excluded from work or be blacklisted for failure to deal with any person or any firm, company, or corporation, or for failure to purchase any item of food, clothing, or other merchandise. A violation of this provision of the Penal Code carries a penalty of a fine of not less than $50 nor more than $200.

In the earlier days of sawmilling, mining, and other such industrial enterprises, the employing company would issue to employees company tokens, checks, or "punchouts" as wages. These could be expended at the company-owned store, but other merchants would not accept them in payment for merchandise. This law was probably enacted because of these practices. If the company issuing the trade tokens, etc., used them to pay the employees on regular pay-days, then the practice would appear to be a clear violation. However, if the company issued the tokens only when the employee called for an advance before payday, and on regular paydays it paid the employees in lawful money or by checks on a local bank that could be cashed for face value, then it hardly could be considered a violation.

Interfering with Labor or Vocation or Lawful Picketing

It is an offense for anyone to prevent, or attempt to prevent, by the use of force or violence, or the threat of the use of force or violence, any person from engaging in any lawful vocation within the state or from engaging in peaceful and lawful picketing. The punishment for this offense is con-finement in jail for not less than thirty days nor more than two years, or by a fine of not less than $25 nor more than $2,000. The same penalty is provided for the offense of gathering one or more persons at or near the place where a "labor dispute" exists and by force, or violence, commit, or attempt to commit, either of the offenses already mentioned.

Highway Traffic Safety Measures

Automobile and truck travel on the highways has reached such a volume that it poses a special danger problem for the operators of those motor vehicles and others, and much property damage results from it. For this reason the legislature has enacted comprehensive and extensive laws to reduce the danger and has set up a Department of Public Safety and a highway patrol system. Drivers of motor vehicles on the highways must qualify for and have in their immediate possession driver licenses, and the vehicles themselves must be registered and licensed and must be certified annually to be in safe mechanical condition for travel on the highways.

The License to Drive

Three kinds of licenses for driving on the highways are issued by the Department: operator's license, commercial driver's license, and chauffeur's license.

1. The operator's license is the one commonly issued to drivers of automobiles and pickup trucks and panel trucks of carrying capacity up to 2,000 pounds. A person 18 years of age or over who has passed successfully the driver's test given by the Department may be issued an operator's license good for four years. The Department issues these licenses so that approximately one-fourth of them will come up for renewal each year. A person 16 years of age or over may be issued an operator's license if he has completed successfully a driver's training course approved by the Department and has passed successfully the driver's test given by the Department. A person at least 15 years of age may be issued a permit to drive if

A. the person has successfully completed the class-room phase of an approved driver education course and has successfully passed all phases of the driver test by the Department, except the driving test. A permit issued on these qualifications is called an instruction permit which can be used only while the person is accompanied by a person sitting on the seat by him who is at least 21 years of age and holding one of the three classes of driver licenses and who has had at least one year of driving experience;

B. the person has successfully passed the Department's driving test and it appears to the department that refusal to issue to the applicant the license would work an unusual economic hardship upon the family of the applicant, or it appears that the license should be issued to the applicant on account of sickness or illness of members of the applicant's family, or that failure to issue the license to the applicant would be detrimental to the applicant or to his or her family.

2. A commercial operator's license, which authorizes the holder to drive trucks as well as automobiles, may be issued to persons 18 years of age or older who pass successfully the test given by the Department, and this license must be renewed annually. A person between the ages of 17 and 18 years may be issued this type of license if he has successfully completed a driver training course approved by the Department and has successfully passed the examination given by the Department. This type of license cannot be issued to a person under 17 years of age.

3. A chauffeur's license may be issued to a person 18 years of age or older who has passed successfully the examination given by the Department, and a person between the ages of 17 and 18 may be issued the license if he has successfully completed a driver training course approved by the Department and has passed successfully the examination given by the Department. One under 17 years of age may not be issued this type of license.

No driver's license of any type may be issued to a person under 15 years of age.

A special combination operator and commercial operator restricted license may be issued to persons between the ages of 15 and 18 years to operate only a motorcycle, motor scooter or motorized bicycle, the horsepower of any of which does not exceed five brake horsepower.

Traffic Laws—Rules of the Road

The Department of Public Safety publishes and distributes for the use of applicants for drivers' licenses a pamphlet containing the information a person must know before he can be licensed to drive on the highways, and it is recommended that all prospective applicants obtain and study this pamphlet before going for the examination. It is not considered necessary to include that information here.

However, since we are all subject to accidents, and we dread their consequences, it seems well to comment on what to do when an accident occurs, because accidents that cause considerable property damage, personal injury, or death bring on tensions and excitement, and in their excitement, people sometimes do things or neglect to do things which they regret.

Accidents Involving Personal Injury

When anyone is in an accident involving personal injury or death, if he is unhurt, he is required by law to stop and give aid. Neglect to give his aid under such circumstances is punishable by imprisonment in the penitentiary for not more than five years or in jail not exceeding one year, or by a fine not exceeding $5,000 or by both a fine and imprisonment. He is obligated to ask what injuries were suffered and to offer assistance. If requested to do so and his vehicle is capable of being driven, he should take the injured person or persons, to a doctor or hospital for treatment. If his vehicle cannot be driven, he should make an effort to find others to take the injured for treatment.

Statements Made at the Scene of the Accident

It is a rule of evidence that statements made by anyone involved in an accident, immediately after the accident, or at the scene of the accident, can be given in evidence by those who hear the statements. Consequently these may be damaging to a person in court if a lawsuit or criminal action is brought against him because of the accident. So often in the excitement immediately following an accident, a person misjudges the facts or the cause of the accident, and he may misjudge them wholly to his detriment. A person involved may feel the urge to immediately confess that it is all his fault, especially if there is personal injury involved or considerable property damage. However, it is wise to refrain from making any statements that would be totally against his interest. He needs to take time to examine as many aspects of the accident as possible. This is not to say he should be rude or bellicose toward the other parties involved. He can be sympathetic and say he is sorry that the accident occurred and otherwise show concern for anyone injured or whose vehicle has been damaged without making statements against his own interest. He may find that there are circumstances in his favor. In fact, he may find that all of the circumstances are in his favor. If this is the case, he owes it to his insurer not to make statements that will cost money unnecessarily, and he owes it to himself not to make his defense more difficult than is necessary.

In most instances, traffic officers will arrive on the scene, for they are supposed to be called to the scene either by someone involved in the accident or some other person. Of course, it is the duty of the officers to make a careful investigation and to take notes so that their testimony of the facts can be used if they are requested by the proper authority.

Generally, an officer will question the parties involved and report the answers in a written statement. Usually, the officer will ask the person questioned if he would care to sign this statement. Of course, if the statement is altogether favorable, one might be glad to sign it, but if the statement is partially or wholly unfavorable to him, it is best that he decline signing it. It is proper for a person to state that though he is fully covered by insurance and expects his insurer to cover any liability he may have in the matter, he would prefer first obtaining his insurer's approval before making any statement and for that reason declines to sign it.

Let us suppose that this accident appears only to involve some damage to the other person's car and that its occupant gave, and signed, a statement saying that he suffered no personal injury. In this case, if the person who appears to be responsible for the accident has an urge to be decent and honorable about it, he may honestly feel it his duty to sign that statement naming him as the party in the wrong. Before he signs this, he should remember that in doing so, he is placing the total liability on his insurer. Once he reports the accident to his insurer, the adjuster will go to settle the claim for damages, whatever they may be. However, the adjuster may now find that the opposite party has obtained a zealous lawyer anxious to make a fee and who has convinced his client that he has sustained a bad back injury; an injury serious enough that it should not be settled for less than a few thousand dollars. For this reason, it is just generally good judgment not to sign any statements that are clearly against one's own interests.

Game and Fish

The game, fish, and oysters within the state boundaries belong to the State of Texas, with the exception of ponds or lakes which lie wholly within privately owned lands. The owner of land can exercise certain protective authority over game animals and birds as long as they remain upon his land, but he can do so because he owns the land, rather than the animals and birds. When these animals and birds wander from his premises, he loses his authority with respect to them. Should this landowner have a pond or lake wholly within his own premises which he stocks with fish, he may fish for them by any means and at anytime of the year and take as many as he chooses since they belong to him.

Game Birds Defined

Wild turkey, wild duck of all varieties, wild geese of all varieties, wild brant, wild grouse, wild prairie chicken or pinnated grouse, wild pheasants of all varieties, wild partridge and wild quail of all varieties, wild pigeons of all varieties, wild mourning doves and wild white-winged doves, wild snipe of all varieties, wild shore birds of all varieties, wild Mexican pheasants or chacalacas, wild plover of all varieties, and wild sand-hill cranes, are declared game birds within the meaning of the state laws.

It is unlawful to kill, catch, or have in possession, living or dead, any wild bird other than a game bird, except those listed as exemptions. The penalty for this offense is a fine of not less than $10 nor more than $200.

Exemptions

The following birds are not protected by law: English sparrows, crows, ravens, buzzards or vultures, rice birds identified as harmful, blackbirds, the goshawk, the Cooper's hawk or blue darter, the sharp-shinned hawk, jaybird, sapsucker, woodpeckers, butcher-birds or shrike, the horned owl, and the starling.

The law does not forbid the purchase and sale of canaries and parrots and parrakeets, or keeping them in cages as domestic pets.

Game Animals

The following animals are declared by law to be game animals: wild deer, wild elk, wild antelope, wild desert big-horn sheep, wild black bear, wild gray or cat squirrels, wild fox squirrels or red squirrels, collared peccary or javelina and the American bison or buffalo. Aoudad sheep are game animals in some Texas counties.

Fur-Bearing Animals

Fur-bearing animals are declared by law to be the property of all of the people of Texas. They include the following: wild beaver, wild otter, wild mink, wild ring-tail cat, wild badger, wild polecat or skunk, wild raccoon, wild muskrat, wild opossum, wild fox, and wild civet cat.

The Parks and Wild Life Department, under the management and control of the Parks and Wild Life Commission (formerly the Game and Fish Commission), administers the Texas game laws. It has the power to regulate bag limits, open and closed seasons, establish game and fish preserves, fish hatcheries, trap and transplant game and fish, etc. It also has charge and direction of all game wardens and game and fish biologists in Texas. Moreover, this department is authorized by law to cooperate with the Federal Game and Fish Authorities in the conservation and propagation of these resources, and through these federal authorities it cooperates with the governments of Canada and Mexico with respect to migratory game birds.

More than half of the counties in Texas are under game regulations imposed by the commission that vary greatly from one region of the state to another. For this reason, no effort is made here to give the reader an analysis of these regulations. They are far too extensive for inclusion. Anyone who wants to hunt, fish, or trap in Texas should consult a game warden in the locality where he intends to hunt, fish, or trap, and should obtain a copy of the regulations covering that area, lake, or stream.

Because the commission can fit the regulations to any particular county, its work is more effective, and biologists can make more effective studies of game animals and game birds in different parts of the state. In counties where wild turkeys are known to exist, the regulations take into consideration the weather and other conditions affecting the normal hatch from season to season. In counties where javelina or peccary thrive, the regulations can fit the needs again, and they can be changed from season to season as the game is affected by natural causes. These same regulations serve no purpose in counties where such game does not exist.

The penalties for various violations are defined in the Penal Code, and the following is given as a summary of them:

OFFENSE	PENALTY
Kill, catch, shoot at, wound, or have in possession, living or dead, any bird other than a game bird (except those shown under exemption above)	a fine of $10 to $200
Exceeding bag limit, or killing game bird or game animal during closed season, or killing game bird or game animal for which there is no open season	$10 to $200
Having in possession more than the possession limit of wild mourning doves, wild quail, Mexican pheasant or chachalaca, water fowl or shore birds	$10 to $200
Kill, wound, shoot at, take, hunt or possess any wild turkey hen	$25 to $100
Using .22 caliber firearm which uses rimfire ammunition in the taking or shooting, or attempting to take or shoot wild deer, wild elk, wild antelope, wild Aoudad sheep or wild desert bighorn sheep	$25 to $200
Hunting or trailing deer with dogs in any area of the state where the use of dogs is prohibited	$25 to $200
Hunting or shooting game birds or game animals from an automobile, airplane, motor boat, sail boat or any or any floating device pulled by motor boat or sail boat	$25 to $200

OFFENSE	PENALTY
Possessing or transporting or selling any live coypu (nutria) without a permit to do so	$10 to $200
Hunting, killing or attempting to kill any wild game bird or other protected wild bird, wild fowl, or wild game animal at night (between one-half hour after sunset and one-half hour before sunrise)	$10 to $200
Selling or buying, or offering to sell or buy, any wild bird or wild fowl, wild game bird or wild game animal	$25 to $200
Hunting game birds or game animals in this State without a license	$25 to $200
Take, kill, wound, shoot at, hunt or possess, dead or alive, any wild female deer, wild fawn deer or any wild buck deer without a pronged horn, or to possess any deer carcass or green deer hide with all evidence of sex removed	$50 to $200
Use deer call, whistle, decoy, call pipe, reed or other device, mechanical or natural, for the purpose of calling or attracting deer, except by rattling deer horns	$100 to $500 or a jail sentence of 20 to 90 days
Violation or any rule or regulation of the Parks and Wild Life Department	$25 to $100

A hunting license is required of all persons who hunt game birds or game animals in this state outside the county where they live; and if anyone hunts deer off the land where he lives a license is required.

Exemptions

Persons who are citizens of Texas under 17 years of age or 65 years of age or over, may hunt deer upon the land where they live without being required to pay the usual license fee. However, before he hunts wild deer or wild turkey, he is required to register with the Parks and Wild Life Department or one of its agents on a form prescribed by the department and shall pay 25¢ for an exemption certificate which will entitle him to hunt game as if he held a regular hunting license.

Fishing

It is the state government's policy not to deny its law-abiding citizens the enjoyment of fishing and taking fish from its waters for their own use, but to make these resources more plentiful and more available to them. The Parks and Wild Life Department attempts to effect these ends through necessary regulations prescribed in connection with the laws that are in effect, and through its state-authorized broad powers it administers and enforces these regulations.

Texas now has many artificial lakes, and it has been found that conditions vary so greatly from lake to lake and from one area of the state to another that it has been necessary to adopt different rules and regulations for some areas, lakes, or streams. For example, Lake Murvaul in Panola County is covered by rules quite different from those applicable to Lake Texoma, Caddo Lake, or Possum Kingdom Lake. But the regulations for these different lakes, or areas, are published by the Parks and Wild Life Department in convenient form and are available free of charge upon request.

In fishing as in hunting, it is suggested that one should familiarize himself with these regulations covering the area where he intends to fish. They are too numerous to include here, however, some basic provisions of the statutes are given below because they have general application.

License to Fish

"It shall be unlawful for any person to fish in any of the waters of this State without first having procured from the Game and Fish Commission (now the Parks and Wild Life Department) or one of its bona fide employees, or a county clerk or an authorized agent, a fishing license, the fee for which shall be Two Dollars and fifteen cents ($2.15) . . ."

Exceptions

"No person under seventeen (17) years of age and no person over sixty-five (65) years of age shall be required to possess the license provided for in this act. No person, or member of such person's immediate family, shall be required to hold the license provided for in this Act when fishing upon property he owns or upon which he resides. No license shall be required of persons fishing with trotline, throw line, or ordinary pole and line having no reel or other winding device attached when fishing in the county of his residence. No other fishing license shall be required of a person who holds a commercial fishing license issued in this State."

From the foregoing it is seen that one fishing with rod and reel, wherever he fishes in this state, except on his own property or where he lives, is required to have the license if he is between 17 and 65 years old.

A person may use a seine not more than 20 feet long for seining minnows for bait.

Commercial Fishing

Commercial fisherman and wholesale dealer's license must be obtained

"...before any person in this State shall engage in the business of a 'Commercial Fisherman', a 'Wholesale Fish Dealer', 'Retail Fish Dealer', 'Bait Dealer', 'Fish Guide'; or use or operate a shrimp trawl, net or seine, oyster dredge, boat or skiff, for the purpose of catching or taking any edible aquatic life from the waters of this State for pay, barter, sale or exchange, the proper license provided for in this act privileging him so to do shall first be procured by such person from Game, Fish and Oyster Commission of Texas (now Parks and Wild Life Department) or from one of its authorized agents."

A summary of the fees for the different kinds of licenses is as follows:

Commercial Fisherman's License	$3
Wholesale Fish Dealers' License, fee for each place of business	$200
Wholesale Truck Dealers' Fish License	$100
Retail Fish Dealers' License for each place of business in each city or town of less than 7,500 population	$3
Each place of business in each city or town with not less than 7,500 and not over 40,000	$10
For each place of business in each town or city over 40,000	$15
Retail Oyster Dealers' License, for each place of business in each city of more than 7,500 population, for sale of oysters only	$5
Retail Dealers' Truck License, permitting the sale of edible aquatic products from a motor vehicle to consumers only	$25
Bait dealers' license for each place of business	$2
Seine or net license for each 100 feet in length	$1
Provided that no net or seine shall be more than 1,800 feet long and the	

meshes shall be not less than 1½ inches
from knot to knot.

Fish Boat License, for any boat equipped with a motor or sail	$6
Skiff License, propelled by oars or poles	$1
Oyster Dredge License	$15
Fish Guide License	$2

Anyone who is required to have any license mentioned above and who proceeds to act without the license is subject to a fine of from $10 to $200.

Commercial Fishing License	$3
Commercial Fishing Boat License	$6

For engaging in commercial fishing without a license or for operating a commercial fishing boat without a license, one may be fined, for the first offense, $100 to $200; for the second and subsequent offenses $500 to $2,000, or may be sentenced to serve not less than five days nor more than six months in jail, or by both the fine and jail sentence.

Size of Certain Salt Water Species

It is unlawful for any commercial fisherman, fish dealer, wholesale or retail, to sell or offer for sale, or to have in his possession any of the following species greater than the maximum length or less than the minimum length specified:

Kind	Maximum Length	Minimum Length
Red Fish or Channel Bass	35 inches	14 inches
Flounder or speckled sea trout		12 inches
Sheephead or Pompano		9 inches
Mackerel		14 inches
Gafftopsail		11 inches

For violation of this regulation a fine of $100 to $200 is provided.

Open Fishing Season All Year Round

In the fresh waters of this state there is no general closed season for fishing by the ordinary method of hook and line or artificial lures. (Art. 927a Penal Code). However, there are many bodies of water in the state where the season is closed by regulation or statute.

There is no upper limit on the size of bass that may be taken in this state, but those caught under 7 inches long must be released, except white bass.

There is a bag limit on certain fresh water fish:

Kind of Fish	Bag Limit
Large mouth black bass, small mouth black bass, spotted bass and sub species, singly or combined	15 of which not more than 10 are longer than 11 inches
White bass	25
Blue catfish, channel catfish and yellow catfish, singly or together	25
White perch or crappie	25

For violation of these regulations, a $5 to $50 fine is provided.

With Respect to Game Wardens

Game wardens have the right, without the necessity of a search warrant, to inspect the game bag or fish bag, automobile, or boat of any hunter or fisherman to determine whether any violation of the game laws has been committed. If anyone refuses to let a warden inspect them he can be fined $10 to $100. If the officer finds that a violation has been committed, he is authorized to arrest the offender and take him immediately before a magistrate. These arrests may be made on Sunday as well as on weekdays.

Presumptions and Prima Facie Evidence

There are certain presumptions of guilt and instances where the circumstances serve as *prima facie* evidence of guilt. For example, if a man is found hunting with a headlight and a gun which is capable of killing deer and it is at night, he is presumed to be hunting deer at night, if deer are known to range in that vicinity. This type of hunting is in violation of the law. If the person is charged with the violation and he makes no defense, he can be punished for hunting deer at night with a headlight. On the other hand, it is no violation of the law to hunt wildcats or wolves with a gun and head-light at night. If a person is charged with hunting deer when in fact he was hunting wildcats or wolves, he should go into court well-prepared to rebut this strong presumption against him. Testimony that at the very time he was stopped by the game warden he had in his possession a wildcat or a wolf and not a deer, and that he was hunting with a shot gun using small shot and not buckshot, might overcome the presumption provided in the law. Certainly, if he has such a good defense he should use it and not remain silent.

There was an actual case where two men had been hunting wildcats with a friend in a distant county. As they were returning home, they passed into a certain area where deer were known to range, and ironically where the game wardens had been trying to catch some hunters who had been killing deer at night. These two men were flagged down by the game wardens, and upon inspecting the contents of their automobile, the game wardens found guns and headlights. They were charged with hunting deer at night with headlights and they paid fines without a trial. But inasmuch as they were not actually doing what they were charged with, they might have overcome the presumption of guilt by a properly prepared defense. Testimony of this friend with whom they had been hunting wildcats and their own testimony that they had been hunting wildcats, and the fact that their guns were unloaded and in cases and that the headlights were in a zipper bag "zipped up" or in a box with string tied around it would have been very strong evidence against the presumption of guilt or the *prima facie* case, and particularly so if the wardens could have been made to admit on the stand that the guns were encased and the lights were boxed or zipped up.

7. Justice and the Code of Criminal Procedure

The Texas Penal Code defines criminal offenses and prescribes the punishment for them. The Code of Criminal Procedure describes how the criminal laws are to be administered, and, as will presently be seen, it gives guarantees to all people within the borders of this state against oppression and wrongful punishment. The theory of the law is that it is better to let the guilty go unpunished than it is to punish the innocent. It is unfortunate that the guilty often find easy escape under these provisions.

Our present Code of Criminal Procedure became effective on January 1, 1966. The objects of the code are declared as "to embrace rules applicable to the prevention and prosecution of offenses against the laws of this state, and to make the rules of procedure in respect to the prevention and punishment of offenses intelligible to the officers who are to act under them, and to all persons whose rights are to be affected by them. It seeks:

1. To adopt measures for preventing the commission of crime.
2. To exclude the offender from all hope of escape.
3. To insure a trial with as little delay as is consistent with the ends of justice.
4. To bring to the investigation of each offense on the trial all the evidence tending to produce conviction or acquittal.
5. To insure a fair and impartial trial.
6. The certain execution of the sentence of the law when declared.

Due Course of Law

"No citizen of this state shall be deprived of life, liberty, property, privileges or immunities, or in any manner disfranchised, except by the due course of the laws of the land."

Rights of Accused

In all criminal prosecutions the accused is entitled to have a speedy public trial by an impartial jury. He has the right to demand the nature and cause of the accusation against him, and to be presented with a copy of the charges. He is not compelled to give evidence against himself, and he has the right to defend himself through testimony, or through counsel, or both. He must be confronted by the witnesses against him, and can exercise compulsory process of law to obtain witnesses in his favor. No person must answer for a felony unless he is indicted by a grand jury.

Searches and Seizures

The law provides that people are safe from all unreasonable seizures and searches of their persons, houses, papers and possessions. No warrant to search any place or to seize any person or thing can be issued without describing it as nearly as possible, nor without probable cause supported by an oath or an affirmation.

Right to Bail

All prisoners are bailable unless for capital offenses when the proof is evident. This provision must not be construed as to prevent bail after indictment found upon examination of the evidence, in such a manner as prescribed by law.

Habeas Corpus

"The writ of *habeas corpus* is a writ of right and shall never be suspended."

This writ means "let's have the body," and is used when some person is being deprived of his liberty, such as, being held in jail without a hearing or trial. It is an order directing the officer or other person holding the person to produce him bodily before the court. By this means the court can then determine whether the person is under lawful arrest and whether he is entitled to a hearing and bail.

Cruelty Forbidden

"Excessive bail shall not be required, nor excessive fines imposed, nor cruel or unusual punishment inflicted."

Double Jeopardy

"No person for the same offense shall be twice put in jeopardy of life or liberty; nor shall a person be again put upon trial for the same offense, after a verdict of not guilty in a court of competent jurisdiction."

If someone is tried in a court that has no jurisdiction, he can again be tried in a court that does have jurisdiction. Once he is tried in the proper court and has gained a verdict of not guilty, he cannot be tried again for the same offense, regardless of how irregular the proceedings may have been.

Right to Trial by Jury

Every person accused of a criminal offense is guaranteed the right of trial by a jury. The accused cannot waive the right of trial by jury if he is charged with a capital felony, one that is punishable by death. If the offense is one that does not carry the death penalty he can waive this right, but then only with the court's consent entered of record in the case and the consent of the attorney representing the state made in writing and entered in the case records. The accused cannot waive the right to a jury trial if he is not represented in court by an attorney. If he has no attorney representing him and he wishes to waive the right of trial by a jury, the court must first appoint an attorney to represent him. If the state intends to demand the death penalty, written notice of its intention must be filed with the court at least fifteen days before the trial date. When the notice is given, the defendant cannot waive the right of trial by jury, and the trial cannot be held until the expiration of the fifteen day period. Note: From the foregoing, one will perceive that the law seeks to protect the accused even against himself.

Liberty of Speech and Press

"Every person shall be at liberty to speak, write, or publish his opinion on any subject, being liable for the abuse of that privilege; and no law shall ever be passed curtailing the liberty of speech or of the press. In prosecutions for the publication of papers investigating the conduct of officers or men in public capacity, or when the matter published is proper for public information, the truth thereof may be given in evidence."

It has been held that the right to speak carries with it also the right to remain silent. Often, in labor disputes, an employer is pressed for reasons for discharging an employee. He does not have to give his reasons, nor does an employee have to give his reasons for quitting his job.

Religious Belief

"No person shall be disqualified to give evidence in any court of this state on account of his religious belief; but all oaths or affirmations shall be administered in the mode most binding upon

> the conscience, and shall be taken subject to the pains and
> penalties of perjury."

Many people feel that it is wrong to swear, even to the
truth of statements made in court; and for this reason the
courts will, to these persons, administer affirmations instead
of oaths. One who affirms falsely is punishable the same as if
he had sworn falsely.

Outlawry and Transportation

> "No citizen shall be outlawed, nor shall any person be
> transported out of the state for any offense committed within the
> same."

In many foreign countries people may be expatriated or
banished from their country; often this is the punishment for
a losing politician.

Corruption of Blood

> "No conviction shall work corruption of blood or forfeiture
> of estate."

A person may be convicted of a heinous crime, but he
cannot be deprived of his property because of it. He can
inherit property and can be inherited from, the same as if he
had committed no crime.

Public Trials

> "The proceedings and trials in all courts shall be public."

Defendant Confronted by Witnesses

> "The defendant, upon a trial, shall be confronted with the
> witnesses, except in certain cases provided for in this Code where
> depositions have been taken."

What To Do When Accused of Crime

An individual accused of a felony is with a few exceptions, arrested and taken into custody by some law officer, the sheriff or his deputy, a constable, a policeman, a United States Marshall, a member of the Federal Bureau of Investigation, or some other officer, and he is generally locked up in some jail. In most cases, innocent people are not arrested and put in jail, for the law requires there must be probable cause for an arrest. But the fact that one is arrested and locked in jail does not prove he is guilty. It does mean, and with few exceptions, that there is probable cause for his being taken into custody. There is still much to do before a person is pronounced guilty. Under our system of law, one is presumed to be innocent until he has been *proven guilty beyond a reasonable doubt.* The burden of proof of guilt rests on the government under whose authority the person is accused of and held for a crime. The proof of guilt must be so convincing that there is no reasonable doubt to the contrary. If the proof falls short of this test, the accused must be set free because probable guilt or any other half-way measures in criminal law are not acceptable.

It is true that there are different sentences or degrees of punishment, but the proof of guilt beyond a reasonable doubt is still required before any degree of punishment can be inflicted upon the accused.

So it is that anyone arrested is still a long way from being convicted of the crime for which he is accused, and our criminal laws, the rules of criminal procedure, the Texas Constitution and the United States Constitution afford the accused a very wide latitude in defending himself. In this respect, his advantages are greater in state courts than in federal courts. Judges in state courts, are not allowed as much discretion of comment as judges in federal courts, and they are just generally more lenient as to the limits a lawyer can go in the interest of his client.

Often a person accused of a revolting crime goes free even though the public expresses disgust at the outcome of the trial; and there are some miscarriages of justice. However, no thinking person could wish to return to that system of trial under which Jesus of Nazareth was handed over to be punished, indeed crucified, because of the shouts of the people even after he had been found innocent. On the contrary, our system of justice is so respected by the people that it is almost unheard of for any public demonstration to follow a verdict.

Anyone accused of a crime should take steps in his own defense. The law provides him the means, but he must exercise them. The first thing he should do after being arrested is to hire a competent lawyer, and this should be done before he makes any statement to the arresting officer, to the press, or to others who may question him. A good answer to all questions would be, "Let me have my lawyer present, and then I shall answer whatever questions he approves." In this way, a lawyer does not have to spend so much of his efforts in trying to overcome the adverse effects of statements made before he gets the case. Often, the accused makes a statement before talking to his lawyer and later repudiates it claiming that he made it under duress. It is indeed difficult, and often impossible, for a lawyer to overcome the adverse effects of confessions by the accused. No one has to make a statement to the arresting officers or to investigators before or after he is put in jail or even in the courtroom. It is basic in our law that no one can be forced to testify against himself.

Therefore, anyone accused should let his lawyer determine which, if any, questions he should answer. Since this is basic right, there is no wrong in holding doggedly to it. There may, in fact, be some advantage in making a statement, but the accused is in no position to judge this advantage, if it does exist. The defense lawyer must be the architect and builder of the defense, and the more serious the charge, the stronger the foundation must be, since the prosecutor will try his best to put the accused in a bad light. The accused needs an advocate to put him in as favorable a light as possible. Indeed, it is midway between these that the jury will try to find the truth. This is not to say that any false representations should be made, but by these opposing efforts both sides of the question of "guilt" or "innocence" are brought before the court, and each side will try to do its best. Whatever the prosecutor brings before the jury will be designed to condemn the accused; whatever the defense attorney brings will be designed to exonerate him. The accused must bear in mind that the arresting officers and the investigators when trying to get answers to their questions and to have him sign a statement are by circumstance on the side of those who seek to convict; and the accused will serve himself well by saying nothing without benefit of legal counsel.

Suppose, however, the accused person is in no financial position to hire a lawyer, or he might be in an area where not even one person knows him and finds himself destitute as far as help from friends is concerned. Nevertheless, there is help at hand if he uses his wits. If truly he is unable to hire a lawyer, and no friends can be called on to do so for him, then he should contact the district judge and request that he appoint him a lawyer, stating he is unable to hire one himself. He should tell the judge his financial situation and let him know that he is accused of a crime that may call for a penitentiary sentence or worse. If those who hold him in custody fail or delay in letting him contact the judge, he should make repeated requests for permission to use the telephone, and each time he should state that he desires to contact the judge and request that legal counsel be provided for his defense. Each time he should keep careful mental note, if he cannot keep written note, when the request is made, the name or description of the person who delayed or refused his request, and what was said each time. This may be useful to his lawyer when he later obtains one. If he cannot reach a telephone, he should request writing materials and state that it is for writing the district judge to request legal counsel. He should be persistent and steadfast in this purpose, for few officers will continue to ignore such requests. There are penalties provided in the law for such repeated and willful failures.

Once the accused has hired a lawyer, or one has been appointed for him, he should then very carefully follow his lawyer's suggestions and instructions. His lawyer will have him brought into a conference room, out of the earshot of others, and it is at this first conference that he must win his lawyer by telling him the truth. He should tell the whole true story, even though he may be embarrassed and ashamed to do so. The lawyer is entitled to have straight answers and it is absolutely necessary, for he can never put his heart into the case until he is sure that he has the whole truth. He must know everything that the accused knows so he can prepare for the onslaughts that will be made upon his client in the courtroom. The accused should bear in mind also, in a case where a lawyer has been provided for him by the court, that the lawyer, even though he is bound by his profession and the appointment to represent the accused regardless of pay, will have a better feeling toward the accused if there is some sincere promise of compensation for his services. The appointed lawyer, of course, cannot demand it, but the accused should avoid as far as possible the risk of making his lawyer feel that he is wasting his time and talents. He should not be too impatient, for the nature of the case may hinder the lawyer from doing all of the things the accused wants him to do. For example, the nature of the offense may make it impossible for the lawyer to provide bail so that the accused could be free pending trial date, or it may be that the accused is such a poor risk that the lawyer could not afford to furnish bail.

But once the lawyer has conferred with the accused and has been given the whole truth and he has accepted employment or has accepted appointment by the judge, he can, and will, go to work with all his skill to "bring his client clear." It may be that the crime is so bad that it is revolting to think of it, but making out a case against the accused is left to the district attorney. It is the business of this lawyer to defend the case, and he will consider it as a matter of personal pride if he can escort his client out of the courtroom a free man.

If it happened that he knew his client was guilty, would he have conscientious scruples and remorse at seeing him go free because of his skill in handling the case? He would not, because his commitment to his client was to do the best he could for him, and because the judge trying the case expected no less of him as attorney for the defense while at the same time expecting the prosecuting attorney to do his best for a conviction. Also, the high calling of his honorable profession demands that he do his best for his client, and our system of justice assumes that a lawyer will, and must, carry his point if he can.

The Mode of Trial in a Criminal Case

Here briefly is the procedure followed in a criminal case, a felony case, in which the accused may be given a penitentiary sentence.

Trial in the District Court.

The trial will be before a jury, and a list of the veniremen must be given to the defendant two full days (48 hours) before the trial begins. When the state and the defendant have announced they are ready for trial, or if they do not announce ready, and the motions for postponement have been overruled, the names of those summoned as jurors will be called. A fine of $50 may be assessed against any juror summoned and not present, and an attachment may be issued by request of either the defendant or the state for an absent summoned juror to be brought immediately before the court.

To those veniremen present in the court, the judge will have this oath administered:

> "You, and each of you, solemnly swear that you will make true answers to such questions as may be propounded to you by the court, or under its directions, touching on your service and qualifications as a juror, so help you God."

The judge will then hear excuses from those who desire to be excused from jury duty, and he may excuse anyone whose reason he considers valid. By consent of both parties, anyone on the venire may be excused. But the judge does not always grant a request to be excused.

Either party may challenge the array, which is the whole panel of prospective jurors, but only on the ground that the officer summoning them willfully did so to secure a conviction or acquittal. It is not often that such a challenge is sustained because it is not often that those grounds exist; but the challenge is available to the party that feels it should be used. If the challenge is sustained, all of the array of prospective jurors will be discharged.

Then a new venire is summoned, and a list of their names is given to the defendant as in the first instance. After the new group has taken the oath, or in case of the original group, if no challenge to the array has been made, or if made has been overruled by the court, the prospective jurors will be tested by the following four questions by the court or under his directions:

1. Except for voter registration, are you a qualified voter in

this county and state, under the constitution and laws of this state?

2. Are you a householder in the county, or a freeholder in the state or the wife of a householder?

3. Have you ever been convicted of theft or any felony?

4. Are you under indictment or legal accusation for theft or any felony?

A prospective juror who gives a "yes" answer to questions nos. 1 and 2 and a "no" answer to nos. 3 and 4 will be qualified, unless subsequent questioning shows he is not. However, each side, first the state and then the defense, will try diligently, by asking questions, to ascertain whether there is still cause for challenging a venireman, and if the attorney for either side finds cause for challenging, he will do so. The judge will immediately rule on the challenge by sustaining it or overruling it. If the challenge is sustained, the venireman is excused; and if the challenge is overruled, the venireman is not yet disqualified.

However, each side has fifteen peremptory challenges if it is a case where the death penalty may be given, ten in a felony case where the death penalty is not asked for by the state. The attorney who sought to disqualify the venireman for cause can still keep him off the jury by using one of these peremptory challenges against him. In this instance, he excuses the venireman without having to give any reason.

There are more than a dozen reasons or causes on which a challenge for cause may be made and without going through the whole list, they are of this nature: that his answers to the four questions asked by the court, or one of them, was not true; that he is a witness in the case; that he was on the grand jury that returned the indictment in this case; that he is insane; that he cannot read and write; that he has a serious hearing defect which makes him unfit for jury duty, etc.

When a venireman has been questioned by both sides, first by the state's attorney and then by the defendant's attorney, and he has not been disqualified and no peremptory challenge has been made against him, then he becomes a juror in the case. After all of the jurors have been selected, the judge will have the following oath administered:

"You solemnly swear that in the case of the State of Texas against the defendant, you will a true verdict render, according to the law and the evidence, so help you God."

The court may permit the jurors to separate and go to their own homes at night until the time the charge of the court is given to them. After that, they stay together until discharged, except for necessary separate sleeping quarters.

Following the jury selection, either side may request that the witnesses be placed "under the rule," which means that the witnesses must remain outside of the courtroom until they are called to the witness stand. This is to prevent them from hearing the testimony of the other witnesses and in this instance, the judge will instruct them not to talk among themselves or to others about matters pertaining to the case, except to the lawyers. Witnesses under the rule are attended by a court officer whose duty is to report to the court any violation of its instructions.

After the jury is seated in the jury box, the stage is set for dramatic clashes between opposing counsel. If the case is well-prepared by both sides, the state has, through its prosecutor and the law enforcement officers, combed carefully to find and have ready to present in court all of the evidence necessary to obtain a conviction of the defendant. They have their witnesses ready to give testimony intended to establish the facts alleged in the indictment, against the defendant and bring about his conviction. This is in direct opposition with the defendant's attorney who has been equally diligent in finding every witness and having him ready to give testimony favorable to the defendant to prove him innocent of the indictment against him, for it may be the defendant's life that is at stake.

It should be kept in mind that the state's burden is to prove to the jury, who will be the judge of the facts, *beyond a reasonable doubt* that the defendant is guilty of the offense as charged. The circumstance of the offense may make this duty extremely difficult for the prosecuting attorney to discharge, though he may be absolutely sure in his own mind that the defendant is guilty. The prosecutor may make such a definite case against the defendant that the defendant's attorney is left with only one hope for his client and that is that he might create a *reasonable doubt* in the minds of the jurors. If he can accomplish only this, his client may walk out of the courtroom free.

The indictment is read to the jury by the prosecuting attorney.

The special pleas, if any, are read by the defendant's attorney, and a plea of "not guilty" is stated to the jury (if the defendant pleads not guilty, which is most often the case).

The prosecuting attorney tells the jury the nature of the accusation and the supporting facts.

The testimony on the part of the state is presented by calling on witnesses whose testimonies are expected to prove the charges against the defendant. Exhibits are introduced into evidence, such as any gun or knife that may have been used in committing the offense, written statements that may have been made by the defendant admitting the crime, and other things which the prosecuting attorney considers necessary to establishing the guilt of the defendant. The defendant's attorney has the right to cross-examine each witness at the conclusion of his direct testimony.

During the presentation of the state's evidence, the defendant's attorney will be alert to object to any testimony, exhibits, or other evidence which he believes should not be presented, or any which he thinks he might have some chance to keep out. He does this by addressing the court stating that he objects to the testimony, and the grounds upon which he bases his objections, such as "it is hearsay," or "it is intended only to inflame the jury against this defendant," or other grounds. The judge will rule on the objections by sustaining or overruling them as and when they are made. If he sustains an objection, the evidence is kept out. If he overrules the objection, then the question is to be answered or the offered exhibit is to be admitted; and in this case the attorney for the defendant will make an "exception" to the judge's ruling. This is extremely necessary to the defendant's case, because if the case is appealed, appeal grounds must be based on some error in the court's ruling or other proceeding in the case. The burden is on the defendant to call these errors to the court's attention as they are made so that the court will have an opportunity to correct them. It is necessary that the defendant's attorney make a good record at the trial and show the particular errors of the court on which he will expect to reverse the case if it goes up on appeal. In the Court of Criminal Appeals, the objections cannot be raised for the first time.

After the state rests, the defendant's counsel states the defenses which the defendant relies upon and the facts expected to be proved in their support.

The testimony on the defendant's behalf is then presented. The defendant may testify but he does not have to do so. As the defense witnesses are examined by the defense counsel, the state's attorney will object to testimony he thinks should not be admitted, and the judge will rule on the objections as they are made, by sustaining or overruling them. If the judge sustains an objection, it means that the question should not be answered or that the exhibit or other evidence should not be admitted. In this case, the attorney for the defendant will enter an "exception" to the court ruling, because he will need this in the record for review if the case is appealed. If the judge overrules the objection, the state's attorney does not make an "exception," because in a review of the case on appeal, such an exception would not help the state. Appeals are taken only by the defendant, not by the state. If the defendant is acquitted in the trial court, the state must be satisfied to set him free. If the defendant is convicted and given a lighter sentence than the state's attorney thinks he should have received, there is no appeal available to the state and the sentence stands.

This is a further example of how far our lawmakers have gone in protecting the accused; and it is based upon the premise that it is better to let the guilty go free than to punish the innocent. The state's attorney may cross-examine each defense witness at the conclusion of his direct testimony.

Rebutting testimony is offered by each side. The court can permit the introduction of further testimony at anytime before the conclusion of the argument, if it considers that further testimony is necessary for justice.

After all the testimony, the judge starts preparing his charge to the jury. Before he gives it, each side is allowed a reasonable time to prepare, in writing, charges and instructions which they desire to be submitted to the jury. The judge will consider these and submit them, or alter them and submit them, or reject all or part of them as he chooses. The defendant's attorney will enter exceptions when necessary to make a good record for his client in the case.

Finally, each side is given a copy of the charge to the jury before it is read to the jury, at which time the defendant's attorney will offer his final written objections to it.

The judge reads the charge to the jury, and in this, he gives them his instructions and tells them what the law is with respect to the case. Then he gives them a copy.

He must not comment on the weight of the evidence or give a summation of or comment on the credibility of the witnesses. The jury is the judge of the facts in the case, but it must accept the law as given by the court. The judge informs the jury of the penalty provided by law in case the accused is found guilty, but he does not instruct them to set the penalty. The jury's first function is to determine from the evidence presented in the trial and the law given them in the judge's charge whether the accused is "guilty" or "not guilty."

The attorneys in the case will offer their arguments after the charge has been read to the jury, and before they retire to consider a verdict. They, with the judge's consent, can arrange the order of argument as they choose, but the attorney for the state has the right to give the closing address.

The attorney on either side may object to the argument of the opposing attorney if he believes it to be improper, and the judge will immediately sustain or overrule the objection. If he sustains the objection, he often will instruct the jury to disregard that part of the argument which was objectionable. But each side has the right of fair comment upon the evidence in the case and to make a summation of it for the jury. The prosecution tries to review it as putting the shadow of guilt upon the defendant and the defense tries to show his client to be innocent. Sometimes these arguments become impassioned and quite moving—sometimes they are overdone. But a well-reasoned and well-presented argument is helpful to the jury. The attorneys on both sides are officers of the court, but they present opposite viewpoints.

The jury retires to the jury room to consider its verdict at the conclusion of the arguments. They are kept together during their deliberations and are not permitted to talk to other people. They elect one of the members as foreman in accordance with the judge's instructions. They may request to have in the jury room any written evidence and exhibits introduced in the case, and they may call on the judge for definitions of words in the charge, and sometimes for further instructions. The judge is generally reluctant to do much more than call their attention to the charge and instruct them to read it and to proceed with their deliberations, because he feels that the charge is complete in the first place and understandable by those qualified to serve on a jury in the second. He is mindful also of the record of reversible errors committed by judges who are too free with instructions to the jury.

The jury, if they can agree, will render a verdict, and they find the defendant "not guilty" or "guilty as charged."

If their verdict is "not guilty," the case is ended and the defendant is immediately released. If the verdict is "guilty," then comes the procedure for assessing the punishment. It may be that prior convictions for similar offenses will subject the defendant to more punishment than that for a single offense. In this case, evidence of prior convictions must be presented to the court by the prosecution, so the judge or the jury, whoever is to assess the punishment, may be properly informed. If it is the jury who is to assess the punishment, the judge will give them a charge on the punishment informing them of the minimum and maximum penalties prescribed by law, and send them back to the jury room to complete the verdict by fixing the penalty. If the jury can agree on the amount of punishment, they return to the court with their verdict written out, and the foreman hands it to the court clerk. The judge calls the court to order and instructs the clerk to read the verdict. The judge then asks the jury if that is their verdict, and generally they indicate that it is. But if there is a dissent, one or more indicating that they did not understand it that way, the judge will send them back to the jury room for further deliberation. Finally, the verdict is complete, and the defendant's punishment is fixed.

At this point, the same as at the time when the jury brought in its verdict of "guilty," the attorney on either side may ask for a poll of the jury and his request will be granted. Then each juror is asked whether the verdict returned into court is his verdict. If all answer affirmatively, then their work is finished. If there is any dissent, they are sent back for further deliberation.

If the jury cannot agree, first whether the defendant is guilty or not guilty, or on the amount of punishment to be assessed, it is commonly termed a *hung* jury, and they are discharged. This calls for a new trial at a later date.

If the defendant is found guilty and his punishment is assessed, the defendant's attorney almost always asks for a new trial. He has ten days from the date of the verdict in which to file his motion with the court asking for a new trial. The court will grant a hearing on the motion and dispose of it by granting it or overruling it. There are ten different grounds on which the defendant's attorney may urge for a new trial. If the judge decides that reversible error has been made in the trial of the case, he will grant a new trial and the whole trial procedure must be gone through again. However, if the judge feels the defendant has had a fair trial and that no valid grounds exist for a new trial, he will overrule the motion.

Generally, the defendant's attorney will give notice of appeal and take the case up to the Court of Criminal Appeals, sitting in Austin. The Court of Criminal Appeals will hear the case *on the record*, which is a copy of the proceedings in the district court, the briefs filed by the attorneys on each side, and the arguments of the attorneys before the court. That court may affirm the judgment of the court below, or it may reverse that judgment and discharge the defendant, or it may reverse the judgment below and send the case back for a new trial. The Court of Criminal Appeals is the "court of last resort" for criminal cases under Texas law. In some instances, an appeal may be carried to the United States Supreme Court on grounds that the defendant's rights under the United States Constitution have been violated.

Who Decides the Punishment, Judge or Jury?

For the past several years there has been confusion as to who decides the punishment, the judge or the jury? In 1965, the legislature wrote new law on the subject, and it appears they wanted to give the accused some possible advantages that he did not previously have by letting him choose between judge and jury to fix his punishment after a guilty verdict. However, the law was poorly written, and among other deficiencies, it failed to make clear whether it would be the judge or the jury who would assess the punishment in a capital case where the death penalty is asked by the state. Because of the provisions of the constitution and opinion by the attorney general, the courts have followed the practice of having the jury (not the judge) assess the punishment when the verdict is guilty and the state has asked for the death penalty.

In 1967, the legislature tried again and wrote, in its amendment of the law, that:

"Article 37.07, Verdict Must be General; Separate Hearing on Proper Punishment.

"1. The verdict in every criminal action must be general. Where there are special pleas on which a jury is to find they must say in their verdict that the allegations in such pleas are true or untrue. If the plea is not guilty, they must find that the defendant is either guilty or not guilty, and, except as provided in Section 2, they shall assess the punishment in all cases where the same is not absolutely fixed by law to some particular penalty.

"2. Alternative Procedure

"(a) In all criminal cases, other than misdemeanor cases of which the justice court or corporation court has jurisdiction, which are tried before a jury on a plea of not guilty, the judge shall, before argument begins, first submit to the jury the issue of guilt or innocence of the defendant of the offense or offenses charged, without authorizing the jury to pass upon the punishment to be imposed.

"(b) If a finding of guilt is returned, it shall then be the responsibility of the judge to assess the punishment applicable to the offense; provided, however, that (1) in capital cases where the state has made it known in writing prior to trial that it will seek the death penalty, (2) in any criminal action where the jury may recommend probation and the defendant filed his sworn motion for probation before the trial began, and (3) in other cases where the defendant so elects in writing at the time he enters his plea in open court, the punishment shall be assessed by the same jury. If a finding of guilty is returned, the defendant may, with consent of the attorney for the state, change his election of one who assesses the punishemnt.

"3. Evidence of prior criminal record in all criminal cases after a finding of guilty:

"(a) Regardless of the plea and whether the punishment be assessed by the judge or jury, evidence may be offered by the state and the defendant as to the prior criminal record of the defendant, his general reputation and his character. The term prior criminal record means a final conviction in a court of record, or a probated or suspended sentence that has occurred prior to trial, or any final conviction material to the offense charged.

"(b) After the introduction of such evidence has been concluded, and if the jury has responsibility of assessing the punishment, the court shall give such additional written instructions as may be necessary and the order of procedure and the rules governing the conduct of the trial shall be the same as are applicable on the issue of guilt or innocence.

"(c) In cases where the matter of punishment is referred to the jury, the verdict shall not be complete until the jury has returned a verdict both on the guilt or innocence of the defendant and the amount of punishment, where the jury finds the defendant guilty. In the event the jury shall fail to agree, a mistrial shall be declared and no jeopardy shall attach.

"(d) When the judge assesses the punishment, and after the hearing of the evidence hereinabove provided for, he shall forthwith announce his decision in open court as to the punishment to be assessed.

"(e) Nothing herein contained shall be construed as affecting the admissibility of extraneous offenses on the question of guilt or innocence."

Index